TELECOMMUNICATIONS
AND
RURAL DEVELOPMENT

Research Team

Project Directors
Jurgen Schmandt, LBJ School of Public Affairs
Frederick Williams, College of Communication
Robert H. Wilson, LBJ School of Public Affairs
Sharon Strover, College of Communication

Researchers
Paula J. Adams, LBJ School of Public Affairs
Lane Darnell Bahl, LBJ School of Public Affairs
Martin S. Bernal, LBJ School of Public Affairs
Oswaldo M. Coelho, LBJ School of Public Affairs
Richard Cutler, College of Communication
Jill Ehrlich, LBJ School of Public Affairs
Sangjae Hwang, College of Communication
Scott J. Lewis, LBJ School of Public Affairs
Julia A. Marsh, College of Business Administration
Dale Phillips, LBJ School of Public Affairs
Harmeet S. Sawhney, College of Communication
Robert Stephens, LBJ School of Public Affairs
Joan Stuller, College of Communication
Liching Sung, College of Communication

Telecommunications
and
Rural Development

A STUDY OF PRIVATE AND
PUBLIC SECTOR INNOVATION

Edited by Jurgen Schmandt,
Frederick Williams,
Robert H. Wilson,
and Sharon Strover

A Joint Project of
The Lyndon B. Johnson School of Public Affairs
and
The Center for Research on Communication,
Technology, and Society
(College of Communication)

The University of Texas at Austin

New York
Westport, Connecticut
London

Library of Congress Cataloging-in-Publication Data

Telecommunications and rural development : a study of private
  and public sector innovation / edited by Jurgen Schmandt . . . [et al.].
    p.   cm.
  "A Joint project of The Lyndon Baines Johnson School of Public Affairs
and The Center for Research on Communication, Technology, and Society
(College of Communication)"
  Includes bibliographical references and index.
  ISBN 0-275-93951-0 (alk. paper)
    1. Rural telecommunication—United States.   2. Rural development—
United States.   I. Schmandt, Jurgen.   II. Lyndon B. Johnson
School of Public Affairs.   III. University of Texas at Austin. Center for
Research on Communication, Technology, and Society.
  HE7775.T34   1991
  384′.0973—dc20   91-10178

British Library Cataloguing in Publication Data is available.

Library of Congress Catalog Card Number: 91-10178
ISBN: 0-275-93951-0

First published in 1991

Praeger Publishers, One Madison Avenue, New York, NY 10010
An imprint of Greenwood Publishing Group, Inc.

Printed in the United States of America

The paper used in this book complies with the
Permanent Paper Standard issued by the National
Information Standards Organization (Z39.48–1984).

10 9 8 7 6 5 4 3 2 1

Contents

Tables and Figure

Preface

This study of rural telecommunications is the third in a series of projects dealing with telecommunications policy undertaken at the Lyndon B. Johnson School of Public Affairs and the Center for Research on Communication Technology and Society (College of Communication) at the University of Texas at Austin. The three projects have been concerned with telecommunications at two levels: the effects of telecommunications advances in our economy and society and the policy framework that has resulted from the divestiture of AT&T. The first project studied state telecommunications policy (see Jurgen Schmandt, Frederick Williams, and Robert H. Wilson, eds., *Telecommunications Policy and Economic Development: The New State Role*, Praeger, 1989). The second project dealt with cities and large telecommunications users (see Jurgen Schmandt, Frederick Williams, Robert H. Wilson, and Sharon Strover, eds., *The New Urban Infrastructure: Cities and Telecommunications*, Praeger, 1990).

Our study of rural telecommunications attempts to assess the potential that telecommunications advances hold for rural America. The research team consisted of ten students from the LBJ School's master's program in public affairs, four students from the College of Communication's Ph.D. program, and one student from the College of Business's master of business administration program. The project management team consisted of two faculty members from the LBJ School and two from the College of Communication. The work was conducted in a year-long policy research project during the 1989–90 academic year.

Our clients for this and the two earlier projects were Texas Telephone Association and Southwestern Bell Telephone Company. As in the past, our clients have been exemplary, offering support and encouragement, providing constructive criticism, and recognizing and honoring the requirement of impartial analysis for university research.

Our work benefited from a conference held in the spring of 1990 at which preliminary results were presented to a group of national experts. The discussion and comments concerning the results greatly improved the quality of the work and we acknowledge their contribution.

This project required extensive fieldwork and interviews with more than 200 individuals. The work could not have been completed without the cooperation of these individuals, and we thank them for their time and ideas. Our report benefited from comments and suggestions from Richard Dietz, Southwestern Bell Telephone; Dr. Ron Knutson, Texas A&M University; R. C. Brown III, Communications, Inc.; Shirley Bloomfield, National Telephone Cooperative Association; Steve Buttress, Kearney State College; and Dr. Heather Hudson, University of San Francisco. While all of their suggestions have not been incorporated in our report, they were very helpful in sharpening the different positions and policy issues involved in this very complex area. We also had input from the National Rural Telecommunications Cooperative, the United States Telephone Association, the Public Service Satellite Consortium, and the National Rural Telecom Association.

We hope this report will be helpful as rural telecommunications becomes a more central issue in our public policy agenda.

1

Introduction

Paula J. Adams and Robert Stephens

In the context of emerging global interdependence, telecommunications infrastructures are becoming an increasingly important component of international, regional, and local economies. During the past 20 years, numerous studies have indicated that telecommunications plays a significant role in the economic viability of nations, states, and cities as global information transfer becomes a primary component of regional economic vitality. Even rural communities are affected by telecommunications infrastructure.

The impact of telecommunications on developing Third World countries has been extensively studied during the last 20 years.[1] However, the potential that telecommunications holds for rural areas in industrialized countries such as the United States is not well understood. This report seeks to help fill this void at a time when maintaining or enhancing the economies of rural regions is especially important.[2]

Our study is the result of growing interest in the United States in how changes in telecommunications and innovation in telecommunications technology can influence rural revitalization. The subject is made more urgent by the calls from different quarters for massive investment in an upgraded rural telecommunications infrastructure and for new expanded definitions of universal services. This investigation examines the role telecommunications currently plays in various aspects of rural America. In order to explore these issues, we first set the context by examining changes in rural America during the 1980s. We then consider some of the telecommunications applications and rural support mechanisms that seem to have contributed to ameliorating certain difficulties faced by distant, sparsely populated regions. Finally, we discuss the rationale behind the research plan adopted here.

CHALLENGES TO RURAL ECONOMIES

Rural areas in the United States are going through a period of economic and social transition.[3] For the first time in history, "rural" and "agriculture" are no longer synonymous. While the economy of rural America once depended on agriculture, farming currently employs only 9 percent of all rural workers and only half as many workers as rural manufacturing does. In the 1980s only 23 percent of the 3,106 counties in the United States could be described as being dependent on agriculture.[4]

The 1980s brought significant changes to rural areas. As Table 1.1 shows, population growth in nonmetropolitan (nonmetro) areas dropped to 1.5 percent nationally, compared to 4.6 percent in metropolitan (metro) areas. An economic crisis was fed by downturns in the natural resource–based industries such as agriculture, forestry, and mining, upon which much of the economy of rural America has been dependent. During this period, net growth in the U.S. economy (both urban and rural) occurred mainly in the service sector.[5] Although the service sector grew in rural America during the 1980s, it

Table 1.1 Population Growth in Metro and Nonmetro Areas, 1970–1987*

	1970-1980	1980-1983	1983-1987
Metro	9.8%	3.5%	4.6%
Nonmetro	15.8%	2.7%	1.5%

*"Metro" is defined here using the 1980 definition that a country must contain either a city with at least 50,000 people or be an urban area with at least 50,000 people adjacent to a county that has at least 100,000 residents. "Nonmetro" is everything else.

Source: U.S. Senate, Committee on Small Business, "Population Trends in Rural and Small Town America Since 1980." Testimony by Calvin Beale, U.S. Department of Agriculture, May 24, 1989.

was not sufficient to offset the jobs lost from the declining natural resource industries (Table 1.2). A persistent income gap between residents in metropolitan versus nonmetropolitan areas widened during the 1980s.[6]

Against the background of declining jobs in traditional economic sectors, large distances between towns and low population densities characterizing rural America create additional barriers. The combination of these two factors increases the difficulty in achieving the economies of scale making many conventional businesses and services viable. Moreover, in the past, rural communities have specialized in the production of just one or two goods. As a result, the economic bases of rural communities are not as diversified and suffer more than their urban counterparts when faced with crises such as drought or a drop in the price of oil. These factors dim the prospects for rural revitalization in the future.

The problems rural America faces in the 1990s run deeper than economics. In comparison to urban areas, much of rural America has inferior physical infrastructure, poor or distressed schools, and poor access to medical services. A comparison of urban and rural socioeconomic indicators during the late 1980s reveals that (1) rural unemployment rates were about 31 percent higher, (2) per capita income in rural areas was about 25 percent lower, (3) rural poverty rates were one-third higher (18 percent compared to 9 percent in 1986), and (4) rural school dropout rates exceeded urban dropout rates.[7] As these figures indicate, the consequences of the economic crisis that rural America faced in the 1980s affected more than jobs and income—it threatened the quality of life. In terms of federal and state aid, the

Table 1.2 Percentage of Employment Growth in Metro and Nonmetro Counties, 1979–1986

| | 1979-1982 | | 1982-1986 | |
	Metro	Nonmetro	Metro	Nonmetro
Farming	.27	-1.79	-1.33	-1.16
Manufacturing	-3.43	-4.21	-0.02	1.41
Construction	-3.16	-3.43	6.38	3.01
Mining	10.94	4.09	-3.97	-6.51
Services	1.63	.95	3.75	2.67

Source: U.S. Department of Agriculture, Agricultural Chartbook (Washington, D.C.: U.S. Government Printing Office, 1990), p. 54.

1980s were also unkind to rural areas. While the 1960s and 1970s brought increased involvement of federal and state governments in local economic development, the 1980s brought a significant decline in the scope of this involvement. For example, intergovernmental transfers (Social Security, Medicare/Medicaid, retirement and disability programs, etc.) in 1977 represented 43 percent of the revenues of rural localities compared to 34 percent in 1962.[8] During the 1980s, under "New Federalism," there was a reduction of intergovernmental transfers from the federal and state governments to local governments. This trend is projected to continue during the 1990s.[9] Additionally, federal farm programs, a large source of income for rural areas, first rose and then declined precipitously in the 1980s, from a high of $26 billion in 1986–87 to $12 billion in 1990–91. Faced with taxpayer resistance and a dwindling tax base during the 1980s, many local governments have been unable to replace funds that previously came from the federal and state governments, rendering rural communities with their smaller tax bases particularly vulnerable.

Despite the passage by the U.S. Congress in 1990 of a rural initiative act aimed at nonagricultural rural economic development, the burden of rural policy-making is shifting from the federal government to public and private institutions on the state and local levels. While many state and local decision makers in the public and private sector welcome the decentralization of decision making, it is important to recognize that they are constrained in their ability to respond to global trends and changes. One of the issues we will examine in this study is how public and private institutions and actors are cooperating and forming alliances in order to foster development, share information, and nurture various investments in rural areas. The role telecommunications plays in ameliorating several of these difficulties is our essential focus.

TELECOMMUNICATIONS INFRASTRUCTURE

The remote nature of many rural communities, combined with their sparse populations, can make advanced telecommunications networks very expensive. Large distances and few users normally mean limited service.[10] Nevertheless, communication is the lifeline of today's business world—especially in the fastest-growing sectors of the U.S. economy—and telecommunications facilities in rural communities often are deficient in advanced technology to store, process, deliver, and use critical information. For example, party lines still exist in some rural areas, and it is estimated that 183,000 households in the United States do not have access to telephone service, although most of that number (97 percent) is due to poverty rather than remoteness.[11] Providing advanced communication services, particularly when they rely on digital switches, is difficult in rural areas. As one investigator noted in 1987,

> A recent study in Washington State indicates that selected telecommunications services, quality of service, and other information technologies were less prevalent in rural cities and surrounding areas than they were in urban areas. For example, only 76 percent of the households in rural locales had one party (private) telephone service compared to 93–97 percent in all other locations. Both rural cities and the countryside are also distinctly less likely to have touch tone, call waiting and telephone answering machines.[12]

The telecommunications infrastructure in the nation's rural areas lags behind that of urban areas in its capabilities. Distance and low population densities discouraged the former monopoly phone system (AT&T) from energetically wiring these regions. In its place independent companies sprang up, sometimes helped by government programs such as the Rural Electrification Administration (REA) and sometimes funded through the cooperative efforts of local residents. An inspection of the telephone service maps of states like Texas or Nebraska, where there are tremendous distances between population centers, reveals that the Bell operating companies (BOCs) generally serve urbanized areas while the more rural regions are served by a quilt of smaller companies and some larger independent companies (e.g., GTE, United Telephone, and Contel).

The Technology

Some rural areas are served by alternative technologies such as radio or satellites. Radio can provide high-quality "connections" and can offer cheaper substitutions when terrain normally would escalate wire line costs. One estimate is that there were about 1,500 subscribers using radio-based telephone services as of 1989. Satellite connections are sometimes used in similar situations. Alaska, with its huge and sparsely populated land mass, has used satellite communications for several years and for several purposes: basic communications, health services, and distance education.

Both line quality and the nature of telecommunications switching technologies are important considerations in characterizing any network. Line quality is sometimes a problem in rural telephone systems because the technology (loading coils, range extenders) needed to maintain quality voice transmissions across long distances actually impedes data transmission. Switching technology determines what sorts of value-added services are available to the user. Both affect not only the commonplace consumer services such as call waiting and call forwarding but also business-oriented services based on facsimile machines and modems. (It should be mentioned that digital switches are preferred for such services because their software can automate many user functions.)

The larger, private independent phone companies such as Contel and United Telephone (many of them serving rural exchanges) are rapidly upgrading to digital switches. Smaller and typically even more rural phone companies are upgrading more slowly, and the BOC facilities serving rural areas likewise are upgrading to digital, only more slowly.[13] Proposals for upgrading switches in rural areas have figured prominently in several BOCs' proposals for rate increases before state regulatory bodies, and since 1982 all REA-financed switch replacements have been for digital technology.[14] Nevertheless, common "user demand" justifications for installing digital switches in rural areas where analog switches still have a considerable functional lifetime are sometimes difficult. Funding technology and systems in areas so sparsely populated, creating a market, and even sometimes generating interest and ideas for using new capabilities can be problematic.

Funding Issues

Telecommunications companies servicing these classically "uneconomic" areas have been protected from the potentially destructive dynamics of the marketplace through various state and federal policies.[15] However, as the effects of divestiture filter throughout the telephone industry, these smaller providers also feel market pressures. For example, business customers in rural areas are able to purchase or lease their own communications systems, often bypassing the local exchange company, which may not have the capabilities needed. Thus the smaller company loses local service charges as well as long-distance and inter-Local Access and Transport Area (interLATA access) charges.[16] Additionally, as cost-based pricing is advocated by larger and more powerful providers, particularly the BOCs, there is an impetus for "every route and service to pay its own way."[17] This means that the various rural service support mechanisms, such as averaging access rates, may dwindle.

The federal government played a key role in encouraging the extension of basic telephone services to rural areas in 1949 through loans provided by the Rural Electrification Administration, created in the 1930s as an agency within the U.S. Department of Agriculture. It gave rural areas access to basic telephone services by providing technical advice and low-cost loans to rural power and telephone providers that could not otherwise afford commercial interest rates. Its phone program began in the 1940s. Several independent phone companies, both privately and cooperatively owned, are eligible for loans from the REA.[18] Although the REA continues to be a primary source of financing for rural telephone companies—in 1988 the REA approved $193 million in loans, of which $166 million was actually advanced[19]—the phone companies believe its awards were curtailed during the 1980s. Budgetary cutbacks under the Reagan administration have adversely affected extending advanced telecommunications infrastructure to rural areas.

In addition to uncertain REA funding there are other difficulties associated with providing rural telephone service. For example, rural companies fear losing the benefits of long-distance rate averaging. The telecommunications industry's practice of averaging the price of accessing long-distance carriers has benefited rural subscribers as they rely more heavily on long-distance calling than their urban counterparts. (Prices are based upon distance rather than transmission cost.) However, greater competition and the trend toward cost pricing may lead to a dismantling of the rate-averaging practice: the Federal Communications Commission (FCC) has already decreased BOC requirements for cost pool contributions. There is additional pressure from long-distance carriers to reduce the access charges they pay to local phone companies, money which benefits rural phone companies through disbursements such as those from the National Exchange Carrier Association. Should such charges diminish, rural telephone companies will see their revenues drop. Finally, rural phone users rely more on intrastate long-distance services, which result in high toll-calling costs for them.

Traditional depreciation policies threaten the ability of local exchange companies (LECs) in rural areas to modernize their facilities in order to participate in the information age. In the past, state regulators have promoted low rural rates by assigning long depreciation schedules to the equipment used by local carriers. This translates into lower telephone rates for customers. However, the allowed depreciation period also affects the ability of rural companies to update their facilities. Setting longer depreciation schedules was an acceptable strategy to keep rates low when "plain old telephone service" was all that rural communities required. Today these policies may inhibit rural telecommunications companies from making critical investments. Additionally, in the postdivestiture era, state regulators have new responsibilities and regulatory latitude in determining how "competitive" (or cost-based) certain services will be and how service obligations are defined and implemented by local exchange carriers. To the extent that rural telephone companies are suddenly thrust into a competitive domain, their ability to provide necessary levels of service may be threatened.

Pressures to upgrade rural service and the potential of reduced support mechanisms are forcing rural phone providers to begin to grapple with marketplace dynamics. The year 1990 marked the beginning of an unprecedented amount of attention directed toward assessing or facilitating the role of telecommunications in development (rural and otherwise), evidenced in the National Telecommunications and Information Administration's *Comprehensive Study of the Domestic Telecommunications Infrastructure*,[20] the Office of Technology Assessment's rural telecommunications study, certain foundation studies,[21] and the continuation of a special Rural Economic Development Loan and Grant Program under the REA program (begun in 1987). New attention is being paid to the variety of alternative service providers in rural areas, including cable television systems, satellite networks, and utility companies, each of which can or already does play a role in delivering advanced services to rural areas. Some of these systems are already seeking ways to contribute to financially strapped rural educational efforts.[22] Or, in competitive response, they oppose the efforts of telephone companies to use the rate base in order to fund plant upgrades in rural areas.[23]

Policymakers must target their efforts toward achieving the most desirable outcomes for rural areas, but without an understanding of which service provider can make the best contribution to rural regions, the policy community's alternatives are unclear. The artificial situation created by insulating rural telecommunications providers from competition has left us with few guidelines. Defenders of the status quo argue that marketplace dynamics will not work in rural areas, suggesting that only continued or enhanced support will contribute to delivering advanced telecommunications services (and facilitating subsequent economic development) to rural areas. Others, particularly those in the alternative service provider category (such as public utilities), argue that they can address some of these rural problems and that competition would enhance the rural infrastructure. How the services available in rural areas can be modernized, how providers can be encouraged to be innovative, and how communities can use telecommunications for their improvement are thorny issues but ones that must be addressed by state and federal policymakers.

There is a consensus that telecommunications has a positive effect on economic development. The nature of this relationship, especially its causal role, is not fully understood and certainly difficult to measure; just how increased competition among rural providers might affect different services is open to speculation. This report will address these issues by examining the roles of both telecommunications providers as well as users in an effort to understand the contributions that innovative telecommunications systems or applications can make to rural life. This information should help policymakers understand some of the situations and regulatory opportunities for telecommunications in rural regions.

STUDY OVERVIEW

Our research on telecommunications and rural economic development sought answers to three primary research questions. First, what sorts of innovative telecommunications applications occur in rural areas? We attempt to determine the origins of each application and the key players responsible for the innovation (e.g., grassroots organizations, local businesses, telephone companies, and policymakers).

Second, what role does telecommunications play in innovation and economic development in rural areas? We try to determine whether the telecommunications infrastructures affect development and what their relationship is to other causal factors. In short, we question whether and how telecommunications may be a catalyst for rural economic development.

Finally, what are the policy and development implications of innovative telecommunications? Since providing advanced telecommunications services to rural communities can be extremely expensive for telecommunications companies, strong incentives to develop them are often lacking. Nevertheless, innovations of various sorts can obtain substantial public support and occasionally overcome some of the rural area's diseconomies. Policies that might influence telecommunications applications are considered.

To address our research questions, we adopted a comparative case study approach. The research is based on 37 case studies of public and private institutions that either deliver social services, run businesses, provide telecommunications services, or promote economic development in rural areas. The case studies do not represent a random sample. To select them, we established an initial data base of more than 100 sites consisting of telephone companies, businesses, and public service and development agencies involved in serving rural areas and using telecommunications in innovative ways. These sites were divided into four functional categories representing key components of rural development and forming the major sections of the report:

(1) telecommunications-intensive rural businesses, (2) public-service agencies such as health and education institutions using telecommunications, (3) telecommunications companies, and (4) rural communities using telecommunications as part of their development strategy. The units of analysis are diverse, including businesses, entire communities, telephone and utility companies, and educational organizations. Figure 1.1 illustrates the location of our sites and Table 1.3 lists them.

The comparative case study method, using a nonrandom sampling design, was chosen after careful consideration of alternatives. Our concern was to identify and understand how new technologies were being utilized in a rural setting. We expect our sites to be atypical or nonrepresentative, and consequently limitations exist when we generalize our findings. Nevertheless, this methodology was deemed the most appropriate for investigating the potential for telecommunications in rural areas.

In the development of the present project, it became clear that the status of small rural telephone companies, cooperatives, and alliances of small telcos (telephone companies) was a topic deserving special attention. Granted that the BOCs and the large independent companies serve the bulk of U.S. customers, there are many very small companies, most distinctive in character, that play a markedly important role in the rural economy. Little attention has been given to these companies in the postdivestiture scene, including their critical role in developing the rural telecommunications infrastructure. Thus we chose to concentrate our resources in this component of the project on these smaller companies, selecting examples of companies, cooperatives, special alliances, and a rural power company offering telecommunications services.

In the section on telecommunications providers, we chose to concentrate on small companies. This by no means diminishes the importance of BOCs in this area, and we reflect the activities of the larger providers in other sections of this report.[24] It is the premise of our study, however, that telecommunications and rural development in America cannot proceed without consideration of the small rural telcos and cooperatives, or the special alliances that they may form in order to serve their customers.

The sites for the cases ultimately selected for this study illustrate the economic and geographic diversity that characterizes rural America. We included communities whose economies are variously dependent on agriculture, manufacturing, retailing, tourism, and public services. We chose at least one site in each of the major geographic regions of the United States: the Northeast, Southeast, Midwest, and Pacific Coast.

Figure 1.1 Map of Rural Research Sites

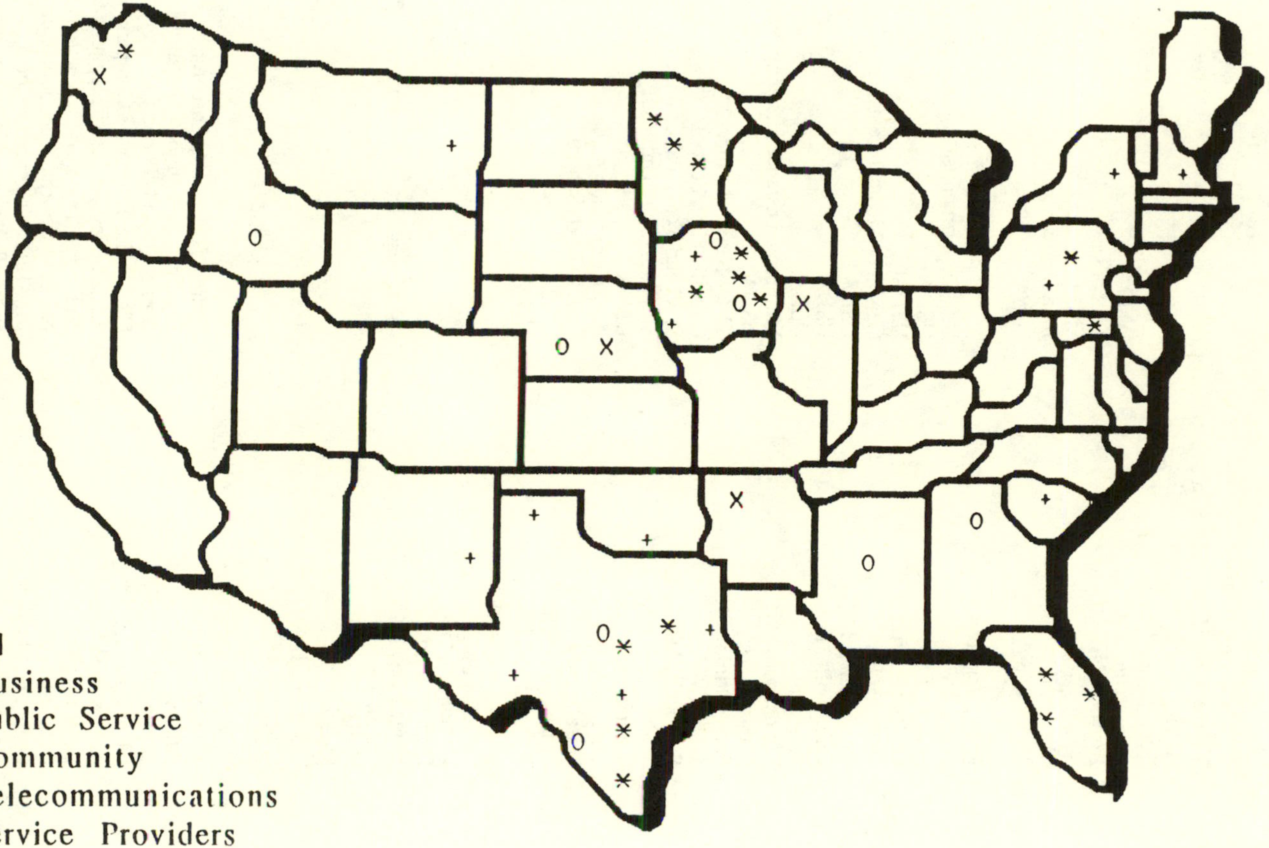

Legend

x   Business
*   Public Service
o   Community
+   Telecommunications
    Service Providers

Table 1.3 Research Sites by Category

Businesses
Bentonville, AR	Wal-Mart
Kearney, NE	Cabela's
	EMRG
Moline, IL	John Deere
Tacoma, WA	Weyerhaeuser

Public Services
Ames, IA	U.S. Department of Agriculture (USDA)
Austin, TX	USDA
College Station, TX	USDA
Danville, PA	Geisinger Medical Center
Des Moines, IA	USDA
Gainesville, FL	USDA
McAllen, TX	USDA
Minneapolis, MI	Minnesota Distance Learning Network
Ottumwa, IA	USDA
San Antonio, TX	TI-IN Network, Inc.
Seattle, WA	Oakville High School
St. Cloud, MN	St. Cloud Technical College
	St. Cloud State University
Tampa, FL	USDA
Thornton, IA	Area Community Cluster
Upsala, MN	Upsala High School
Washington, DC	USDA
Winter Park, FL	USDA

Communities
Dahlonega, GA
Demopolis, AL
Eagle Pass, TX
Hutto, TX
Hailey, ID
Kearney, NE
Thornton, IA
Ottumwa, IA

Telecommunications Service Providers
Albany, NY	Taconic Telephone Corporation
Alpine, TX	Big Bend Telephone Company
Bretton Woods, NH	Bretton Woods Phone Company
Clear Lake, IA	Clear Lake Telephone Company
Clovis, NM	Eastern New Mexico Telephone Cooperative
Dalhart, TX	XIT Rural Telephone Cooperative
Gibsonia, PA	North Pittsburgh Telephone Company
Glendive, MT	Mid-Rivers Telephone Cooperative
Henderson, TX	Eastex Telephone Cooperative
Kerrville, TX	Kerrville Telephone Company
Rock Hill, SC	PalmettoNet
West Des Moines, IA	Iowa Network Services
Walters, OK	Cotton Rural Electric Cooperative

Our research utilized three sources of information: government documents, published literature, and more than 100 interviews—both telephone and personal—with representatives of the major players at each site. Prior to the fieldwork, research teams conducted in-depth studies of the issues involved in each of the four fields. Students then traveled to various sites across the country to gather data.

Communication between students and research sites was maintained throughout the writing process to ensure accuracy in the data. Feedback was also offered from professionals in the telecommunications industry during a conference held by the project in the spring of 1990; these ideas were incorporated into the final report.

The following is a brief overview of the four service categories around which this study is organized.

Doing Business in Rural America

The engine of economic growth and development in rural areas will ultimately be fueled by private business. In order to compete globally, businesses require access to telecommunications infrastructures that enable them to respond to the ever-changing global marketplace. Traditionally, urban areas have had more communications resources than rural areas, giving them a distinct advantage for attracting, maintaining, and creating business.

We present five cases in which the extension of advanced telecommunications to rural areas enabled businesses to locate in rural areas, or enabled other traditionally rural industries to be more efficient by competitively exploiting certain rural resources and markets. In studying these businesses we examined the following issues: What advantage does telecommunications provide for businesses operating in rural areas? How did businesses choose their telecommunications systems? How have these industries and their telecommunications uses affected local economies in rural areas?

Public-Service Delivery

Competing in the global marketplace requires that rural communities have a healthy and educated work force. Solid health and educational systems ensure that citizens will stay in rural areas. We selected case studies that illustrate how telecommunications resources are being utilized to overcome distance barriers for medical, educational, and information service delivery. Our research into the use of telecommunications for public-service delivery was aimed at answering the following questions: How have rural communities used telecommunications to gain access to public services? Which public and private institutional arrangements are most conducive to rural public-service delivery?

Issues for Rural Telecommunications Providers

In order to assess the problems faced by those who install and maintain the rural telecommunications infrastructure, we studied 16 telecommunications companies serving rural areas in an innovative fashion. A key player in rural economic development is the rural telephone company. As mentioned earlier, low-cost REA loans and other support mechanisms in the telecommunications industry have traditionally enabled telcos to serve rural areas. Today, rural service providers are concerned that these support mechanisms may disappear. Simultaneously, rural telcos face pressures to upgrade their technology.

Our research questions included the following: How do rural telcos interact with their communities? What challenges are faced by rural telecommunications companies? How do rural telcos approach innovative services?

Telecommunications and Community Development

The role of telecommunications in rural economic development was one of our initial research topics. To study the issue we selected six rural communities in which development projects had been implemented and in which telecommunications was found to have either made an important contribution to or hindered these development efforts, and we attempted to answer four questions: What role does telecommunications infrastructure play in community development efforts? How did these innovations affect local actors and the community development process itself? What was the origin of both the telecommunications and community development innovations? What is the relative importance of a viable, modern telecommunications system in improving the quality of life and economic standing of the community?

This volume is organized in terms of the four major sets of cases discussed above: telecommunications-intensive businesses in rural America, public services using telecommunications facilities, rural telecommunications providers, and telecommunications-related community development efforts. Each chapter reports on its unique cases and is organized around our broad questions concerning the types of innovations that are feasible in rural areas, their role in local economic development, and their policy implications. A final chapter compiles our findings and synthesizes the themes that cut across the specific sites. We comment on the process of innovation in rural America and offer some broad policy recommendations that focus on how telecommunications providers or certain telecommunications applications might contribute to revitalizing rural communities.

NOTES

1. J. Saunders, R. Warford, and Bjorn Wellenius, *Telecommunications and Economic Development* (Baltimore: Johns Hopkins University Press, 1983). For additional bibliographic information, see Heather Hudson, *When Telephones Reach the Village: The Role of Telecommunications in Rural Development* (Norwood, N.J.: Ablex, 1985).

2. Telecommunications infrastructures in industrialized countries such as the United States have several essential building blocks already in place, including both wire-based and wireless services. Industrialized nations are more integrated into the global economy through advanced telecommunications resources than are Third World nations still struggling to extend basic telephone services to rural residents within their own countries. Moreover, rural dwellers generally have at least some basic level of telephone service and often an advanced level of television or video service. Therefore, this study assumes that the telecommunications needs of rural areas in the United States may not be able to rely on analyses or reasoning that made sense for developing nations and suggests different strategies and approaches than those applied to rural communications in less developed nations.

3. We understand there is debate concerning what exactly constitutes "rural" (population density, the presence of farming, population size); for the purposes of this study, rural America is defined as areas comprising fewer than 50,000 inhabitants located outside of metropolitan statistical areas (MSAs). By this definition, rural America encompasses about 25 percent of the nation's population and 90 percent of its natural resources.

4. Sue H. Jones, ed., *Options in Developing a New National Rural Policy* (College Station, Tex.: Texas A&M University, May 1989), p. 6.

5. D. Brown, J. Reid, H. Bluestone, D. McGranahan, and S. Mazie, eds., *Rural Economic Development in the 1980s: Prospects for the Future*, Rural Development Research Report No. 69 (Washington, D.C.: U.S. Department of Agriculture, September 1988), p. 135.

6. M. Henry, Mark Drabenstott, and Lynn Gibson, "Rural Growth Slows Down," *Rural Development Perspectives* 3, no. 3 (June 1987), pp. 25–30.

7. Jones, *Options*, p. 6.

8. Brown et al., eds., *Rural Economic Development*, p. 22.

9. Robert Tannenwald, "The Changing Level and Mix of Federal Aid to State and Local Governments," *New England Economic Review*, May/June 1989, pp. 41–55.

10. The non-traffic-sensitive components of telephone service must be borne by rural carriers as they are by urban carriers. This portion of telephone service costs does not vary with volume; consequently, with few subscribers in rural areas and the large distances between them, physical plant costs can be very high.

11. Edwin Parker, Heather Hudson, Don Dillman, and Andrew Roscoe, *Rural America in the Information Age: Telecommunications Policy for Rural Development* (Lanham, Md.: University Press of America, 1989), p. 67.

12. Don A. Dillman and Donald M. Beck, "Information Technologies and Rural Development in the 1990s," States' Agenda for Rural Economic Development Conference Proceedings, Lexington, Kentucky, 1987.

13. Parker et al., *Rural America in the Information Age*, chap. 5.

14. U.S. Department of Agriculture, Rural Electrification Administration, "Comments of the Rural Electrification Administration," in U.S. Department of Commerce, National Telecommunications and Information Administration, *Comprehensive Study of Domestic Telecommunications Infrastructure* (Washington, D.C., January 1990), Docket 91296–9296, p. 9.

15. For example, in Nebraska small independent companies are protected from any competition (they have an exclusive territorial franchise) and at the same time are entirely unregulated in the rates they charge their customers.

16. Local access and transport area is a telephone service region, incorporating local exchanges, usually smaller than a state. Typically they are serviced by a given telephone company for local service and by interexchange companies for some intraLATA and all interLATA service.

17. U.S. Department of Agriculture, Rural Electrification Administration, "Comments of the Rural Electrification Administration," p. 2.

18. In 1988, 26.2 percent of REA borrowers were cooperatives, 73.2 percent were commercial companies, and 0.5 percent were public bodies. Among BOCs serving rural America that do not use REA loans, US West has by far the largest rural service area obligation.

19. U.S. Department of Agriculture, Rural Electrification Administration, *1988 Statistics Report, Rural Telephone Borrowers*, REA Bulletin No. 300–4, p. xiv, table 4; interview with Joe Bryant, Automated Information Systems Division, REA, Washington, D.C., November 7, 1990.

20. U.S. Department of Commerce, National Telecommunications and Information Administration, *Comprehensive Study of the Domestic Telecommunications Infrastructure* (Washington, D.C., January 1990).

21. The Office of Technology Assessment is undertaking a study at this time entitled *Information Age Technology and Rural Economic Development*. The Aspen Institute has sponsored several studies attempting to comment on the role of telecommunications for rural areas, including Parker et al., *Rural America in the Information Age*, as well as additional studies still under way at this writing. Other related work includes Jurgen Schmandt, Frederick Williams, and Robert H. Wilson, eds., *Telecommunications Policy and Economic Development: The New State Role* (New York: Praeger, 1989), and Jurgen Schmandt, Frederick Williams,

Robert H. Wilson, and Sharon Strover, eds., *The New Urban Infrastructure: Cities and Telecommunications* (New York: Praeger, 1990).

22. For example, a new cable service provided by Whittle provides schools with the technology to receive its educational public affairs cablecasts. Some members of the National Rural Telecommunications Cooperative are facilitating regional course sharing through their wire-based networks.

23. For example, state cable television associations in Texas and Tennessee recently have opposed overearnings dispositions in which utility commissions ordered phone companies to use the disputed revenues (overearnings) to upgrade their networks. See, for example, Rachel Thompson, "FYI: Tennessee Adopts Massive High-Tech Plan," *Multichannel News* 11, no. 33 (August 13, 1990), p. 1.

24. Two earlier studies examine the BOCs in some detail. See Schmandt, Williams, and Wilson, eds., *Telecommunications Policy and Economic Development*, and Schmandt et al., *The New Urban Infrastructure*.

2

Doing Business in Rural America

Martin S. Bernal, Joan Stuller, and Liching Sung

INTRODUCTION

In the 1980s, rural America witnessed the decline of natural re-source–based industries, traditionally rural America's mainstay, even though, in terms of income production, these are still the most important industries in rural America. (Natural resource–based industries account for approximately 20 percent of the income of all nonmetro counties.[1]) While growth in the service sector—a prominent feature of the national economy—has benefited the rural economy, it has not been able to replace the decline of traditional industries.

Structural shifts in the economy are driving such changes. The rural economy is now more closely linked to the national and global economies, thus making it more sensitive to macroeconomic conditions and global competition. Agriculture has become more efficient, so it employs fewer people and its products cost less. Other natural resource-based industries were hit hard during the recession of the early 1980s, even as rurally based manufacturing faced intense competition from offshore sites with lower labor costs. The effects of industrial transformation on rural America can be seen in slow job growth and high unemployment rates. Between 1979 and 1986, although employment in agriculture remained stable, counties depending on mining and energy extraction saw their total employment decline by 9.5 percent, and manufacturing employment grew only 2.7 percent.[2] High unemployment rates generally have plagued rural areas. In 1986, more than 1,000 rural counties had unemployment rates of 9 percent or higher.[3]

The nonagricultural businesses in rural areas are dominated in terms of employment by affiliates of large corporations, particularly their manufacturing plants. According to recent statistics, branch plants provide more jobs and more job growth than do small independent businesses in rural regions. For the period 1976 to 1980, 68 percent of new jobs in rural areas came from corporate branches and subsidiaries.[4] Small independent businesses, so-called Main Street businesses, operating in nonmetro areas do provide great numbers of jobs, but they are often unstable, particularly because they are subject to constraints on their access to capital. Consequently, their potential for adding jobs is questionable. Businesses that have survived for more than five years, however, appear to be more resilient and may create some job growth.

In examining how telecommunications might affect businesses in rural areas, then, we must look at branch plants, without overlooking the abilities of resourceful, smaller firms, particularly those that have some longevity, to exploit new telecommunications opportunities. Since business services and computer and data-processing services are among the service industries most likely to grow in the near term, those located in rural areas may provide particularly useful data on how telecommunications might be used to a rural location's advantage. Evaluating the use of telecommunications technology in relation to other factors undergirding small businesses—venture capital, the entrepreneurial climate, and innovativeness—should provide us with a useful perspective.

Telecommunications has been a fundamental infrastructure for the newly emerging economy.[5] The issue explored in this chapter is what new economic opportunities for rural America are offered by this new infrastructure. With advancements in technology, it has become feasible and attractive for nontraditional businesses (such as telemarketing) and other industries (such as high-tech manufacturing and telecommunications) to locate in rural areas. Telecommunications has also allowed businesses to operate more effectively and efficiently in order to become more competitive or simply to remain competitive. For example, manufacturers whose interests traditionally have been focused in rural areas, such as John Deere, which sells agricultural implements, or Weyerhaeuser, whose principal raw material is found in forests, can operate more effectively in rural areas and can significantly reduce costs through telecommunications. These firms are even able to remain competitive in the international market. Sometimes new opportunities are within reach with the help of telecommunications technology. For example, retailing businesses, such as Wal-Mart, have been very successful in exploiting rural markets through innovative uses of telecommunications.

Telecommunications has provided benefits and has become an enabling service for all sorts of firms, giving them the capability to conduct business in innovative ways, both externally and internally. For example, a business can customize its telecommunications requirements by building its own phone system to communicate within the firm and with the outside world. In the process, a firm may actually become a telecommunications provider rather than a customer.

In an effort to delineate the impact of telecommunications on business operations in rural areas, three industries that have significant operations in rural areas are studied in this chapter. These industries are manufacturing, retailing, and telecommunications-intensive industries. The role of telecommunications in these businesses' operations in rural areas and the implications of their increasing reliance on new technology are examined in an effort to answer these questions:

1. What advantages do telecommunications provide for corporations operating in rural areas?
2. What are the factors affecting rurally based companies' decisions to adopt certain telecommunications technology?
3. What are the consequences of corporations' adopting more privately owned telecommunications?

A modern telecommunications infrastructure is not the only requirement that a business needs to decide where it will locate and how it will conduct its business. Nonagricultural businesses in rural areas must overcome a number of problems and obstacles endemic to such regions, notwithstanding certain built-in advantages that rural locations enjoy. A rural area must satisfy certain requirements for a firm to locate or stay there, including favorable transportation costs, an adequate labor force, adequate infrastructure (e.g., water, power, and telecommunications), and the conditions associated with the locality itself. The influence of some of these factors is considered below.

Transportation Costs

Transportation costs have greatly decreased in the past 50 years. This decrease can be primarily attributed to the development of modern highway (state and federal), air, and rail systems (which have been extended to many rural areas) as well as improvements in automotive and aircraft technology. Today it is possible to transport almost anything overnight (i.e., with Federal Express, United Parcel Service, and U.S. Mail) to almost anywhere in the country and almost anywhere in the world. Thus, transportation factors are not as significant as they used to be in determining where a business is located, and it is now more feasible for a business to locate in a rural area. For a large manufacturer, however, transportation costs can still be significant, especially if the manufacturer needs to transport many materials from many places to its plant. Telecommunications-based or -oriented companies whose products are electronic services need not be as concerned with traditional transportation costs. They are primarily concerned with the cost and availability of phone service, particularly the inter-LATA costs and digital capabilities of the local phone provider.

Adequate Labor Force

Having a sufficiently large and appropriately skilled labor pool is vital to a business wherever it locates. Many of the growing sectors, particularly the advanced-technology sectors, require a well-educated labor pool. In a rural area, satisfying these requirements can be difficult. Therefore, certain types of businesses (i.e., very large, labor-intensive, high-skill, research-oriented firms) are automatically limited by the availability of suitable labor. The problem of labor-force size, in some cases, can be negated by combining the labor resources of a number of rural towns that are in proximity.

The problem of adequate education or training, however, may be difficult to overcome. Educational attainment in rural areas still lags behind that in nonrural areas,[6] although rural schools can provide excellent public education systems (K–12). Even if the labor pool is not educated or trained in the particular need of a business, the solid educational foundation provided by schools in many rural areas will allow businesses to train workers easily. The strong work ethic for which certain parts of the country are known may offset training deficits. Many businesses consider this attribute to be very valuable because it translates into higher productivity and lower absenteeism.

Adequate Infrastructure

The lack of an adequate infrastructure is another problem faced by many businesses in deciding where to locate. Roads, utility services, basic city services (i.e., protective services), and telecommunications are among the basic needs of businesses. While most rural areas have a complete infrastructure, problems arise when the requirements of the business are greater than the capacity of the rural area—for example a large manufacturer may need too large an amount of electricity or water.

A related problem exists in rural areas that have an outdated infrastructure. Many rural areas lack recent advances in telecommunications technology such as digital switches and fiber optic cables.[7] (Chapter 4 provides many case studies of rural telephone companies and their attempts to deal with the changing technological and regulatory environment.) Having an adequate telecommunications infrastructure can affect a firm's location decision if telecommunications is a very important component of the business. Not only having the proper physical equipment and technology but also being able to use it efficiently and at a low cost is of great importance.

It is important to note that a town lacking an adequate infrastructure, but with qualities that satisfy some of the firm's other high-priority requirements, might still attract a business to the area if the firm is able to build the necessary infrastructure itself. For example, a manufacturer might build its own power generator, or a telemarketing firm (telemarketing firms are intensive telecommunications users) might decide to bypass entirely the local telephone company and provide its own services by purchasing appropriate technology. In fact, the mere commitment of a firm to move to a rural area might cause an infrastructure provider (like a telephone company or power company) to build or install the necessary equipment.

Rural small businesses are particularly captive to the local exchange company. They are not large enough to make extensive investments in their own phone systems and therefore must accept what the public-switched network can provide. If this sector of the economy is to grow and prosper, its telecommunications requirements must be met. The lack of local expertise or knowledge concerning what sorts of telecommunications facilities or capabilities exist can impair small businesses. Moreover, in those cases where local exchange companies are not well equipped to work with local small businesses—where they are inexperienced at marketing, where their own system may not have necessary upgrades, where system investment is problematic—small rural business enterprises will not be able to capitalize on potential efficiencies achievable through telecommunications.

Local Conditions

The final major variable that a business considers when deciding where to locate is the locality itself. A business might look at the customer base in the rural town or the surrounding region if the business hopes to sell its products there. A company might also consider whether the town is growing and whether it can grow with the company. The quality of life that a rural town offers may also be a major consideration. The availability or proximity of good medical, educational, and recreational facilities will make a rural area more attractive to a business. Finally, the accessibility of the rural area may also play a major role. Being reasonably close to a major metropolitan area might be critical to a firm that conducts most of its business there. Having access to a major highway, railroad, or airport might be important to a firm that transports its products into outside markets.

RESEARCH OVERVIEW

The three rural industries investigated here include examples of manufacturing, retailing, and telecommunications-intensive services (telemarketing and processing) (see Table 2.1). Each has adapted to some of the environmental constraints (or opportunities) noted above, using telecommunications in advantageous ways.

John Deere Company, the largest farm equipment supplier in the nation, and Weyerhaeuser, the number-one private paper producer in the world, were chosen as manufacturing cases. Because of the nature of the companies' resources and their client base, these businesses must remain in rural areas. Both Deere and Weyerhaeuser lease private dedicated lines for two-way voice and data communication. In addition to the terrestrial lines, Deere also uses satellite capacity to link itself to a few of its remote dealers. Weyerhaeuser, in contrast, established its own telephone company to connect two of its rural plants.

Table 2.1   Telecommunications Applications in Three Rural Areas

	Telecommunications Applications			
	Inventory	Marketing	Training	Management Systems
Manufacturing				
John Deere	*			*
Weyerhaeuser	*			*
Retail Trade				
Wal-Mart	*		*	*
Telecommunication-Intensive Services				
Cabela's		*		
EMRG		*		

Wal-Mart was selected as a retailing case. Headquartered in Bentonville, Arkansas, the rurally based giant has grown in the past ten years from a relatively unknown regional chain to the second largest and most profitable retailer in the discount department store industry. A large part of Wal-Mart's success can be attributed to the company's ability to capitalize on advanced telecommunications technologies, particularly satellites, which it uses to link 1,600 retail and wholesale stores, headquarters, and distribution centers, thereby bypassing the public-switched network.

Recently, many telemarketing firms have located in the rural Midwest, particularly Nebraska, which has the most deregulated state telecommunications policy in the country. Electronic Marketing Resource Group (EMRG), a relatively small company that processes 40 percent of the nation's college financial-aid applications, and Cabela's, the world's second largest mail-order sporting goods outlet, were studied as examples of telecommunications-intensive firms. Both companies are located in Kearney, Nebraska, a small town 200 miles west of Omaha. These companies were selected because they demonstrate the ability of telecommunications to overcome distance and to bring economic potential to rural areas. They are also good examples of how the presence of telemarketing firms can help draw advanced telecommunications infrastructure to rural areas.

MANUFACTURING

The growth of large manufacturing companies in the twentieth century has involved the spatial dispersion of multiplant production units, throughout the country and the world. The communications needs for the management of such far-flung operations have been a driving force in telecommunications development. Improvements in telecommunications technologies in the late 1960s and early 1970s made it feasible for large manufacturers to move branch plants into rural areas to enjoy cheaper labor and better amenities. Although this trend slowed in the 1980s due to foreign competition and lower offshore labor costs, the advancements of recent years in transmission technologies provide U.S. manufacturers the opportunity to gain a competitive edge in the marketplace. Telecommunications has enabled certain manufacturers to maintain operations in dispersed locations, especially locations in remote rural areas. Several resource-based industries (e.g., oil, pulp, mining) use modern communications systems to track their field operations. The need for corporate headquarters to exchange information with branch manufacturing plants and to be informed of current inventory information is ably met by advanced communications systems. Getting products delivered in time for sale is vital to the success of many of these businesses. These activities depend on an effective communications network.

In the early 1980s, the appearance of high-capacity T-carriers provided a solution for corporations that needed to transmit large volumes of data and voice messages between headquarters and branch plants. In the mid-1980s, the development of the very small aperture terminal (VSAT) satellite offered similar advantages but also allowed companies to privatize their communications networks since they would own the antennas and lease satellite time.

The early application of satellite communication required a huge and relatively expensive earth station as well as dedicated satellite capacity.[8] As the technology improved, the size of the dish decreased and the price dropped. The first VSAT earth station with a two-foot dish for data reception was introduced in 1981. The existence of the very small aperture earth terminal made it cost efficient to bring satellite communication directly to the end user's location[9] and offered U.S. corporations an alternative to leased-line communications.

The nature of VSAT technology requires a controlling master station to communicate with numerous remote stations. The capabilities and operation of a master station create the concept of network service.[10] VSAT communications uses fall into three categories: data, video, and voice. In the early 1980s, the primary users of VSAT were the financial and news and media industries for two-way data and one-way video transmission.[11] The technology improved significantly during the next few years. By the mid-1980s, the applications for VSAT communications networks spanned from data to video to voice.[12]

Two-way voice and video are also possible at a higher earth station and satellite capacity cost. Standard video requires a full transponder in terms of both bandwidth and power, with a significant effect on earth station cost. Voice applications are almost exclusively limited to "closed network" requirements, where a private network is advantageous from a cost or availability standpoint; but the voice traffic, by design, is limited to supporting communications from the corporate headquarters to the branch locations.[13]

Corporations embrace VSAT technology for specific applications relevant to their competitiveness and growth. The technology that was initially implemented in the finance and banking industries has expanded to support two-way applications in retail, hotel, and data-processing industries. Today, large businesses are persuaded to install VSAT networks mainly for their ability to provide cost-effective bypass transmission alternatives.[14] The FCC's deregulation of Ku-band satellite frequency has played an important role in boosting the use of VSAT systems (which primarily use Ku-band frequency), particularly among large corporations. Because distance is relatively irrelevant to satellites, the VSAT network is ideal for companies with a central control unit and a large number of nodes. In the meantime, break-throughs in research on fiber optics provided a transmission tech-nology with almost unlimited capacity. These technologies have allowed manufacturers to remain in rural areas and have become strategically valuable for their operations. Deere & Company and Weyerhaeuser offer illustrative information on how telecommunica-tions can aid rural manufacturing.

CASE STUDY: DEERE & COMPANY

According to Deere & Company's 1988 annual report, Deere & Company is "the free world's largest producer of agricultural equip-ment since 1963." With 1988 income of about $179 million,[15] Deere's consolidated group includes manufacturing plants in Kernersville, South Carolina; Horicon, Wisconsin; and Coffeeville, Kansas, and a retailing force of employees who visit and service small dealers in several countries[16] and facilities as far away as Mannheim, Germany. John Deere Credit Company sells property and life insurance and is said to be the carrier of choice for outboard marine boats. Another Deere subsidiary develops, builds, and markets diesel and rotary engines for off-highway use.[17]

Deere is primarily involved with the manufacture and distribution of farm implements such as tractors, harvesting machines, and other machinery that works the soil. An industrial section builds bulldozers, tractors, and forestry products such as log skidders, and a lawn and grounds care group makes lawn mowers and tractors for home and landscape maintenance. Deere & Company uses voice and data com-munications to connect employees and franchisees throughout its headquarters, factories, and distribution centers.

Telecommunications Uses

Deere has four categories of telecommunications needs. The first is corporate office management and integration, which includes local area voice and data ties through its headquarters in Moline, Illinois. The company's communications network carries current sales, finan-cial, personnel, manufacturing, and distribution figures in supporting the primary business.

A second category of telecommunications focuses on coordinating manufacturing. Deere's administration facility must exchange information with its manufacturing plants in Waterloo, Davenport, Dubuque, and Des Moines, Iowa; Silvus and Moline, Illinois; Horicon, Wisconsin; Coffeeville, Kansas; Greenville, Tennessee; Saltillo and Monterrey, Mexico; Welland, Ontario, Canada; Mannheim, Germany; and its joint venture with Hitachi in Kernersville, South Carolina. These production centers also trade design information with each other as part of the innovation process.

The third category involves the inventory management system's use of telecommunications to transmit and receive voice and data for use by marketing and warehouse branches. Providing current inventory information is vital to these branches; each party must know what is available to sell. Such information might include the status of special-order tractors proceeding through a manufacturing plant or the availability of a specific axle needed to repair a broken corn planter.

The fourth type of telecommunications use at Deere concerns communicating with franchisees. These units are independently owned by dealers. The success of a Deere retailer often depends upon order-processing speed; the owner must be able to locate Deere parts and equipment and ensure quick delivery to the customer. Deere promises overnight transmission of merchandise to purchasers and makes available a 24-hour telephone line to take overnight orders.

Deere's systems illustrate how large businesses use and integrate communications facilities. All Deere divisions must trade voice and data to administer the business. In addition, segments exchange manufacturing and inventory information to serve the Deere client.

Segments of the Deere communications network are privately controlled, including VSAT dishes, telephones, dedicated lines, and microwave transmissions. To supply telecommunications services, Deere has a nine-person group, excluding one outside consultant, and a two-person staff (one full-time and one half-time) centered in Mannheim, Germany. The telecommunications department reports to the John Deere Information Systems (JDIS) Division, which is led by its vice-president of engineering, information, and technology.

Role of Telecommunications

The telecommunications department provides continuous voice and data transmission connections to and from each Deere-related operation. It is linked to nearly every department within the company. Telecommunications and other JDIS corporate sections often take each other's trouble calls. However, each section within JDIS has a separate hardware agenda. For telecommunications, the focus is on securing the most cost-efficient equipment for transmitting and receiving voice and data communications. Yet Deere also must provide prompt parts replacement and delivery information to potential customers through its dealer communications. Substandard customer service risks losing parts, and eventually tractor, sales to more expedient competitors.

Telecommunications equipment is obtained in two ways. First, an annual budget covers the purchase of some equipment as well as regular maintenance, telephones, software, and related appliances. Specific allocations are made for special large purchases (separate from the operating budget), although these sums can be preempted by other more immediate needs of the company. Such needs might include subsidizing a dealer for VSAT or new microwave relays if top management's approval is obtained.

Organizational decision-making style varies from place to place. While Deere makes deliberate and careful decisions, other companies make decisions in a faster, less planned manner. Organizationally, Deere also makes decisions in a top-down fashion. For example, it does not inform managers of its long-term corporate plan. This can cause problems when certain parts of the company need or expect support from top management. The telecommunications department has a good history of careful purchases and cost-saving choices, so management executives often quickly approve choices made by the telecommunications unit. Major hardware investments must gain approval through a much slower process.

Adopting Technology

The telecommunications management at Deere believes advanced technology is essential to the future success of the company.[18] The company has implemented advanced manufacturing processes in its assembly lines, utilizing "just-in-time" technology. "Just-in-time" systems for managing inventory and delivering products are in vogue among top industrialists nationally and internationally. They invoke careful planning in order to have what is needed available at exactly the right time and place. In addition, advanced technological processes allow tractors to be built to purchasers' specifications. Utilizing telecommunications technology is also part of Deere's plan. But although Deere employees have adopted voice mail and computer terminals, other innovations have not been as easily accepted by personnel and management.[19]

William Coopman, Deere's telecommunications manager, cited two examples of difficult or unsuccessful adoptions. One involved a VSAT network; the other was corporate video. Deere knows that Caterpillar Corporation, one of its competitors, is two generations ahead in its communications system with its franchisees or dealers. Caterpillar initiated a multidrop network of lines direct to its dealers and later replaced it with a VSAT system. Deere too would like to move from telephone to VSAT for customers' orders. Five Deere distributors have begun using VSAT dishes to expedite inventory replenishment.[20] For Deere, a complete conversion to VSAT for franchisees would benefit both the company's and dealer's profits. Coopman said, "The dealers who have gone on [VSAT], they've saved money [from their telephone bills] and the response time is better. . . . To me, satellite makes all the sense in the world where you don't have the terrestrial facilities or you have to disseminate the same information to many people."[21] However, if he had to choose between equally capable terrestrial or satellite systems, he would choose the more reliable land-based links.

Nevertheless, adopting VSATs has proved to be a difficult process. Company officials have not given the telecommunications department approval to replace its phone service to dealers. "Even though a system was completely planned, the company had not decided on how it would subsidize installations at dealers' sites,"[22] Coopman said, adding that management likes the current telephone system and does not yet understand the need for a more advanced network.

Deere is not replacing the existing network with VSAT as Caterpillar did when it replaced drop lines with VSAT. Caterpillar management had already accepted a need for superior communication and response time to dealers. Unlike Deere, Caterpillar dealt only with replacement of obsolete technology, not with initial adoption. Changing its conservative system to an advanced technology means a radical shift for Deere. If VSAT is adopted, Coopman said, Deere will own all dishes within its system, "so we control the level of technology."[23] The decision to invest in new technology when existing equipment works well enough is a difficult one, particularly for a company like Deere that operates on a lean budget. The company's purchase of used telephones at 18 cents apiece is perhaps emblematic of its thriftiness—a quality not always in harmony with innovation.

In the second situation (corporate video), the John Deere Television department was created to improve intercompany communication through internally produced conventional and slow-scan video. One application for video was editing of a newsletter betwen two publicity departments, one in Illinois and the other in Germany, in addition to more routine teleconferencing applications.

Corporate video conferencing, however, was unsuccessful. Coopman said people do not want teleconferencing in place of meetings, which come with certain bonuses. Another problem may have been timing: "I think we were too early. Senior management had trouble understanding it, accepting it . . . we were looked at as those crazy people who were playing with technology."[24] Such an attitude is not uncommon among companies when faced with new technological options. Adoption of new technology is clearly related to the company's corporate culture.

Deere has successfully used many other telecommunications innovations. For example, it installed a private overseas line between its Moline and Mannheim plants through Overseas Telecommunications, Inc.[25] Along with the five dealer VSAT dishes, Deere also implemented a T-1 carrier network. Deere also uses teletype (electronic or E mail) and dedicated lines (for incoming 800 numbers and outgoing WATS [Wide Area Telephone Service] lines). A microwave system links its Waterloo, Iowa, plant with the Moline headquarters. Pagers, mobile radio, Centrex service, fiber phone lines in the Waterloo plant, PBX (private branch exchange) equipment, personal computers, and an IBM mainframe together are utilized to run the Deere phone network.[26]

It seems clear that the telecommunications department can pave the way for technology decisions. For example, the department helps make site decisions when Deere opens new plants. At one potential plant location, the telecommunications envoy noticed that the nearest pay telephone was five miles away. This became a clue to a potential problem: the local phone company's lines stopped at that point. Moving to the location would have meant a $5 million infrastructure investment for Deere because microwave relays would have been needed to meet corporate requirements. Deere chose another location for the plant.[27] While the development implications and constraints of inadequate telephone service will be discussed in more detail in later chapters, it is worthwhile to note that a rural location will be at a decided disadvantage if it cannot meet the telecommunications requirements of firms searching for potential sites.

The Public and Private Networks

Public phone companies are the backbone of Deere's intercompany service. Since satellite communication has not been extensively utilized and since microwave and fiber optics have limited uses to the company, outside carriers are patronized. Therefore, Deere is not as concerned about obsolescence of privately owned equipment as some companies might be. The goal of the telecommunications department is to purchase VSAT and other appropriate equipment in time to remain competitive with its competition. Until large hardware purchases are made, obsolescence will remain a minor problem.

Deere's telecommunications network is comprised of dedicated private lines, private Centrex switches, VSAT dishes, company-owned fiber phone lines, and microwave communications links. None of these facilities are available for use to the public, and some of them remove potential revenue for the local exchange carrier. Nevertheless, there are several public advantages accruing to Deere's system.

For example, the company has provided the Moline community with information it needed to intervene during local telephone rate cases, before the state regulation commission, regarding message rate service, rate hikes, and exchange boundaries.[28] Illinois, which is primarily served by Illinois Bell as the intraLATA carrier, has a regulatory environment that encourages competition.[29] Several services have been designated as competitive and are deregulated. The state's public utilities commission, the Illinois Commerce Commission (ICC), can exclude from regulatory review services such as private-line services not used to originate or terminate switched services, cellular radio, and high-speed data transmission.[30]

In this environment Deere privately negotiated its Centrex contract and its local area network with Illinois Bell. The ICC accepted this arrangement, which was based upon the company's buying power and use. The headquarters town may also benefit from Deere's presence because MCI and US Sprint are considering putting a point of presence in Moline to gain Deere's service.

CASE STUDY: WEYERHAEUSER

Weyerhaeuser uses data and voice communications to connect employees in its two Tacoma, Washington, headquarters with 81 other domestic sites. These locations include 14.8 million acres of productive timberland in North America, which supply logging camps, milling and processing facilities, and papermaking factories. Weyerhaeuser, after the recession of the 1980s, has diversified and also owns a mortgage company with two main California locations.[31] A firm with diverse businesses scattered geographically, Weyerhaeuser has initiated several advantageous telecommunications applications.

Unlike most companies, Weyerhaeuser's telecommunications department does not serve each company facility. The group is organized under Weyerhaeuser Information Systems (WIS), which operates as if it were a separate company. Weyerhaeuser employees are considered customers, not users. Employees' cost centers are charged for each service provided by WIS and are not discouraged from patronizing another supplier that can offer quality service at a lower rate. WIS, however, attempts to meet prices of competition if it can. WIS, in effect, attempts to sell both to customers within and outside Weyer-haeuser.[32] Weyerhaeuser is one of several corporations following this "service bureau" approach to management information services.

WIS is divided into several divisions, including the information systems division and parallel divisions for manufacturing systems, telecommunications services, and financial services and administration.[33] Like many other large corporations, Weyerhaeuser's basic approach is to maintain its large-capacity "pipelines" where the quantity of use justifies it. It is moving toward software-defined networks for more lightly used communication traffic patterns and could soon be doing a great deal of its interLATA business with one large carrier. The following sections detail some aspects of WIS's telecommunications network.

Telecommunications Uses

The Weyerhaeuser Data Network (WDN) is a part of the Telecommunications Systems Division (TSD). The operations group of WDN includes a private "telephone company"-like group which operates buried cable along railway right-of-way in Valiant, Oklahoma. WIS customers in the telecommunications division are currently limited to Weyerhaeuser employees. No excess capacity is currently sold to outsiders.[34]

WDN's hardware links 4,600 lines by a series of connected T-1 carrier multiplexed lines that feed from Weyerhaeuser facilities through the public-switched network. Because the national public telephone network was designed with its strongest backbone from northeast to southwest (New York to Los Angeles), and Weyerhaeuser uses lines northwest to southeast (from its Tacoma headquarters to its southern facilities), the company's connection costs are higher than if the conventional direction were used by Weyerhaeuser. Consequently, T-1 and 800 lines are heavily utilized. Long-distance carriers include US Sprint, which provides a virtual private network, and AT&T, which supplies a software-defined network.[35]

In Tacoma, Weyerhaeuser uses a Centrex switch provided by US West. It is serviced by three remotes which, in total, serve 4,600 lines. The Tacoma Weyerhaeuser telecommunications staff, which maintains these lines, includes three installers, two outside contractors, four operators, and analysts and engineers. One person's sole job is processing the company's monthly 400 adds, moves, and changes.

An important data link for Weyerhaeuser is between headquarters and its mortgage company in California. The location in Woodland Hills contributes to Weyerhaeuser's total profit, and its data needs are substantial. Duplicate communications systems were designed for that service, with one set of T-1 lines to avoid the earthquake-prone portions of California west of the San Andreas fault.[36]

Company policy strongly supports the establishment of the necessary technological infrastructure. During a site visit to Weyerhaeuser's Longview paper-processing facility, it was apparent that putting hardware into place is a function of the local budgeting process, with local plant managers responsible for implementations at each facility. However, progressive telecommunications practices were evidently supported by management at each location.

However, these systems may change. The US West–owned Centrex contract expires in 1991. An internal Danray switch, owned by Weyerhaeuser, is obsolete, and Weyerhaeuser needs more functionality to accommodate greater user needs. James Davis, Weyerhaeuser telecommunications systems project manager, said his local area network may find an integrated digital service network too slow and too costly for its needs. (About four billion billable characters move through the lines each month, largely between Tacoma and other company locations.[37])

Key Telecommunications Concerns

Richard Sherwood, a Weyerhaeuser telecommunications project manager, mentioned four key issues faced by TSD. First, "restoral versus repair" invokes the issue of placing redundant lines so that, if one wire fails, only a few minutes of connection time would be lost. Since many plant processes are automated and computerized, long outages could be devastating. The company does not have three days to locate and repair broken lines. (A redundant system with immediate restoral has provided over two months of perfect service to Weyerhaeuser Mortgage Company in California.)[38]

The second issue is the cost and availability of bandwidth. Weyerhaeuser decided it needs 56 kilobytes (KB) for its communications, but most rural local telephone companies cannot supply this. In addition, the Canadian rates are much more expensive than U.S. rates, leading to high costs for Weyerhaeuser when interfacing systems from the United States to Canada. However, in 1992 the expiration of Canadian tariffs may lower the high telecommunications costs in Canada.[39]

A third difficult area, related to the second, is T-1 line sharing. Weyerhaeuser has been leasing portions, or fractions, of lines for different needs, such as combining data and voice in separate fractions. Leasing an entire line, if combining the separated functions, was found to be more expensive than leasing just the total of the fractions.[40]

Finally, local area network (LAN)/wide area network (WAN) inter-facing is problematic. It is difficult to connect one network to another because different network systems controllers, or protocols, do not necessarily interface with each other. Controlling systems or software may conflict and cause impossible linkages.[41] At the Tacoma WDN Network Control Center, this difficulty manifests itself through a series of systems controllers. Several panels, each running and diag-nosing a separate group of wires, are needed to control Weyer-haeuser's voice and data networks. An umbrella system that could combine the functions of the several, separate controllers and proto-cols is desirable.[42]

Adopting Technology

WIS is headed by Vice-President Susan Mersereau, who gained a reputation in 1985 with her cost-effective implementation of applica-tions support. The company sought decentralization and Mersereau provided the tools. Mersereau maintained the few centralized depart-ments, which include telecommunications, central computing, and personnel applications support.[43]

Mersereau's technological leadership and agenda have been em-braced by the company. Weyerhaeuser remains a leader in the adop-tion of new telecommunications technologies, using the most current equipment to support its main businesses of forest products and paper.

Although Weyerhaeuser has adopted many new technologies under the profit center concept, not all new equipment is readily accepted. One example is videoconferencing. Although Weyerhaeuser tested high-quality facilities for this site-linking technology, employees did not immediately use it. Richard Sherwood said videoconferencing may succeed for areas in which travel is prohibitive (where it takes a day to approach the location) and for repetitive uses.[44] Additionally, as technology costs drop and user friendliness increases, overall use is likely to grow, according to Sherwood. The paper company, for example, is going to install videoconferencing equipment in its major mills and sales locations as a direct result of an initial test pilot program conducted in 1990.

Relationship with the Public Network

Mersereau contributes to several community organizations in-volved with telecommunications by serving on an advisory board for the governor of Washington State, sponsoring participation in the local AT&T large users group, and maintaining TRACER, a group of large telecommunications users in Washington actively supported by Weyerhaeuser.[45] Because of this participation, Weyerhaeuser can affect the outcome of tariff decisions by the Washington Utilities and Transportation Commission (WUTC). The WUTC regulates "intraLATA toll service as a noncompetitive market," where all alternative providers "must enter the network via access through the local exchange carriers."[46] TRACER "has maintained an active role in part because it feels the WUTC is more inclined to favor small consumers," and its participation is a leveling influence.[47] Weyerhaeuser's position is similar to that of many large businesses, both rural and urban. To the extent that it can find cheaper or better telecommunications service and avoid the access charges of local service, Weyerhaeuser believes it should do so. While this attitude is perfectly understandable, there are negative implications for the local network, which loses customers, and for small businesses, which are not able to bypass. This point will be discussed more fully in subsequent chapters.

RETAILING

The discount retailing industry traditionally has operated in metropolitan markets due to population density advantages. Yet this type of retailing service also has a place in rural communities and may be a profitable niche for the industry if some of the problems faced by rural areas are overcome.

A major problem for rural retailing is obtaining merchandise because manufacturers and distributors do not rush to get goods to stores in remote areas. One solution is for the retailer to provide the distribution capabilities so that the stores can order regularly and receive merchandise quickly. If stores can have guaranteed delivery, they do not need to build a large storage room, thus facilitating better stock position and keeping costs down. However, a good distribution system is not viable without a good communications network, especially when greater shipping distances are involved.

In addition to distribution difficulties, retailing in rural areas has problems similar to those in other multilocation businesses—keeping headquarters informed of current sales, financial, and personnel data. When these problems, often exacerbated in relatively remote settings, are overcome by innovative communications technologies, rural communities can be profitable venues for retailers. Rural markets do offer a few distinct operating advantages, such as lower rents, a moderate-wage labor force, a more loyal customer base, and a productive work force.

CASE STUDY: WAL-MART

Located in a small town in northwest Arkansas, west of the Ozark Mountains, Wal-Mart Stores, Inc., quietly runs a retail empire. The Bentonville-based general merchandise discounter is a familiar name to most people, particularly in the Midwest and South, where the discount store is almost omnipresent.

Since the first Wal-Mart discount store opened in 1962 in Rogers, Arkansas, the company has been on a fast track. Wal-Mart has climbed from a relatively unknown regional chain, operating only 276 stores in 11 states in 1979,[48] to the nation's largest and most profitable retailer, operating over 1,700 stores in 36 states.[49] Since 1990, Wal-Mart not only has surpassed the stagnating Sears, Roebuck & Company as the leader in retailing, but has expanded its territory into California and New York states, making the chain a true national merchant.[50] The 29-year-old retailer's spectacular growth and expansion is a remarkable story and has drawn national recognition in recent years. The secret behind the story is technology,[51] which allows the company to exploit rural markets and to gain a foothold in urban centers as well.

Wal-Mart's discount stores are typically located in small rural towns, although more outlets are being opened in and around metropolitan areas. The rural setting has the advantages of lower operating costs, the loyalty of a committed work force, and better amenities. Even more significant is that the dispersed and remote environment perpetuates the need for Wal-Mart to integrate modern communications technologies. Wal-Mart is one of the first chains to recognize the potential of small towns; it has found enormous profit and growth opportunities in the out-of-the-way markets that others have ignored. Advanced communications technologies have played an important role in the company's ability to reap the windfall of rural markets. Innovative telecommunications technologies such as satellites have turned rural barriers into advantages. Companies like Wal-Mart are proof that businesses can be run effectively in small towns.

Wal-Mart has a corporate culture that is very innovative. It encourages employee involvement in all stages of the innovation process. This corporate culture is also reflected in its use of innovative technology. It was the first major retailer to adopt the universal product code (UPC) as the marking technology for merchandise that was already being bar-coded by manufacturers for sale in supermarkets. The bar-code scanning system not only speeds up checkouts but allows the company to track merchandise.[52] Wal-Mart also uses computer-aided design to help chart marketing strategies. Its extensive utilization of computers in its headquarters has facilitated fast internal communication. Yet the cream of the company's technology is not any of these. The technology Wal-Mart is most proud of is VSAT, which Wal-Mart initiated in 1985.

The business satellite network features a central hub facility with a very small aperture terminal at each branch outlet. Wal-Mart's initial trial system reduced data and voice costs significantly, justifying more widespread use of VSAT in company operations. The company then capitalized on its investment by searching out and developing several other benefits that could accrue from using the technology.[53] By 1991 Wal-Mart's VSAT network supported two-way data and voice communications between its headquarters in Bentonville, Arkansas, and 1,590 Wal-Mart stores, 178 Sam's Wholesale Clubs, 4 Hypermarts, and 18 distribution centers across the country. In addition, the VSAT network transmits training and promotional video from headquarters to each operation unit.

Adopting Technology

The remote location of Wal-Mart's headquarters and the large number of its retail outlets made telephone service costly. In addition, the terrestrial telephone facilities in these rural locations were not always reliable. With increasing competition and the company's commitment to growth and expansion, Wal-Mart opted for a VSAT communications network that included all major communications components: voice, data, and video. In 1985 the company began a pilot program of a VSAT network that would provide two-way voice and data and one-way video transmission. The initial test turned out to be very successful. Wal-Mart completed installation of the nation's largest private satellite communication network in 1987.[54] This VSAT network provides the discounter with faster and more reliable data transmission and voice messages at less cost than the previous leased-line communications.

The voice use of Wal-Mart's VSAT network is probably the most unique and cost-effective application. It is unique because to date Wal-Mart is the only corporation that utilizes VSAT for telephone purposes on such a large scale. There are at least two reasons for the lack of interest among VSAT users for this specific application. First, the voice takes up a large bandwidth from the satellite and requires sophisticated and expensive equipment.[55] Second, there is a slight delay associated with a satellite-transmitted telephone call. Wal-Mart, however, is able to utilize the satellite bandwidth in such an efficient way that both data and voice can share the same satellite capacity. Furthermore, Wal-Mart uses VSAT only for internal communications—between headquarters and branch outlets. Since Wal-Mart owns all its retail outlets, the company can require its employees to use VSAT for voice communications despite the undesirable delay.

Since the satellite is not distance-sensitive, it is ideal for Wal-Mart's multilocation operations. Moreover, the costs of satellite transponders are fixed and not affected by the volume and length of phone calls. Wal-Mart estimates that the VSAT network saves two-thirds of its long-distance telephone costs.[56] Further, it allows the company more control over its communications. The company no longer has to rely on the 400 telephone companies that it previously dealt with for voice communications. Wal-Mart still uses the public-switched network as a redundant system for emergency purposes.[57]

The private network simplifies the dialing procedure for any extension within the system. Using a six-digit number, an employee at headquarters can simply dial directly any Wal-Mart store. If an employee from a store needs to call headquarters, he or she has only to dial a four-digit extension number to reach a certain department or executive in the General Office, the company headquarters facility. The VSAT phone system in a store is programmed to reach only the Arkansas headquarters; thus communication between stores through VSAT is inhibited.

In the data network, the previously leased multidrop network has been completely replaced by the satellite system.[58] VSAT provides two-way data transmission that is much faster, more reliable, and of higher capacity. The link between Wal-Mart's high-capacity computers and the VSAT network keeps headquarters informed of all transactions in each store at every minute. Unlike the previously used leased-line network, the VSAT network also allows stores to place orders simultaneously, speeding up the ordering process.

Video is a more recent form of communications supported in Wal-Mart's VSAT network, and it is used to provide video training, to facilitate teleconferencing and marketing applications, and to deliver executive addresses. Each Wal-Mart store, Sam's Wholesale Club, Hypermart, and distribution center receives biweekly video motivational or instructional messages from Wal-Mart executives. Although the VSAT network has the capability to transmit two-way video, Wal-Mart uses it only for one-way broadcast delivery.

Wal-Mart has already realized a return on investment through lower communications costs in voice and data. The discounter has also capitalized on its investment by searching out and developing other benefits that can accrue from using the technology. In 1988, it added to its satellite system a credit authorization system, which is referred to as "point-of-sale" in the industry. In this application, it takes five seconds, on average, to verify a credit card; previously, the same procedure required a phone call that took about five minutes.[59]

The satellite network has also been used to test a truck location system whereby each delivery truck's exact location would be relayed to headquarters every 15 minutes.[60] Although Wal-Mart has not really pursued this application, VSAT does have the ability to provide a truck-tracking system. In 1990 Wal-Mart launched a broadcast background music system that piggybacks a Muzak-type background music system on the VSAT network. All Wal-Mart shoppers can listen to the same music regardless of which store they are in.

Configuration of Wal-Mart's VSAT Network

Wal-Mart's VSAT network is now one of the world's largest, operating 1,700 VSAT antennas at retail and wholesale outlets, headquarters, and distribution centers. With the demonstrated success of this network, several other retailers have embarked on similar programs. For example, K mart, Wal-Mart's primary competitor, has announced plans to launch a comparable system. In 1990 the retailing industry represented 24.8 percent of the VSAT market.[61]

Wal-Mart leases a Ku-band satellite transponder 24 hours a day for two-way voice and data transmission between each store's computers and the main network in Bentonville. The voice application takes up 45 percent of the available bandwidth while data transmission uses only 30 to 40 percent. The background music system uses the same transponder.[62] The company leases a second Ku-band satellite transponder to transmit its biweekly video messages. This transponder is leased only on an hourly basis. Both data and voice signals are digital while the video is analog. In its voice application, VSAT allows 84 simultaneous channels.

In Wal-Mart's Bentonville headquarters, a ground-mounted 9.1-meter satellite dish is responsible for transmitting and receiving all the data and voice signals. It also transmits the one-way video information and is used for the music signals. Although this earth station has the capability of receiving video information, the company does not yet utilize it in a two-way mode. Another 3.5-meter dish is placed next to the main dish. This satellite dish supports the health claims network for the 325,000 Wal-Mart employees nationwide. There are four smaller dishes ranging in size from 1.8 to 2.4 meters mounted on the rooftop of the General Office buildings. Their functions vary— from receiving training programs to diagnostic testing and troubleshooting.[63]

The majority of Wal-Mart's retail outlets are equipped with 1.8-meter or 6-foot dishes. Although a VSAT dish can be as small as two feet, a larger dish is required to receive video signals.[64] These dishes are mounted on the rooftop because most of Wal-Mart's store facilities are leased buildings in shopping centers, and ground installations were deemed impractical. The decision was made to use nonpenetrating mounts on rooftops, which reduced costs associated with any heavy site preparation.[65]

Advantages of the Technology

According to Jay Allen, the former manager of Wal-Mart's satellite department, there are four major advantages to the VSAT system.[66] First, it is flexible. The system allows easy and quick addition of sites. One can also change baud rate with a keystroke and add new applications, such as a bandwidth channel, without worrying about overtaxing the system. Second, it is cost effective. Allen estimated that if Wal-Mart tried to use phone lines to do what it does now with the satellite, there would be a 300-percent increase in cost. (On average, the satellite-transmitted phone calls cost as little as four cents per minute.) Third, the VSAT system is efficient, offering a coupling of real time and batch processing in a bandwidth-efficient way. And, finally, VSAT is fairly reliable and allows control over the communications medium by its user.

In addition to the advantages mentioned by Wal-Mart's engineers, VSAT networks have some benefits over terrestrial networks. Satellite transmission is not distance-sensitive, and therefore it is ideally suited to carry traffic over long distances to many different locations. Another advantage is that VSAT network management systems are easier to use than systems that manage terrestrial networks. The latter usually involve both the interexchange carrier and the local exchange carrier. With a VSAT system users can get a single network management system.[67]

Wal-Mart's VSAT network also greatly facilitates the company's ability to operate the most sophisticated inventory control system in the industry.[68] Wal-Mart practices the manufacturing industry's "just-in-time" concept for its inventory control through the VSAT network, the company's high-speed computer system, which "links virtually all the stores to headquarters and the company's 16 distribution centers, electronically logs every item sold at the checkout counter, automatically keeps the warehouses informed of merchandise to be ordered and directs the flow of goods to the stores and even to the proper shelves."[69]

Such in-depth inventory control helps detect sales trends quickly and speeds up market reaction time substantially. Furthermore, the automatic replenishment system reduces storage room, increases merchandise turnover, and reduces costs. Wal-Mart has so fine-tuned communications between its stores, suppliers, distribution centers, and its trucking fleet that to resupply a store with a product takes only a day.[70] Wal-Mart stores get 75 percent of their merchandise through the company's 16 distribution centers[71]—eliminating middleman costs. The automated communications network helps Wal-Mart keep distribution costs at about half of those of most other chains.[72]

How important is the satellite network to Wal-Mart's operation? According to Allen, Wal-Mart stores are heavily dependent on it: "They would not be able to provide the dynamic services with the price pointing without it. The way that Wal-Mart does business is tremendously benefited by the addition of a real-time satellite communication system."[73]

In an extremely fast-changing environment, technologies are easily outdated. Wal-Mart is aware of the threat of technological obsolescence and, despite its use of the most advanced technologies, is still looking for better ones. Wal-Mart recognizes that the competitive edge that VSAT provides is only short term and would like to explore more opportunities on the technological frontier. The company has an interest in an integrated digital service network, believed by its engineers to be the stepping-stone to the future.

Public Consequences

Retailers' use of bypass technologies that give them flexibility and lower costs has rebound effects on traditional communication providers and on the communities in which the businesses operate.

Impacts on the Public Telephone Network. Because of the presence of Wal-Mart's headquarters in Bentonville (population 10,000), MCI has established a point of presence (POP) in the community. This is significant because competitive long-distance carriers usually do not serve a town this small due to limited demand. However, the large quantity of long-distance communications that Wal-Mart generates justifies MCI's investment. As a result, the city of Bentonville enjoys equal access to a non–AT&T long-distance carrier, a luxury for most small rural towns. Telephone companies did not favor the development of privately owned communication networks because it cut into their revenue. Their function as the sole telecommunications-service provider for the large user is being displaced as they integrate with a user's private system.

Furthermore, telephone companies are now more in tune with businesses' communications needs. As the telecommunications industry becomes more competitive, telephone companies will offer inducements for large users to employ their services. They are also receptive to playing a supportive role in large users' privately built communications networks and are willing to negotiate tariffs. Telephone companies now are more willing to integrate with large corporations' private communication systems, such as Wal-Mart's VSAT network, because the hybrid technologies are available and more and more large corporations are establishing their own private networks.[74]

Economic Impacts on Rural Towns. When a Wal-Mart store opens in a small or medium-sized town with little population growth, there will be an economic impact on other local businesses. Kenneth Stone, an economics professor at Iowa State University, recently studied the impact of Wal-Mart stores on other businesses in Iowa.[75] According to this study, after a Wal-Mart store moved into a town the total retail business increased—an increase that was primarily Wal-Mart's gain and that was at the expense of existing merchants. According to Stone, "There will be some beneficial 'spillover' sales accruing to some firms, primarily restaurants and building materials firms. However, several existing merchants will suffer losses of sales unless they make adjustments to compete in the new environment."[76] Stone's study also found that Wal-Mart stores took business away from downtown stores. Shops on the main streets of smaller towns closed down after Wal-Mart moved in. "It appears that Wal-Mart stores are holding customers in the local area to shop for general merchandise to a greater extent than before, thereby causing fewer shopping trips to the city."[77] Moreover, Stone found that Wal-Mart had greater economic impacts on smaller towns, which suffered more than larger cities.

Another economist, Professor Phil Taylor of the University of Arkansas, has reached similar conclusions. He found that a business was better off if it was located next door to Wal-Mart rather than 20 miles away, primarily because the presence of the Wal-Mart store changed the traffic pattern.[78]

However, a competing study by researchers at the University of Missouri (sponsored by Wal-Mart) suggests that when Wal-Mart moves into a rural town, almost everybody in the area benefits.[79] This study examined the economies of the 14 rural counties where Wal-Mart opened stores in 1983–87. Critics argue that the study covered only a period in which the national economy boomed. Furthermore, it did not compare the economies of counties that had a Wal-Mart store with those that did not.[80]

Although the Iowa and Missouri studies draw conflicting conclusions about Wal-Mart's economic impact on rural towns, both reinforce the importance of Wal-Mart's operation to local economies in rural towns.

TELECOMMUNICATIONS-INTENSIVE BUSINESSES

With the dramatic improvements of telecommunications technologies and the convergence of the telephone and the computer, a host of information-based business operations has emerged. These business activities, often referred to as "back office" operations, include answering 800 numbers, processing credit cards, and processing insurance claims. These information-based businesses can be operated at any location as long as it is equipped with the proper telecommunications infrastructure. Telecommunications developments have enabled such economic activities to decentralize, making it possible for rural economies to participate more actively in the overall economy.

One example of a new telecommunications-based industry is telemarketing, which in recent years has spread rapidly throughout rural areas, particularly in the Midwest. Many telemarketing companies prefer to locate in the Midwest because of the country atmosphere and clean environment, the cheap labor force, the strong work ethic, and the flat midwestern accent—considered desirable for phone work. Consequently, telemarketing may be an increasingly important industry in rural development. The telemarketing concept entails the intelligent and systematic use of telephone communications to improve marketing and retailing productivity. Specialized calling and routing capabilities, as well as recent developments in computer technology, have led to cost-effective telemarketing technology.

There are two types of telemarketing: inbound and outbound. With inbound telemarketing, a client calls the company, presumably in response to a catalog or advertisement. Inbound telemarketing relies on 800-line services. Outbound telemarketing is very different. With outbound telemarketing, a potential market is targeted for direct sales. A phone list of the target market is obtained, and only those customers who are expected to respond are contacted. Consequently, outbound telemarketing generally relies on the discounted dedicated WATS lines. Outbound telemarketing is often used to offer additional services or products to existing customers.

The operation of telemarketing firms or other telecommunications-based information businesses in rural areas may bolster and diversify local economies, even if much of its labor is part time. These businesses provide an alternative for some of the economically depressed communities to survive and even to grow. However, such information businesses require a modern telecommunications infrastructure to handle high-volume telephone traffic efficiently, and unfortunately most rural areas are poorly equipped to meet these needs.

CASE STUDY: ELECTRONIC MARKETING RESOURCE GROUP (EMRG)

Electronic Marketing Resource Group (EMRG) is a telecommunications-based business successfully operating in a rural area. Located in Kearney, Nebraska (population 25,000), this small company of 35 employees provides software, consulting, and data-processing services primarily for college financial-aid offices. EMRG currently controls approximately 40 percent of the national federal Pell Grant electronic processing market.

David T. Waldron founded the company in 1983 not as EMRG but as Software Marketing Associates (SMA), a small software-developing company with Waldron and his wife as its only employees. EMRG did not come into existence until 1985, when Waldron acquired the small electronic financial-aid data-processing companies Advanced Process Laboratories (APL) and M-Data, Inc. EMRG was founded as a parent company under which SMA, APL, and M-Data are organized.

EMRG has continued to grow and diversify. In 1987, EMRG acquired two more small financial-aid data-processing firms (Financial Analysis Service and CompuGrant), which were consolidated with APL and M-Data to form one EMRG company, EDTECH, Inc. Currently, three separate companies and one division comprise EMRG: (1) Software Marketing Associates; (2) EDTECH, Inc.; (3) Executive Management Services (EMS); and (4) the Direct Marketing Center (DMC), a division.[81] It is fundamentally a data- or information-processing firm.

SMA designs and maintains specialized financial applications software. Clients that purchase SMA's products are financial-aid offices of universities, colleges, and trade schools. Other major clients include national insurance companies. One specialized product is a custom-designed program on microelectronic computer chips for handheld computers and desktop calculators used to determine financial-aid eligibility. In FY (fiscal year) 1989, SMA collected maintenance revenue of $100,000 from one national insurance company account alone. Revenues doubled for FY 1990. Marketing for SMA's products is conducted primarily through direct marketing via telecommunications. In fact, all of EMRG's companies use such direct marketing.[82]

EDTECH was formed in 1987 as the education division of the company. As noted above, its formation consolidated four other companies (APL, M-Data, Financial Analysis Service, and CompuGrant) that had been acquired by EMRG. EDTECH provides electronic student financial-aid processing for universities, colleges, and trade schools. EDTECH uses telecommunications to communicate between the client, itself, processing centers, and national data banks. Student aid applications are "batched" or processed by a computer for transmission to the federal Pell Grant data center in Iowa City.[83] EDTECH generated nearly 85 percent of EMRG's total revenue for FY 1989.[84]

EMS is the consulting arm of EMRG. EMS was originally a division of EMRG and was later incorporated as a separate company in January 1989. As of October 1989, EMS was operated as a Nebraska corporation with an office in Reston, Virginia. EMS was created to continue EMRG's diversification and to expand its business function from that of marketing products (software) to that of providing services (transaction processing and consulting).[85]

Another recent addition to EMRG is the Direct Marketing Center. Formed in FY 1989 as a division of EMRG, DMC has become a significant profit maker through direct marketing, customer services, and database services for all EMRG companies. To date, it has been dedicated to EDTECH. DMC has grown from one person to the current staff of eight. The unit also runs an automated telemarketing group, providing both inbound and outbound marketing; it is also experimenting with an automated voice-response system. In 1989, DMC handled 41,272 calls and generated $2,000,000 in revenue. Seven of the eight persons in the unit are on the phone "telemarketing" the company's services through business-to-business telemarketing.[86]

Adopting Technology

The story behind EMRG's presence in Kearney is very different from that of a large business that systematically examines the entire country for an ideal place to locate. (Community development in Kearney is discussed in more detail in Chapter 5.) EMRG could have been operated anywhere, as long as an adequate telecommunications infrastructure was available. The major factor governing the decision to locate EMRG in Kearney was the quality of life Kearney had to offer, a factor that may become increasingly important for small and medium-sized information businesses. EMRG's founder, David Waldron, first went to Kearney in 1983 after selling his small calculator franchise store and software design operation in Denver, Colorado. He and his wife decided that a large city was not the place where they wanted to rear their children. Instead, they preferred an area much like where they had grown up. (Waldron's wife grew up in Aurora, a small town 90 miles east of Kearney.)[87]

Waldron's company experienced rapid growth and diversification in Kearney, and much of the company's success can be attributed to Waldron's ingenuity. Several other factors have also been critical. One major player has been the community of Kearney. For example, the acquisition of APL and M-Data were in part financed through Community Development Block Grant monies provided through the Buffalo County Economic Development Council. In return for a $250,000 loan, EMRG agreed to provide Kearney with 26 jobs. Moreover, Kearney now owns 10 percent of EMRG.[88]

EMRG works closely with the Buffalo County Economic Development Council and the Kearney Chamber of Commerce, of which Waldron is a member. Together they have helped to attract larger telecommunications users (e.g., telemarketers, WATS Telemarketing, and Cabela's), which in turn have attracted more telecommunications infrastructure to Kearney. Bringing telemarketers into town was a planned strategy, and the strategy has worked.[89] As discussed in the next section the presence of Cabela's in Kearney led AT&T to install a point of presence (POP) at Cabela's; the switch is actually located in the company's building, possibly the first POP in a private business.[90] EMRG should also benefit from the POP. It will soon be able to connect or "piggyback" onto AT&T lines and consequently reduce telephone costs considerably. At times EMRG overwhelms the capacity of the local GTE phone system. To connect to some long-distance switches 40 miles away in Grand Island, GTE must rely on lines owned by US West. Thus far, US West has not seen any reason to expand those lines, so there is a capacity bottleneck in the local exchange service. US Sprint's high-capacity transcontinental line runs just two blocks from EMRG's front door, but US Sprint will not connect Kearney for a "small" customer.[91] Limited telecommunications capacity can hurt a business like EMRG. In one instance, Waldron passed up the opportunity to bid on a major federal database contract, in part because the GTE phone system would not have been able to handle the volume.[92]

Another major factor that has allowed EMRG to grow and continue its presence in Kearney is the local state college. Kearney State College provides Kearney, the surrounding rural areas, and the entire state with well-educated people. (The state college became affiliated with the University of Nebraska in 1990.) Waldron notes that while the individuals he hires are not adequately trained for specific jobs in his company, they are well educated and thus easily trained.[93] EMRG's employees mainly come from Kearney and the surrounding communities, and some have been recruited from out of state. Most EMRG jobs require a high level of education because many of the jobs are technical.[94] Thus, Kearney State College is an important resource for EMRG.

The importance of Kearney State College for the future of the local communities and businesses is well recognized by Kearney's community and business leadership. The importance of technology and telecommunications is also acknowledged. With this in mind, local community leaders, business leaders, and college officials together developed a telecommunications management program at Kearney State College where a student can earn a bachelor of science in telecommunications management.[95] It is important to note that the business leaders of Kearney are also the town's community leaders; they all work together to develop business, jobs, and opportunities for the town—the growth and success of EMRG exemplifies such a total town commitment. This facet of Kearney is examined further in Chapter 5.

Advantages of Technology

The advantages of telecommunications technology for EMRG are quite obvious. Without it, most of EMRG's business activities simply would not exist. Nevertheless, the new technology provides added benefits beyond cost savings.

The technology itself can be used to create and design new products or new operations. EMRG has been able to grow by diversifying its business operations. Waldron reports that EMRG is currently developing an automated voice-response system for the Direct Marketing Center. In fact, all of EMRG's companies continually develop new products.[96]

Telecommunications technology also offers the user the ability to expand in-house operations that would otherwise be contracted to outside firms. For example, EMRG does its own business-to-business marketing via the telephone.[97] Not only does marketing its own products result in substantial savings, it also helps make EMRG more competitive.

Public Consequences

EMRG's presence in Kearney has been very beneficial to the community. The company offers relatively high-paying jobs, with wages averaging over ten dollars an hour, although it does not employ a great number of persons (approximately 35).[98] Nevertheless, there is great potential for the expansion of EMRG and other telecommunications-oriented businesses in Kearney. EMRG's case demonstrates that small businesses can thrive in rural areas by using telecommunications. However, the leadership provided by knowledgeable and resourceful people cannot be underestimated in evaluating the net contribution of technology.

CASE STUDY: CABELA'S

Cabela's represents another example of a telecommunications-oriented business successfully operating in a rural area. Cabela's is a phone-order catalog house and thus an inbound telemarketer. It advertises itself as the "world's foremost outfitter of fishing, hunting, and outdoor gear."[99] Cabela's began operations in 1962 in Sidney, Nebraska, a small rural town of about 6,000. Dick and Jim Cabela started the business by printing flyers and selling fishing flies through the mail.[100]

By the late 1980s, Cabela's had grown into one of the country's largest mail- and phone-order outdoor outfitters. Moreover, with the phenomenal growth in the inbound telemarketing business, Cabela's outgrew the labor resources of Sidney. In 1987, Cabela's opened a new and larger telemarketing center in Kearney, Nebraska. In addition to the telemarketing center, Cabela's opened a warehouse, shipping facility, and a large retail store. In 1988 and 1989, Cabela's experienced a growth rate of 15 to 20 percent a year. During the Christmas season, Cabela's receives so many orders it has to subcontract its inbound telemarketing to Aurora Telemarketing in nearby Aurora. Cabela's is also considering opening a second telemarketing site.[101]

The business employs 300 people during the summer and up to 500 during the winter Christmas season. About 90 percent of the employees are part time; 55 to 60 percent of them are college students, and the rest are either persons working for a second family income or farmers' wives. Thus, most employees are women. Employees primarily come from Kearney, but some commute from surrounding towns as far as 20 miles away. To work at Cabela's, a potential worker does not need a high level of skills or education but does need good communication skills and a strong work ethic. Familiarity with keyboards and typing is also helpful since workers use a computerized ordering system.[102]

Adopting Technology

Cabela's decided to locate in Kearney for a number of reasons, the primary one involving the community of Kearney. Kearney's Chamber of Commerce and the Economic Development Council developed a package to lure the company to the town. Kearney was recruiting telemarketing firms at a time when Cabela's was looking for a new site in Nebraska. With headquarters already in Nebraska, the company wanted to stay in the state.[103] Kearney had a building where Cabela's could start immediate operations. It had been vacated by a manufacturing firm (Rockwell) but was owned by the Kearney Chamber of Commerce.[104] The city also contributed to the company's decision to locate in Kearney by changing some local service jurisdictions. For example, the building was located outside the city limits, but the city incorporated the area into its fire district in order to obtain a more favorable fire rating for the building. This created an insurance rate savings for Cabela's.[105]

Cabela's specifically looked for a rural area for several reasons. The firm was founded in a rural area, and its founders were committed to the development of rural areas. Furthermore, labor costs were cheaper in Kearney than in Omaha, where there was a bidding war on telemarketing labor. The average wage in Kearney was between five and six dollars per hour, while in Omaha the average wage was eight dollars per hour.[106] In addition, a large part of Cabela's large part-time labor requirement was easily met by Kearney State College's student population of approximately 10,000.[107]

It is interesting to note that the telecommunications infrastructure did not play a major role in this particular location decision. Nevertheless, in the future it definitely will. Cabela's now realizes that with better technology (such as a POP), substantial benefits, especially in cost savings, can be obtained. In considering locations for its next telemarketing site, Cabela's will examine access to long-distance carriers.[108]

In sum, Cabela's chose to locate in Kearney for three reasons: (1) Kearney's recruitment package (especially the availability of a building), (2) the pool of available low-wage labor, and (3) commitment to remaining in rural Nebraska.

Advantages of Telecommunications

Like EMRG, Cabela's has adopted telecommunications technology to help improve its method of doing business. One interesting adaptation involving the company's ability to shift automatically the inbound phone load to a telemarketing subcontractor. Through telephone lines and with the aid of a computer, the telemarketing manager at Cabela's can input into the computer the percentage of phone calls to be routed to the subcontractor if the load of phone calls is too great for its own telemarketing center to handle.[109] The company's entire system is computer operated. Special software has been purchased by Cabela's, while other software has been developed in House. The system is sophisticated enough to monitor every telemarketer. The telemarketing manager can use a computer terminal to check, among other things, who is on the phone, how long they have been on the phone, and the number of calls they have handled. The automatic call distribution system automatically distributes phone calls to telemarketers who are available to answer calls.[110]

Of particular interest is AT&T's POP in the company's building, the only one in the Midwest. As noted above, Cabela's, the Kearney Chamber of Commerce, and the Buffalo County Economic Development Council worked together to bring AT&T to Kearney. The volume of business generated by Cabela's lured the carrier into Kearney, where the company handles over 2 million calls each year. The POP was very attractive to Cabela's because it offered enhanced capabilities that GTE, the local carrier, could not provide—primarily an automatic call-distribution system that helps reduce costs and improves efficiency. While GTE tried to provide Cabela's with the needed equipment, it resisted the automatic call-distribution technology Cabela's management wanted. GTE claims that it tried very hard to work with the modern telemarketer,[111] but Cabela's felt that GTE was not up to date in technology and could not provide the desired maintenance and advisory services. AT&T, on the other hand, could. The POP has benefited Cabela's by lowering its telephone bill for 1989 by 24 percent, compared to 1988 figures. In addition to the enhanced capabilities, the POP allows Cabela's to connect with the other network services. The POP also allows for future expansion and provides better sound quality.[112]

Public Consequences

The presence of Cabela's in Kearney has been favorable to the city in a number of ways. First, it has brought new telecommunications infrastructure to the region which may benefit other users who choose to connect to the POP. Even though bypass of the local exchange carrier is a loss that may be felt in the local network, benefits accrue to the city and will continue to do so. For example, EMRG plans to piggyback on the POP at Cabela's with considerable savings. Other manufacturing firms in the region are also investigating connections to the POP.

Second, the presence of Cabela's has filled a labor market niche. Kearney State College students can easily find jobs in telemarketing. Cabela's provides jobs for housewives and farmers who want a part-time job as well.[113]

Finally, Cabela's has increased the pay scale for entry-level jobs in Kearney. The starting salary, while considerably lower than that of telemarketing firms in Omaha, still exceeds the minimum pay at other likely job sites for part-time work.[114] Consequently, fast-food restaurants have had to increase their wages in order to attract workers.

While the company's telemarketing jobs have benefited Kearney, telemarketing as a means for economic development in rural areas is limited. The overwhelming majority of jobs created by telemarketing firms are part time and require a part-time labor force that many rural areas simply do not have. In this respect, Kearney is an exception; it has the good fortune of having a state college that can provide a large part-time labor pool. Most rural areas do not have this luxury.

CONCLUSIONS

Our initial research questions focused on assessing (1) the advantages of using telecommunications for doing business in rural settings, (2) the processes that rurally based businesses use to evaluate and adopt telecommunications technology, and (3) the impact on community and infrastructure when companies adopt more privately owned telecommunications systems. Through various case studies of rurally based businesses, our first finding is that the advantages of telecommunications go beyond cost savings. Second, we found the size of a company and the nature of its operation dictate what kind of telecommunications systems the company adopts. The corporate culture also plays an important role in the company's ability to capitalize on telecommunications technologies. Third, private industry's bypass of the public network may eventually affect the public interest. Finally, we found that the coming information age may bring opportunities as well as threats for rural businesses. The details of these findings are discussed in the following sections.

Telecommunications Advantages

Although the greatest initial advantage of private telecommunications to businesses is cost-effectiveness, the benefits of telecommunications far exceed financial savings. Investment in privately owned telecommunications allows corporations more control over their communications. This is best demonstrated by Wal-Mart's VSAT network. The system relieves Wal-Mart of dependence on both long-distance and local telephone companies for data and voice communications.

Internally purchased equipment also provides flexibility for enterprises. A company that budgets, develops, and controls its communications equipment cannot be limited by a telephone company's equipment. This freedom refers to both equipment and hardware management. Neither the local nor the long-distance carrier can halt internal communications through equipment obsolescence, malfunctions, or time delays if the company controls its own lines and switch. This situation also aids adaptiveness. A company can fill needs more quickly and expand more easily if it controls its communications network. Again using Wal-Mart's VSAT network as an example, the system allows easy and quick addition of new service sites as well as new applications. This feature allows Wal-Mart to grow at a rate of 200 stores each year and allows new applications such as credit-card authorization and Muzak to piggyback on the system.

More significant, developing telecommunications systems can also make money for a corporation. Two identifiable products can be marketed: excess capacity and new, internally created software usable by other companies. Sale of company-owned resources can turn a telecommunications department or capability into a profit rather than a cost center. For example, Weyerhaeuser Information Systems operates as an independent company to provide phone services. Although WIS users are currently limited to Weyerhaeuser employees, the division can act as a competitive phone service provider to customers outside of Weyerhaeuser. Other sections of WIS, such as software development, are created and marketed for outside users. Another example is the AT&T POP at Cabela's. While not owned by the company, the facility may ultimately contribute to cost savings among other users who connect to it. These examples are above and beyond simple transmission uses.

Process of Adopting Technology

In our study of the processes businesses use to adopt telecommunications, we found that the scope of business determines the type of telecommunications technologies that corporations adopt. The businesses studied here can be categorized into three groups according to their size. The first is national and multilocation businesses such as Wal-Mart, John Deere, and Weyerhaeuser. Both Wal-Mart's and Deere's dispersed locations and large number of branch outlets make VSAT an ideal technology. The leased-line network is less efficient when companies have hundreds of branch outlets. Although Deere has not fully utilized VSAT, the company's plan is to link most of its dealers by satellite in five years. Weyerhaeuser, although belonging to the same size category, has slightly different communications needs because it stays in rural areas for resource and distribution purposes and maintains a more limited number of branch outlets.

The second category is the midsize business such as Cabela's, whose operation is totally created by telecommunications technology. Although Cabela's does not have the resources or the need to build an entirely private communications network, its large telecommunications requirements impels the company to search for the most cost-efficient communication means. The volume of business generated by Cabela's also gives it leverage to shop around among existing telecommunications providers. The result is a system that partially alters the public network by bypassing the local carrier.

The third category is small businesses such as EMRG. Small companies are necessarily more reliant on the public network. They do not have the clout or the leverage to bargain with telecommunications providers. One way for these "small potatoes" to enjoy better-quality telecommunications services is through partnerships—for example, piggybacking on infrastructure already built by others. EMRG plans to build a direct link to the point of presence at Cabela's.

We also found that the corporate culture plays an important role in companies' abilities to capitalize on advanced communication technologies. Attitudes from management can strongly enable or limit the development of new technology-based systems. We found that management's attitudes range from highly innovative and risk taking to conservative and cautious in adopting new telecommunications equipment. In the case of Wal-Mart, management welcomes and accepts new ideas that will facilitate the company's operations. The company's innovative corporate culture is reflected in its implementation of technology. It was the first major retail chain to adopt the UPC bar code scanning system and VSAT, and it has earned tremendous profits from both innovations. Another innovative example is Cabela's, whose management had the technological insight to bring in the AT&T POP, which benefits not only the company but the entire community.

John Deere, on the other hand, represents a more conservative school of companies in adopting technologies. Deere is behind its primary competitor in adopting VSAT. Even though a complete conversion to VSAT for franchisees would eventually benefit both the company and its dealers, the company is slow in making this decision. One reason is that the management is used to the land line system and has not yet understood the need for a more advanced network. The management structure is designed to encourage deliberate and careful decisions on equipment purchases and this inhibits the company's ability to respond quickly to new technology. Deere's reticence to adopt technology is also reflected in the failure of the videoconferencing experiment for intercompany communications.

Management philosophy has great effects on the decision to choose, develop, implement, and use telecommunications equipment. Although the companies we studied have different corporate cultures in adopting technology, they all shared the recognition that the public network ultimately would not be able to accommodate their needs and that they would have to plan for meeting their infrastructure requirements themselves.

Relationship with the Public Network

The trend among corporations to adopt and develop private communications infrastructures reflects the inadequacy of the public telecommunications network for dealing with the needs of multisite companies or businesses with highly specialized communications needs. Corporations that need complex long-distance connections are finding limits in the public telecommunications infrastructure primarily because it lacks the ability to tailor systems to their requirements with the speed they need. This is more profound in rural areas than in urban areas since public telecommunications systems in urban areas often start with more advantages. While locations with inferior telecommunications systems suffer disadvantages, the technology itself allows companies, principally large ones, to overcome disadvantages in a location that is otherwise attractive by bypassing the local telecommunications network.

Each company reviewed in our study found a combination of methods to deal with the problem of an inferior telecommunications system. Some of the solutions included altering the public infrastructure and creating a private network. For example, John Deere and Weyerhaeuser "built" their own communication networks by leasing dedicated lines from telephone companies. Another example of altering the public network is Cabela's. The AT&T POP basically bypasses the local telephone carrier. However, AT&T has leased a fiber-optic line from GTE as part of this operation, maintaining some benefits for the local carrier. Some other solutions are more drastic, such as Wal-Mart's VSAT network, which can virtually bypass the public infrastructure. Furthermore, the five miles of fiber-optic cable that Wal-Mart built in Bentonville to connect three nearby distribution centers with headquarters indicates that the company is working toward further privatizing its communications system.

Internally purchased communication networks move capital investments from the public to the private sector and reduce telephone companies' income. Bypass limits the ability of the public network to keep up with private networks, although arguably private companies' needs for network security, redundancy, and all the special features of their consumer premises equipment outdistance the capabilities of many public networks. A local telephone carrier, especially one in a rural area, is not always equipped or prepared to provide such services. For example, Cabela's purchased its own switch because GTE's switch was not designed to handle the high volume of phone calls that the telemarketer receives. There is some evidence that when telephone carriers do have the ability to provide the services customers need, they do not know how to market their services because they are new to that endeavor.

Valid concerns exist about the ability of the public network to offer service on a par with enhanced corporate systems. Although few companies totally avoid the public-switched network, the trend appears to be toward more rather than less bypass; this is true despite the fact that both Deere and Weyerhaeuser lease dedicated lines from the Bell companies to build their own networks, thereby bringing additional high-quality and high-capacity systems to the public network. For the corporation using private telecommunications, the resulting cost savings and additional advantages in flexibility and efficiency are compelling.

Further, the private systems are technologically "distant" from the public-switched network. These new and internal systems may contain protocols that cannot communicate with those of the public network. Issues such as network and technology compatibility and control will arise, although the countervailing trend toward more modular hardware means that it may be more readily integrated with existing equipment. If the private and the public networks continue to move in different directions, the result will be a double-tiered system of telecommunications. As the private systems advance further due to competition, the public-switched network may lag farther behind.

Rural Businesses in the Information Age

The information age represents both opportunities and challenges for rural businesses. Technologies have changed the way business is conducted in rural areas. For large corporations with substantial financial resources, innovative communications technologies allow them to consolidate operations in both rural and urban areas. If used strategically, technology will facilitate their operations in dispersed and remote areas. This is best demonstrated by Wal-Mart, whose advanced communications system enables it to exploit rural markets.

Because of the nondiscriminatory nature of technology, the information age also represents opportunities for so-called footloose businesses that require only good telecommunications infrastructure in order to operate. Business start-ups, such as EMRG, with technological know-how can survive and succeed in rural areas. The same technologies, on the other hand, may represent threats to traditional small businesses, such as mom-and-pop grocery stores. Wal-Mart's ability to take away downtown business in rural communities exemplifies this challenge.

To meet the challenge associated with the coming information age, small businesses need to adjust themselves to the new environment. Their ability to survive in the future is dependent on their ability to take advantage of technologies. For those who do not have the financial resources or the need to build private telecommunications networks, one way to take advantage of technology is through partnerships. Small businesses can pool their resources together and aggregate their telecommunications demands to create an infrastructure to compete with large corporations in the modern age.

NOTES

1. U.S. Congress, Joint Economic Committee, *Rural Development in the 1990s*, 100th Cong., 2d sess., September 28, 1988, p. 259.

2. D. Brown, J. Reid, H. Bluestone, D. McGrarahan, and S. Mazier, eds., *Rural Economic Development in the 1980s: Prospects for the Future*, Rural Development Research Report No. 69 (Washington, D.C.: U.S. Department of Agriculture, September 1988), p. vii.

3. Ibid.

4. J. Miller, "Rethinking Small Businesses as the Best Way to Create Rural Jobs," *Rural Development Perspectives* 1, no. 2 (February 1985), pp. 9–12.

5. Jurgen Schmandt, Frederick Williams, Robert H. Wilson, and Sharon Strover, eds., *The New Urban Infrastructure: Cities and Telecommunications* (New York: Praeger, 1990).

6. David L. Brown and Kenneth L. Deavers, "Rural Change and the Rural Economic Policy Agenda for the 1980s," *Rural Economic Development in the 1980s*, ed. Brown et al., pp. 20–21.

7. See Brown et al., eds., *Rural Economic Development in the 1980s*, p. xiv.

8. Edwin Parker, "Future Perspectives on Satellite Communication," *Telecommunications* 21, no. 8 (August 1987), pp. 47–48.

9. Ibid.

10. Ibid.

11. Steven Salamoff, "VSAT Technology for Today and for the Future—Part 4: Real World Applications Prove Benefits," *Communications News* 25, no. 1 (January 1988), pp. 38–42.

12. Ibid.

13. Parker, "Future Perspectives," p. 47.

14. Salamoff, "VSAT Technology," p. 39.

15. Deere & Company, *1988 Annual Report* (Moline, Ill., December 6, 1988), p. 3.

16. Interview with William Coopman, Telecommunications Manager, Deere & Company, Moline, Ill., January 12, 1990.

17. Deere & Company, *1988 Annual Report*.

18. Interview with Coopman.

19. Ibid.

20. Each of these five dealers, according to Coopman, has sales in excess of $2 million per year. These initial dishes were partially subsidized and are wholly owned by Deere.

21. Interview with Coopman.

22. Ibid.

23. Ibid.

24. Ibid.

25. "Deere Links U.S., Germany," *MIS Week*, January 8, 1990, p. 8.

26. Interview with Coopman.

27. Ibid. Telecommunications became part of the site team because Deere is very cost-conscious. At the beginning of the decade, 34,000 employees at Deere were laid off to save the company. Deere now chooses to maintain a lean management and employee structure. Deere, therefore, is a company that makes slow, conservative decisions, keeps a lean employee structure, and has a strong telecommunications personnel backbone. Its department seeks the hardware of its competitors to stay equal in its industry.

28. Ibid. Coopman said, "We were the force leading the community . . . we were the major founder of the effort."

29. Jurgen Schmandt, Frederick Williams, and Robert H. Wilson, eds., *Telecommunications Policy and Economic Development: The New State Role* (New York: Praeger, 1989).

30. John Horrigan and Darren Rudloff, "Illinois," in *Telecommunications Policy and Economic Development*, ed. Schmandt, Williams, and Wilson, pp. 68–70.

31. M. Beauchamp, "Lost in the Woods," *Forbes*, October 16, 1989, pp. 221, 224; Weyerhaeuser Telephone Directory, vol. 2, 1989.

32. D. Gabel, "Systems Integration: MIS Stakes a Claim in New Service Field," *Computerworld*, October 10, 1988, pp. 95, 102.

33. Interview with James Davis, Project Manager, Weyerhaeuser Data Network, Telecommunications Systems Division, Tacoma, Washington, January 2, 1990.

34. Ibid.

35. Ibid.

36. The locations served by this redundant network, which Davis called "the longest T-1 span in the United States," reconnect at the company's Walnut Creek and Woodland Hills, California, locations.

37. These computer strokes by users are billable to a cost center and are not a corporate expense. Interview with Davis.

38. Interview with Richard Sherwood, Project Manager, Weyerhaeuser Data Network, Telecommunications Systems Division, Tacoma, Washington, January 2, 1990.

39. Ibid.

40. Ibid.

41. Ibid.

42. Ibid.

43. "Susan Mersereau: On Running MIS as a Profit and Loss Center," *Journal of Information Systems Management* 7 (Winter 1990), pp. 94–96.

44. Interview with Sherwood.

45. TRACER stands for Telephone Ratepayers Association for Cost Effective and Equitable Rates. See K. Strayer and D. Twenhafel, "Washington," in *Telecommunications Policy and Economic Development*, ed. Schmandt, Williams, and Wilson, p. 244.

46. Ibid., p. 242.

47. Ibid.

48. Arthur Markowitz, "Where Profits Come Home to Roost," *Discount Store News* 28, no. 23 (December 18, 1989), pp. 29–32.

49. Telephone interview with Jane Arend, Director, Public Relations, Wal-Mart Stores, Inc., Bentonville, Arkansas, April 17, 1991.

50. Ibid.

51. Arthur Markowitz, "Widening Technology Gap over Rivals," *Discount Store News* 28, no. 23 (December 18, 1989), pp. 203–4.

52. Ibid.

53. Ibid.

54. Markowitz, "Widening Technology Gap," p. 203.

55. Telephone interview with Tom Newell, Manager of Satellite Department, Wal-Mart Stores, Inc., Bentonville, Arkansas, February 24, 1990.

56. Interview with Jay Allen, Former Manager of Satellite Department, Wal-Mart Stores, Inc., Bentonville, Arkansas, January 3, 1990.

57. Ibid.

58. Salamoff, "VSAT Technology," p. 40.

59. Markowitz, "Widening Technology Gap," p. 203.

60. Ibid.

61. Bob Vinton, "VSATs: Undaunted by Fiber," *Communications Week*, January 22, 1990, p. 45.

62. Interview with Allen.

63. Ibid.

64. Interview with Newell.

65. Salamoff, "VSAT Technology," p. 40.

66. Interview with Allen.

67. Vinton, "VSATs: Undaunted," p. 45.

68. "Wal-Mart Stores—Penny Wise," *Business Month* 132 (December 1988), p. 42.

69. Ibid.

70. Markowitz, "Where Profits Come Home," p. 29.

71. Ibid.

72. Lisa M. Keefe, "Guess Who Lost," *Forbes*, September 7, 1987, pp. 60, 62.

73. Interview with Allen.

74. Ibid.

75. Kenneth E. Stone, *The Impact of Wal-Mart Stores on Other Businesses in Iowa*, Working Paper (Ames, Iowa: Iowa State University, October 1989).

76. Ibid., p. 15.

77. Ibid., p. 15.

78. Interview with Phil Taylor, Professor of Economics, University of Arkansas, Fayetteville, Arkansas, January 3, 1990.

79. "To Wal-Mart or Not to Wal-Mart," *The Economist*, March 7, 1990, p. 66.

80. However, what makes this study particularly controversial is the fact that the university received $10,000 from Wal-Mart for the research.

81. Interview with David Waldron, President, Electronic Marketing Resource Group, Inc., Kearney, Nebraska, January 12, 1990.

82. EMRG, *1990 Company Review* (Kearney, Neb., 1990), pp. 1, 8.

83. Ibid., pp. 3, 7.

84. Ibid., p. 7.

85. Ibid., pp. 4, 9.

86. Ibid., p. 10.

87. Interview with Waldron.

88. Ibid.

89. Interview with Steve Buttress, President, Buffalo County Economic Development Council, Kearney, Nebraska, January 8, 1990.

90. Interview with Tim Miller, Director of Telemarketing, Cabela's, Inc., Kearney, Nebraska, January 7, 1990.

91. William Fulton, "Getting the Wire to the Sticks," *Governing* 2, no. 11 (August 1989), p. 34.

92. Ibid.

93. Interview with Waldron.

94. Ibid.

95. Interview with Greg Dunn, Instructor, Kearney State College, Kearney, Nebraska, January 12, 1990.

96. Interview with Waldron.

97. Ibid.

98. Ibid.

99. Cabela's, Inc., *Cabela's* (Kearney, Neb., 1989) (brochure).

100. Interview with Miller.

101. Ibid.

102. Ibid.

103. Interview with Bruce Blankenship, Director, Kearney Chamber of Commerce, Kearney, Nebraska, January 8, 1990.

104. Ibid.

105. Ibid.

106. Interview with Miller.

107. Ibid.

108. Ibid.
109. Ibid.
110. Ibid.
111. Interview with Kay Bauman, Vice-President, Nebraska Operations, GTE North, Inc., Columbus, Nebraska, March 9, 1990.
112. Ibid.
113. Ibid.
114. Interview with Blankenship.

3

Public-Service Delivery

Paula J. Adams, Scott J. Lewis,
and Robert Stephens

INTRODUCTION

Problems with Rural Service Delivery

Rural populations traditionally have lagged behind urban populations in receiving basic health and social services.[1] Despite evidence of increased needs, recent decreases in population, demographic changes, and the rising costs of social services have strained the ability of many communities to provide a basic level of care for their residents.

Many researchers have documented the fall of America's family farmer. Along with agriculture, other labor-intensive industries that once thrived in the rural environment have declined. The economic instability following these changes has led, in part, to a decline in population in rural America. Declines in population have added to the traditional rural problem of developing a population base large enough to support services.

While rural population figures are falling, the percentage of elderly residents living in rural areas has increased. In areas of declining population, the elderly are often left behind because of economic and life-style choices. The elderly have "characteristics that make them a major challenge for rural health and social service providers. They have lower incomes, less mobility because of poorer transportation facilities, and poorer health status than their urban counterparts."[2]

The cost for providing services in rural areas has increased dramatically. Schools face problems in recruiting teachers and providing students with the modern facilities needed to provide educational equity with their urban counterparts. Rural hospitals provide most of their care to Medicare patients and face strict cost controls from the federal government. Businesses that remain in rural areas must be able to access information efficiently to compete in the market. Compounding the problem is the large proportion of rural residents who live at or below the poverty level.

The development and adequate use of human resources is important for the future of rural America. Quality education, adequate health care, and efficient information links to rural residents are a necessary foundation for the revitalization of a depressed rural economy. This chapter examines the role of telecommunications in providing education, health, and information services to rural residents and includes innovative examples of service delivery that promise a better quality of life in rural communities. The case studies to be examined and the technology in each are provided in Table 3.1.

Telecommunications Solutions

Given the nature of the emerging global economy, it is becoming evident that an educated work force is essential if the nation is to survive economically in the 1990s and beyond. While urban schools move ahead with innovative programs, schools in rural areas are unable to provide a wide array of vocational and college preparatory classes. Telecommunications technology offers educational oppor-

Table 3.1 Public-Service Delivery: Case Studies in Education, Health, and Computer Networks

	Technology	Purpose
Education		
Minnesota Distance Learning Network	interactive television over fiber optic system	training
TI-IN Network, Inc.	satellite	training
Health		
Geisinger Medical Center	computer system	information network
Computer Networks		
Agricultural Marketing Service	multiple	information dissemination
Computerized Information Delivery Service	computer network	information dissemination

tunities to students in remote areas via interactive and broadcasting services without transporting students. The benefits of this technology reach beyond school-age students; rural residents also benefit from satellite or fiber-optic distribution of programs.

The use of telecommunications can also play an important role in providing adequate health care in rural America. Telecommunications can link rural clinics and regional hospitals or health centers, allowing a specialist the opportunity to consult with a health care provider concerning diagnoses and treatment plans. Applications of telecommunications for health care provide cost-effective and medically efficient service in rural areas.

Finally, in the age of an increasingly integrated world economy, the ability of rural business owners to access information on prices, markets, clients, suppliers, and consultants is vital to their survival. New management techniques and continuing education are also important elements in the new economy. Telecommunications can help give rural businesses access to the nation's market system.

An important policy issue is who should supply the telecommunications innovations discussed in this chapter. So far as "public" solutions are concerned, a logical case might be made that the public-switched network be expanded to provide new services for education, health, or rural information services. Currently, some of these applications are supported by special services purchased from the local or interexchange company, but in others—as in the case of satellite-based distance learning—the main services bypass the public network. As we shall see in the examples, there may be a case for expanding the definition of universal service to include the provision of an advanced telecommunications infrastructure for public service to rural areas.

Case Studies of Innovation

The two innovative education systems that we chose to study were the Texas-based TI-IN network and the Minnesota Distance Learning Network. The TI-IN and Minnesota networks are technologically and organizationally different, but both have been successful since their inception. Adopted by many school districts, they have grown quickly in a short period of time. TI-IN uses satellite technology that is capable of transmitting over entire continents at the fixed cost of launching satellites and establishing downlinks. The Minnesota network uses fiber optics to provide state-of-the-art interactive voice and video transmission. Because the Minnesota system requires point-to-point transmission, it is used mainly for relatively close distances. Conversely, the TI-IN network is centralized and transmits from only a few locations.

Hospitals also have adopted several strategies to combat the problems they face in the rural environment. The Geisinger health care system developed a network of outpatient clinics to secure a strong referral network. These clinics link 45 communities with Geisinger Medical Center through an advanced telecommunications system that provides administrative services, patient information, diagnostic support, and lab results.

Finally, our U.S. Department of Agriculture study examines computer data systems and courses on two computer networks. Each represents a different model and serves a different function. The first system, Agricultural Marketing Service, plays an important role in maintaining and enhancing the international competitiveness of U.S. agriculture. The second system, Computerized Information Delivery Service, still struggles to identify its objectives.

EDUCATION

Overview of Distance Learning

Distance learning can be defined as teaching-learning arrangements in which a portion or all of the learning interactions occur via the transmission of educational or instructional programming to geographically dispersed individuals and groups.

History of Distance Education. The forerunner to modern distance learning began in Australia in the 1880s, when printed correspondence courses were used to educate people in isolated areas.[3] In 1938, educators concerned with the distant learner formed the International Council for Correspondence Education. Instructional television was a much-touted distance learning model in the 1960s, although it fell far short of early expectations. In the mid-1970s, NASA (National Aeronautics and Space Administration) teamed with the National Science Foundation and the National Institute of Education to reach isolated schools in the Rocky and Appalachian mountains via satellite technology. Today, telecourses and educational programs reach many distance learners in diverse settings. The Soviet Union, Germany, England, and China all have adopted distance education for students in higher education.

In the United States, adult distance education has been embedded in the corporate, military, and university continuing education sectors for many years. The rapid expansion of distance learning efforts in the past five to ten years was brought about by the advent of video teleconferencing technologies, which allowed two-way interaction. A national education network, first begun in 1984 by a group of concerned Texans, has now become so popular that nearly 6,000 students nationwide are enrolled in approximately 20 for-credit courses. "Fewer than 10 states were promoting distance learning in 1987," reads a report on distance education prepared by the Office of Technology Assessment. "One year later, two-thirds of the states reported involvement in distance education."[4]

The availability of computers in schools and the ability to connect them have expanded opportunities for two-way interaction between distant locations. Recent technological innovations, including the widespread adoption of fiber optics, have increased even further the capabilities for two-way interaction.

Recent developments in distance learning. Structural, economic, and demographic changes in rural America have left small rural schools with declining student populations and limited financial and educational resources. Many rural school districts, because of resource constraints and decreasing population, are unable to provide challenging curricula for their students who face increasing requirements for college admission. Without advanced studies, these students are not able to compete in higher educational environments.

In addition, decreasing populations in rural school districts often promote school consolidation or busing. While these measures are logical in some cases, in others they threaten the stability of rural communities. School consolidation and the transporting of students and teachers are disruptive and politically unpopular, since the local school is considered the heart of the community in most rural areas.[5] If the community is to thrive and grow, so too must the school.

Distance education can provide these schools with the curricular resources needed to remain operational. This technology is being used by more and more rural school districts across the country. Providing courses for underserved or advanced students is a principal application of distance learning for K–12 education.

Applications for distance learning reach far beyond teacher-classroom interaction. Rural school districts may use their facilities for continuing education for teachers, administrators, and school board members. Broadcasters may also provide programming pertinent to the rural community itself, such as economic development issues, government aid programs, and state and federal education programming. In short, the applications for distance learning are limited only by the need, imagination, and enthusiasm of rural communities.

Sources of distance education. Business and higher education, traditional users of distance learning, are now providing educational programming and services for the K–12 market. Schools are engaging in innovative partnerships and choosing from a range of technical and programming alternatives. New coalitions across state and district boundaries as well as new networks of educators and geographically dispersed schools are being established, providing opportunities for collaboration and resource sharing among many groups. Telecommunications technologies make it possible to aggregate local, state, regional, and even national needs. This aggregation, and the expanding education and technology needs of schools, has brought a widening array of providers to the educational market.

Many of these providers are members of the traditional public education community, while others are from the private sector. They supply the K–12 community with a variety of programming, services, and hardware. Teachers and outside experts can be provided by other districts, the higher education community, or the private sector. Hardware and software companies offer programming and technical assistance. Public and commercial broadcasting stations, cable and local instructional television systems, local or regional telephone companies, and satellite distributors can provide the means to connect different sites. Although most schools will continue to offer much of their own instruction, many are likely to turn to outside suppliers to obtain educational and telecommunications resources.[6]

Technologies. The primary use of current distance learning technology is to replicate the experience of face-to-face instruction. The features of traditional instruction retained are live instruction, teacher-student interaction, and student-student interaction. These qualities distinguish this application of educational technology from previous attempts, particularly educational television, where interactivity was virtually impossible.

Live experiences heighten the interest of many students and sharpen classroom activities by demanding that teacher and student be ready to begin class at a specified broadcast time. This demand of timeliness is sometimes problematic, however, since different school districts have different time schedules.

The modern concept of distance education is fairly simple. Distance learning networks employ one- or two-way video, computer, and/or audio transmissions from a central location to geographically separate ones. By combining audio and video technologies, rural school districts can provide courses that students otherwise would be unable to take. Two-way interaction between students and teachers takes several forms, depending upon the technology used. Microwave transmission and satellite both provide one-way video from teacher to student, and two-way audio typically allows students to speak with teachers over a portable telephone. Fiber optics, by contrast, provides two-way video and two-way audio; all participants in the classroom activity can hear, speak to, and see each other.

Although there are conflicting opinions regarding whether a multiple-point broadcasting service or a switched network is better suited for distance learning, each technology should be considered relative to the service needed. Microwave is capable of covering long distances, but microwave transmitting towers are vulnerable to aboveground disturbances. A satellite broadcast can transmit over entire continents to multiple sites at the fixed cost of launching the satellite and establishing receiving sites, thus producing substantial economies of scale. Weather problems may create transmission difficulties. Finally, fiber optics provides state-of-the-art, fully interactive service in both voice and video transmission but requires switching. It is often used for shorter distances, since the network must connect all service users. Fiber optics installation is usually more expensive than a satellite network. New opportunities for audio conferences and computer conferences over the telephone are also becoming possible.

Funding and cost. Solutions for financing distance education are as varied as technical solutions. Funding can come from bonds, grants appropriated by the government, taxing on videotape rentals, or private assistance.

The Minnesota Distance Learning Network

History. Distance learning in Minnesota began in 1983 when educators and citizens in Eagle Bend, Minnesota, became concerned about the possible closing of their school. Distance learning was found to be an innovative way to provide their children with the courses they needed. They started a one-way interactive television learning system via microwave technology. The effort was initiated without any support from the state; funds were collected from a variety of sources, such as technology and course integration grants.[7] The success of the first project ignited an interest in distance learning throughout the state. Private companies, school districts, cable companies, and legislators all became involved in the creation of a statewide distance learning network. As additional schools employed interactive television systems, telephone companies made long-term investments in the system by replacing microwave technology with buried fiber-optic cable. As a result of the involvement of telephone companies in distance education, an economic and educational partnership formed between technology providers and school districts.[8]

The grassroots movement in Eagle Bend was so successful that now almost all rural schools in Minnesota are linked or have access to the interactive television network. The delivery of instructional programs via interactive television is now emerging as the best alternative for secondary education (primarily grades 10 through 12). Interactive television allows school districts the opportunity to offer courses that they previously could not offer because of low enrollments or lack of certified staff in particular curricular areas. Many school districts in the State of Minnesota have created local and regional distance education applications to share their existing pool of teachers and staff resources without transporting students or instructors.[9] When distance learning was first put into operation, union teachers raised concerns about the possibility of being replaced by technology. On the contrary, distance learning has created jobs.[10]

TI-IN Network, Inc., the Texas-based provider of instructional programs through satellite technology, heavily marketed its programs in the State of Minnesota during the initial stages of Minnesota's distance learning projects. There was, however, a consensus among policymakers and educators that Minnesotan children should be taught by Minnesotan teachers.[11] In addition, the Department of Education in Minnesota did not view TI-IN as an effective means of information delivery. The Department of Education wanted to promote active learning and did not see one-way delivery systems (one-way video, two-way audio), such as TI-IN, as capable of supporting active learning. The Department of Education mandated a smaller class size for distance learning than for regular classes, which is about 20 or 30 students. Furthermore, the Department of Education did not want the programs originating out of state because of curricula and logistical controls.[12]

Interactive video systems are used in 150 of Minnesota's 436 public schools; these 150 are regionally clustered within 19 interactive television cooperatives and include some postsecondary schools. As interactive video evolves, the ultimate union of public schools with Minnesota's 5 universities, 7 state universities, 19 junior colleges, and 33 area vocational technical institute campuses will require a ubiquitous facility.[13]

Technology. In 1987, Minnesota's legislature approved the formation of the Task Force on Instructional Technology to position the State of Minnesota as a leader in educational, support, and governmental services in the 1990s and beyond. The telephone companies, the Minnesota Telephone Association (MTA), and its 94 member companies play a unique role in providing a state-of-the art network, which will ultimately be fiber optic and digital based.[14]

The task force uses the most advanced form of technology in distance learning, employing interactive video systems. These systems typically use fiber with laser transmission, enabling classrooms to view and be viewed by all other classrooms as well as the instructor over studio-grade quality circuits. Fiber optics is a cost-effective transport technology and provides capabilities beyond those previously limited by analog transmission and expensive bandwidth. The fiber-optic cable is buried underground and provides for full two-way interactive audio and video communications.[15]

Each interactive classroom has three (or four) monitors on a cart in front of the students so that they can watch the instructor and the students at other sites. The teacher operates from a podium surrounded by three (or four) ceiling-mounted monitors and various controls for selecting which of three camera signals to transmit. There are also three (or four) cameras in the classroom. One of the cameras is focused on the students, one is on the instructor, and the third (or fourth) is an overhead camera mounted on the cart so that the instructor can use it in place of the blackboard. There are also a computer and a videocassette recorder (VCR) in each classroom.

Generally, each room is equipped with three television cameras, two microphones, and eight television monitors. The annual lease cost of existing telecommunications projects in Minnesota for connecting higher education campuses in rural areas of the state ranges from $900 to $1,200 per mile when acquired on a ten-year contract basis. The average annual lease cost per site is $23,650 to $31,550.[16]

Upsala High School. Upsala High School was chosen as part of our study because it is part of a cluster of educational cooperatives. Upsala High School has a student population of 430. It is a member of the Mid-State Educational Telecommunications (MSET) Cooperative, which was formed by eight districts to provide technological service and support to its members. These members consist of Holdingford, Little Falls, Long Prairie, Onamia, Pierz, Royalton, Swanville, and Upsala. MSET is working jointly with such companies as Upsala Telephone, Wilde Construction, and Pirelli Optronics to provide telecommunications and technological services to its member schools.[17]

MSET has established a two-way interactive television hookup to all eight member districts by means of fiber-optic cable. Each of the eight schools has one classroom outfitted as a television broadcasting studio so that class can originate at any of the schools. The host or origination location is changed daily if not hourly. Every connected location in the system is a host site at some time.

Through the LITESPAN network, MSET has the capability of participating in live college preparatory courses. LITESPAN, a network originating from St. Cloud State University, provides freshmen-level courses to eligible high school juniors and seniors. The system allows for full two-way interactive access between any of the eight communities and St. Cloud State University. The existing network has been expanded to include Brainerd Community College, St. Cloud Technical College, and several other postsecondary institutions in the central Minnesota region.[18]

With the use of fiber-optic cable, each community can share educational classes and programming. Community members can participate in a wide variety of classes without traveling any farther than their local school. MSET is able to generate a program from any of the high schools and send it out to any or all households in the eight communities that have cable television. MSET is also investigating potential uses of the interactive system for local businesses. Local professionals such as firefighters, nurses, and bankers can obtain valuable in-service information in their local communities without lengthy travel.

In many schools, the system is used for nearly every period of the school day and in the evenings for college classes as well. The system is sometimes used for early morning sessions, and faculty and administration meetings are conducted during many free segments. School administrators use the system's facsimile machines to communicate between schools.[19]

St. Cloud Technical College. The Mid-Minnesota Telecommunications Consortium (MidTeC) consists of the technical colleges of St. Cloud, Willmar, Anoka, Alexandria, Pine City, and Hutchinson. MidTeC is the first totally postsecondary organization in the state to unite on the concept of distance learning. MidTeC member colleges have an interactive classroom capacity of 12 to 16 people. At some schools this is a classroom dedicated just to distance learning. Others are now sharing a multiple-use classroom. A majority of campuses have auditoriums or teleconferencing rooms that can accommodate up to 150 persons and thus serve as an interactive television facility on a somewhat limited basis.[20]

The purpose of MidTeC is to serve 1.7 million citizens over the age of 16 in a 16-county service area. These citizens include but are not limited to day students, extension students, nontraditional students, postsecondary students, special needs students, teaching staff, displaced workers, the incarcerated, the handicapped, nonprofit groups, senior citizens, farmers, and merchants.[21] The six member campuses are each located within a 60-mile radius of the most central school, St. Cloud. By using this regional approach, MidTeC encourages more cooperation among campuses and enhances programming opportunities for the citizens in or near their communities.

The MidTeC network uses fiber-optic cable to connect the member technical colleges. Both audio and video signals are sent and received at all sites simultaneously. The classroom equipment is similar at each site, having an instructor station (a large desk) that houses a switcher.

With the switcher, the teacher can select which camera will be used to transmit to the remote sites. There are three cameras: the camera on the instructor, the camera on the class, and the graphics camera. The students at the remote sites generally keep the classroom camera trained on them; however, they can also use their camera switcher, if needed.

St. Cloud State University. St. Cloud State University (SCSU) established a two-way, interactive television network to serve the educational needs of central Minnesota. This distance learning network began operations in the fields of special education, administration, music education, and early childhood education. The network enabled over 1.7 million citizens to gain access to higher education in their local communities by providing direct linkages from SCSU to Willmar, Alexandria, Brainerd, Cambridge, and the Minneapolis/St. Paul metropolitan area. In addition, secondary linkages expanded service to communities surrounding these contact points.

SCSU provides a five-spoke optical network. Each route selected coincides with efforts by schools to build and operate regional two-way television systems. The opportunity for these regions to secure assistance from SCSU enhanced their operation. Furthermore, opportunities exist for expanded service beyond the identified areas to other citizens of Minnesota at a relatively low cost simply by adding additional clusters. It permitted schools and other organizations wishing to become a part of this system to do so at a cost-effective price.

The system provides simultaneous full-motion video and audio from SCSU to each remote site and full-motion video and audio from each remote site to SCSU. An additional two-way audio channel is available for voice conversations and for sending computer information to and from the remote site.

There are several educational institutions and resources that share distance learning in both undergraduate and graduate education. In the realm of undergraduate education, SCSU has been offering general education classes at Hutchinson, through extension, since 1979. Through telecommunications technology, SCSU is able to expand general education classes to other districts where the limitation of class size would not support an on-site program. Telecommunications technology is also able to provide upper-level courses to three community colleges: Willmar Community College, Brainerd Community College, and East Central Community College in Anoka-Ramsey. In cooperation with school districts in each of the five areas, courses are offered at the freshman level to eligible high school juniors and seniors. This allows students to interact with on-campus college students without taking time out of the school day for travel. Courses are offered in general education areas that meet SCSU requirements or that are easily transferable. Calculus, art, theater appreciation, and Chinese or Japanese culture are examples of the types of courses that enrich the high school curriculum and provide access to expertise less apt to be available in the districts.

The graduate program differs enough that, after core courses are completed, it is difficult to find courses in the many areas of emphasis chosen by students. Extension courses provide the core classes on site, and these are supplemented by more specialized offerings transmitted from the central campus. Reconsolidation of school districts, through telecommunications, provides the necessary number of students for advanced courses. The telecommunications network provides a structured way to provide training for elementary education, math, science, and other potentially scarce areas. The telecommunications network allows the university to offer educational opportunities to all persons in the service area. In addition, SCSU offers noncredit courses, seminars, and workshops to serve the business and professional community as well as a training program designed to assist participating faculty in using the network.

With a two-way interactive television network, the university's small business development center is better able to serve effectively the needs of central Minnesota's rural entrepreneurs. This network enhanced the center's ability to educate and help the rural small business entrepreneur.[22]

TI-IN Network, Inc.

History. TI-IN Network, Inc., is a privately owned, for-profit company. Its organizational structure is centralized, with headquarters in San Antonio, Texas. Lloyd Otterman is chairman and chief executive officer of TI-IN and works with a board of directors representing investors. In addition, TI-IN maintains seven middle- and upper-level managers who oversee various aspects of TI-IN operations and promotions. The network uses satellite technology to broadcast distance education classes across the continental United States.

TI-IN was created in 1984 and grew very rapidly during its first five years. A pioneer in the field of satellite distance education, the network was initiated by a group of concerned citizens in Texas for the sole purpose of effecting positive change in rural school districts. While TI-IN broadcasts were initially limited to the state of Texas, the network quickly expanded and by 1990 serviced 950 sites in 30 states.[23]

TI-IN offers an impressive spectrum of courses from which teachers, students, and administrators may choose. At the most basic level, TI-IN provides advanced course work in mathematics, science, and foreign language, three subjects that are critical for higher education preparation. In addition, TI-IN offers specialized training programs for teachers, administrators, and school board members. Student enrichment programs are also extremely popular, the purpose of which is to familiarize students with various cultures and performing arts.

Technology. TI-IN's impressive capacity for growth results directly from the use of satellites.[24] With satellite technology, the broadcast "footprint" covers extremely large distances. Consequently, implementing service in new areas is simple from a technical standpoint, involving only the installation of downlink equipment. With this equipment, efforts for further improvements can focus on methods of serving incoming phone calls to the technical assistance center, giving students better access to teachers. Additional options being studied include more telephone lines and a voice mail system.[25] TI-IN researchers are considering a new electronic mail system, allowing teachers, students, facilitators, and administrators access to the TI-IN information distribution center.[26]

Financing. For schools unable to afford the approximately $5,000 to $6,000 annual TI-IN subscription fee (the price is a function of the number of courses used and the number of students participating), it is worth noting the establishment of the United Star Schools Network, a subsidiary organization of TI-IN. The network serves 316 eligible schools in 20 states. Student instruction and teacher training are provided through the established satellite system. The $9.7 million grant from the U.S. Department of Education's $32 million Star Schools Program equalizes access to educational resources by overcoming geographic barriers.[27]

In addition to TI-IN, five other participants constitute the partnership. They include the California State University at Chico, Education Service Center Region 20, Western Illinois University, Mississippi State University at Starkville, and the North Carolina Department of Public Instruction.

Despite the establishment of the United Star Schools Network, financing remains a pressing issue for distance learning advocates. The United Star Schools Network cannot meet the national demand, and many schools remain hard-pressed to afford distance learning services.

Distance Education Findings

During our research into the Minnesota and TI-IN distance education networks, we observed two primary differences between the networks in the classroom environment and teacher certification. In addition, several themes surfaced repeatedly during our analysis, many of which provided unanticipated answers to our research questions. These themes include expanded applications for distance education, the effectiveness of distance learning, distance education and economic development, the importance of linking networks, and the role of telephone companies in constructing distance learning networks.

Classroom activity. In format, TI-IN classes are quite different from Minnesota Distance Learning Network classes. For TI-IN courses, transmission to field sites travels through satellite, and a facilitator is present in every classroom to supervise student activity. Satellite connections link student-held portable telephones to teachers at the broadcast site. While students can see their instructor, they cannot see students in other classrooms. Similarly, teachers cannot see their students.

TI-IN's two-way audio transmission also follows a clear etiquette. Because only four students can be on the phone with their instructor simultaneously, rules are established regarding who should speak and when. These rules vary between teachers and courses. Often teachers call on specific students or request participation from a particular class. TI-IN also provides 800 numbers for students and administrators to contact teachers during scheduled office hours.

Conversely, the Minnesota Distance Learning Network provides audio and video interaction between all sites at all times through its use of fiber optics. No special etiquette is necessary since teachers can hear and observe activities in all classrooms. Consequently, the Minnesota system resembles a typical classroom atmosphere to the highest degree possible.

Interstate versus intrastate teacher certification. Whereas Minnesota Distance Learning Network instructors are required to be certified only in Minnesota, TI-IN instructors must be certified to teach specific courses in every state receiving TI-IN broadcasts. Mandates differ drastically from state to state, and teachers sometimes scramble to meet requirements ranging from tuberculin tests to specified course work. Because states require teachers to be certified annually, the process becomes never-ending, increasingly complicated, and expensive. Although state legislatures and education agencies are slowly realizing the inefficiency of this system, change is gradual.

Expanded applications for distance education. Expanded applications are pertinent to both centralized and decentralized systems (Minnesota and TI-IN, respectively). However, specific applications may be better suited for specific organizational structures. For example, centralized systems are well suited for macro-level programming, where sponsors such as government agencies affect multiple regions. Decentralized systems, however, are well equipped to service individual communities and their immediate neighbors.

The effectiveness of distance education. There are no data comprehensively documenting the long-term success or failure of learning through interactive television. Clearly, distance education is no substitute for teachers in the classroom. However, in rural communities where financial resources are limited and teachers cannot be attracted to teach advanced courses, distance learning provides a powerful medium for helping students to access material that otherwise would be unavailable. If given a choice between studying advanced mathematics, science, and foreign languages over a distance learning network or entering colleges and universities without adequate preparation (or being denied entrance), students clearly will prefer the former.

It also should be noted that distance learning programs tend to work best with students who are highly motivated and independent; such characteristics promote success in any environment. Consequently, the nature of student-teacher interaction in a distance education setting often produces interesting benefits. First, since students must take the initiative to speak with instructors for help and work more autonomously in other aspects of the learning process, they are especially encouraged to think critically and independently. Second, because student interaction frequently involves linking classrooms from opposite ends of the country, students using the TI-IN network quickly develop new social skills while trading perspectives on critical issues with students in other geographic regions.

Distance education and economic development. Distance education has clear implications for rural economic development. First, students who excel in higher education have the option of returning to rural communities to make a variety of socioeconomic contributions. Of course, distance education is not the sole precursor to community involvement. Distance learning does, however, encourage rural students to pursue higher education, which *is* fundamental for development.

Second, distance learning can, in many cases, substitute for consolidation of rural schools. Although school consolidation is sometimes highly efficient and appropriate, it can also be economically crippling or politically infeasible for many rural communities; in towns with small populations, schools are extremely important in that educators may represent a large percentage of a rural work force. The advanced course work provided by distance learning allows rural schools to meet state education requirements, providing challenging curricula that prepare students for higher education. Such effectiveness can make consolidation unnecessary, a relationship seen most clearly in the Minnesota Distance Learning Network.

Finally, the aforementioned community development programming can make major differences in rural economic development, given matches between community needs and distance programming. The applications for community development programming are endless, ranging from continuing education for physicians to tax and finance information from the Internal Revenue Service. Clearly, distance education provides a wealth of new possibilities for rural economic development. In an age where access to information can make the difference between economic progress and recession, distance learning provides new mechanisms to bridge the information gap.

The importance of linking networks. In addition to financial pressures, the fragmented nature of the distance learning industry threatens the long-term adoption or expansion of distance education networks.[28] Despite TI-IN's national presence, distance learning is a relatively unknown concept to American educators. Adequate communication between potential distance education users and providers is lacking. The result is a large number of incompatible distance learning networks, since little thought is given to interregional compatibility of policy, technology, or application. Administrators must be educated on the applications for various technologies and begin planning networks on a macroscale. Without such planning, promising solutions for rural schools threaten to break down in an overly fragmented system.[29]

In addition to the overall goal of constructing interfacing distance education networks, administrators must address several smaller considerations: (1) evaluating the instructional needs of specific schools, (2) determining the amount of money available for distance education, and (3) identifying and comparing the distance learning systems that meet identified needs.[30]

The role of telephone companies in constructing networks. Telephone companies provide a great deal of momentum for distance education planning. As the Minnesota Distance Learning Network illustrates, telephone companies are essential providers of distance education technology, of which fiber-optic cable is only one example.

While telephone companies can make significant contributions to distance education networks, the networks can also benefit the telephone companies. Although fiber-optic cable is often prohibitively expensive in rural areas, establishing distance learning networks provides the incentive for telephone companies to install the necessary technology. Both rural townships and the telephone companies servicing them benefit in that telephone companies enhance their public image by contributing to education and rural communities gain access to advanced technology. Once fiber is laid for distance education, it easily can be used for multiple technological applications associated with rural economic development.

Ultimately the question of whether to invest in satellite-based, multiple-point distribution systems or in the switched network delivery of education materials may be answered by a policy that encourages both. The "long-haul" distribution of education materials, especially where two-way video is not critical, may be done best by satellite distribution, including services where downloading is done onto tape media for later replay. The switched network can then be used for local distribution, perhaps combined with "live" interactive classroom activities.

HEALTH CARE

Current Hospital Challenges

As a result of changes in the federal government's Medicare reimbursement policies, improvements in transportation opportunities, changes in the practice of medicine, and shortages of health care providers, almost every rural hospital in the country faces financial distress. Today's challenge to rural health care leaders is to define new institutions and delivery methods that preserve the level of care needed to meet a community's needs in a cost-effective manner.

Reimbursement. In 1983, the Health Care Finance Administration proposed the Prospective Payment System (PPS) to curtail the spiraling costs of the Medicare program. Under this system, rural hospitals are frequently not reimbursed for the full cost of a Medicare patient's treatment. In addition, the complicated formulas used to calculate reimbursements are very taxing on hospital administrations, especially in small, rural hospitals.

In 1988, the Robert Wood Johnson Foundation initiated the Hospital-Based Rural Health Care Program. The program's goals include the promotion of cost-efficient management through shared data and billing systems. The program is being conducted in 13 different rural hospital consortia across the nation.[31] Early program success shows the value of consolidated services and implies a logical implementation of telecommunications services. The increased need for data shared among facilities combined with centralized information services can be handled by a telecommunications network.

Transportation. Many rural citizens now have reasonable access to large urban hospitals. An improved highway system allows residents to drive past their local community hospitals for what they perceive to be superior care in urban medical centers.[32] Ambulances are virtual rolling emergency rooms with advanced equipment and highly skilled personnel administering immediate care.[33] Where available, Life Flight® helicopters have decreased emergency response times dramatically and often carry residents to trauma centers that specialize in emergency care. These advances have reduced the necessity for each community to have its own primary care facility.

To maintain their market share, rural facilities must continue to attract patients that they can prudently treat. By participating in consortia with other hospitals, rural facilities can concentrate on specialized services. Through a communications network, hospitals can pass on referrals to member hospitals and coordinate services among member facilities.

Practice of medicine. Advances in medical science have moved the delivery of many services from hospital beds to outpatient treatment rooms. Treatments that required several days in the hospital as recently as five years ago are now performed in outpatient clinics. Technological changes have led to a significant decrease in hospital use in other ways. Since the 1940s, the estimated need for hospital beds has dropped from 4.5 to 1.5 beds per 1,000 persons. Compounded by declining populations, rural hospitals find themselves operating facilities that are not designed to take advantage of today's medical practices. Facilities constantly struggle to keep up with the technology and services necessary to maintain quality care.[34]

One program designed to take advantage of these changes is the Medical Assistance Facility (MAF) Program in Montana. These facilities provide acute care for up to 96 hours prior to transfer to a hospital. The MAF thus represents "an option for acute medical care in isolated rural areas that is more comprehensive than an underutilized rural hospital."[35] To be successful, health care providers must link these smaller MAF facilities with their larger centers to provide the most efficient care possible.

Health care providers. There are serious deterrents to recruiting physicians and other health care providers to rural areas. Physicians who practice only 15 miles outside of a modest-sized town are paid 20 to 40 percent less for the same services that local physicians perform in town.[36] The lack of a physician network to share after-hours duty as well as isolation from professional colleagues play major roles in the burnout of physicians who practice medicine in rural areas. Finally, the rural setting calls for medical generalists. Providers in the rural setting must treat a wide variety of patient needs. Most of today's physicians and nurses are trained in specialties required by the larger hospitals. This training does not always transfer well to the rural setting, where there may not be enough patients for such specialization.

When community facilities are linked in a telecommunications network, economies of scale can be developed that can provide a critical mass needed for specialization. Using one method, "hub and spoke," a hospital can develop a referral network large enough to operate efficiently while maintaining locally controlled physician and clinic facilities. Large networks offer rural providers stability that could not be attained on their own and support after-hours services and professional consulting.

Successful Strategies

Developing new delivery strategies has been the subject of recent research by many of the nation's leading health care policymakers. To maintain their link to the nation's health care delivery system, many rural communities have been forced to institute new strategies.

ARCH. Local control is an important aspect of many community hospitals. The Affordable Rural Coalition for Health (ARCH) demonstration project, funded by the W. K. Kellogg Foundation, helps rural hospitals shift their focus from acute care to locally controlled health care centers. The ARCH process requires community involvement through the development of local networks. These networks provide communities the opportunity to mobilize the resources of the community's organizations and provide a level of care the community can realistically support.[37]

Partnerships. The need for local control is important because of the special needs of rural communities and the importance of the hospital as a defining institution in many rural communities. There are sucessful examples of rural hospitals that have developed relationships with larger, urban hospitals that allow them to maintain local control as well as achieve stability through the urban center. In western Washington State, Virginia Mason Medical Center in Seattle is part of a group of 15 rural hospitals. The medical center provides educational services, group purchasing, and consulting services to member hospitals. Virginia Mason's participation results in referrals from member hospitals, although referrals are not a requirement of membership. Local hospitals maintain principal control of their facility and gain the benefit of belonging to a formal partnership with other hospitals.[38]

Rural HMOs. The financial distress of many hospitals has forced some communities to develop taxing entities to keep their hospitals open. An alternative to this form of fund-raising is the establishment of rural-based health maintenance organizations (HMOs), owned and operated by the hospitals. Hospital costs are spread throughout the community, and residents of the community make a commitment to the hospital and incorporate this cost into their health insurance. The increased information and administrative requirements for the HMO can be handled by a telecommunications system linking referral clinics throughout the area with the hospital.

New technology. Diagnostics and automated patient records are areas in which telecommunications can play an increasingly important role in health care settings. As text-based terminals are replaced by high-resolution, graphical workstations and voice-input devices, health care personnel will more readily incorporate the technology into their daily interactions with patients, increasing their efficiency.

The Geisinger System

One hospital that has overcome the disadvantages of its rural environment is the Geisinger Medical Center in Danville, Pennsylvania. The Geisinger system of a regional network of outpatient clinics combines the efficiency of a large referral medical center with locally distributed clinics, providing comprehensive health care services to a mostly rural population of over 2 million.

Organization. In 1915, Abigail A. Cornelison Geisinger founded the George F. Geisinger Memorial Hospital in memory of her late husband. Today the hospital offers comprehensive health care based on a physician group practice concept.[39]

The Geisinger system is comprised of the Geisinger Foundation and its nine affiliated entities. The foundation is a parent organization to the system's entities and oversees their health-related business activities. The foundation's 14-member board is also involved in initiating and administering grant and philanthropic support for Geisinger entities.

Geisinger Medical Center (GMC), a nonprofit corporation, owns and operates a 577-bed medical center in Danville. This regional referral center is the system's flagship facility. GMC offers six clinical centers: the Cancer Center, the Children's Hospital Center, the Heart Center, the Kidney Center, the Neuroscience Center, and the Trauma Center. GMC is a Level One Regional Resource Trauma Center and operates a Life Flight® rapid-response, air-ambulance retrieval program.[40]

Geisinger System Services (GSS) provides management and consulting services to Geisinger system entities. Geisinger's Information Systems Department, included in GSS, provides telecommunications equipment and consulting for the system.

The Geisinger Clinic employs Geisinger's multispecialty salaried physician group. The clinic employs 457 physicians at 46 sites in 35 communities. Clinic physicians provide skilled services in 65 areas, including acute intervention in myocardial infarction, laser surgery, magnetic resonance imaging, and sleep disorders.

Founded in 1972, Geisinger Health Plan is one of the nation's oldest and largest rural health maintenance organizations. It serves 78,478 members in 17 Pennsylvania counties.[41]

Administrative uses of telecommunications. As a referral center, GMC depends on the Geisinger doctors in its surrounding rural area to send patients to GMC. To ensure continued referrals, the system pursues formal relationships with doctors in its service area. To establish these relationships, the Geisinger Clinic began purchasing physician practices throughout the region in 1982, and, as a result, the doctors in these practices are employed by the clinic. Doctors see an advantage to belonging to the clinic because of Geisinger's financial security and reputation.[42]

To support the administrative needs of its 46 sites, GSS installed a consolidated billing system. Although individual medical records are kept at each site, the billing system contains basic demographic, insurance, and medical information on patients. Sites are tied to the computer in Danville through dedicated leased lines.[43]

The efficiency of the system has developed around a hub-and-spoke concept, with Danville and Wilkes-Barre in the hub and the spokes represented by the hospitals throughout the region. Local control is an important aspect of the clinic's success. Doctors are not required to refer their patients to GMC, located in Danville. When a local community hospital can provide adequate service, doctors refer patients to that hospital. The six physicians in the town of Bloomsburg, for example, can refer their patients to Bloomsburg Community Hospital. When Bloomsburg's services are inappropriate or specialists are needed, patients are referred to GMC. Sending all of these patients to Danville would place a serious financial burden on the Bloomsburg hospital.[44]

An underutilized service available to the clinics through the telecommunications network is an electrocardiogram (EKG) reporting system. Physicians in the field have the ability to transmit EKG reports from their clinics to specialists at GMC. However, the system is rarely used. According to Bill Byron, the administrative director of operations for the Geisinger Clinic, when physicians diagnose questionable EKG readouts, they tend to send their patient to the GMC specialists anyway, whether or not the EKG is sent through the telecommunications system.[45]

Diagnostic and patient care. Another telecommunications service offered by Geisinger is the Lifeline® program. According to Kim Edwards of Geisinger's Lifeline® Services, almost 100 elderly residents receive equipment for their homes that automatically contacts the hospital when a special button is activated. This gives elderly or disabled patients who live alone or isolated from others an opportunity to contact the hospital in emergencies.[46]

The Geisinger Health Plan (GHP) is another system entity that capitalizes on the telecommunications system, the reputation of Geisinger's name, and the rural nature of the area. Because rural penetration of health maintenance organizations is much less than in urban areas, competition is much less. Geisinger has carved a niche in the market that helps support the regional network of the clinics and GMC in Danville. Today, GHP accounts for 18 to 20 percent of clinic business, with higher percentages in the clinics closer to Danville. GHP's projected five-year growth is substantial. The billing system and communication network are important to the efficient operation and information requirements of a large health maintenance organization.

Regional lab network. The Geisinger system generates about 8 million test results a year. To manage this volume, Geisinger has been implementing since 1985 a regional laboratory network that will handle all of the test results generated throughout Geisinger's regional network. When fully operational, the Laboratory Information System will consist of a series of six hubs. These labs will take specimens, run tests, and feed results into telephone lines connected to the Danville computer. Physicians will then receive reports from the on-line system.[47]

Dr. Jay Jones, the Director of Chemistry for the Geisinger Clinic, said many of the components of a regional health care system fit perfectly with a regionalization of the laboratory. Once coding is standardized, split specimens can be sent to Danville and facilities in the field. This setup can assure quality control and optimal use of equipment. Currently, seven minivans travel over 35,000 miles a month, moving reports and transferring specimens. This expense can be reduced dramatically with the real-time transfer of information. Looking toward the future, Jones anticipates microworkstations with personal computers linked by local area networks at each site. Integrated software for appointments, testing, and lab work will increase the efficiency of the operation.[48]

COMPUTER NETWORKS

The Rural Information Infrastructure

Don Dillman, a prominent researcher in the field of rural telecommunications, asserts that one important feature of the emerging rural information infrastructure is the ability of individuals to access readily and use information technologies when needed.[49] Indeed, in this age of an increasingly integrated world economy, the economic viability of rural communities will be linked to the ability of a farmer, a rural business owner, or a public decision maker to access from distant places information on prices, markets, potential clients and suppliers. Access to information is one of the central prerequisites for the functioning of an efficient market system.

Information can be defined as any message or signal that, when communicated, relates some fact or knowledge about the state of the world. It is important to distinguish between information and data. Data are empirical measures of reality that become information when they are compiled, processed, and organized so that they can have value to a decision maker, whether the decision maker is a farmer, a shipper, a small businessperson, or an officeholder.

Five factors affect the value of information that is available to public and private decision makers: timeliness, accuracy, efficiency, relevance, and accessibility.[50] Information can be enhanced on all five of these factors through its delivery on computer networks. Therefore, computer networks could help rural economic development by enabling public and private economic players to use information that will help them to find economic niches in the global economy.

In this section we examine two computer and telecommunications systems that are operated by the U.S. Department of Agriculture (USDA). Each of these systems represents different models with distinct functions. The older and more established system plays an important role in maintaining and enhancing the international competitiveness of U.S. agriculture, while the latter system is struggling to define its role and objective.

While conducting the research for this section, we examined other networks operated by state agencies. We focus on the USDA networks because they encapsulate many of the findings we uncovered in the state networks.

The Agricultural Marketing Service and the Market News Service

Since 1920, the Agricultural Marketing Service (AMS), a department within the USDA, has operated the Market News Service (MNS).[51] The primary objective of the MNS is to serve as the eyes and ears of the agricultural commodity industry by collecting and disseminating price and shipping information for agricultural commodities from almost 130 field offices nationwide. The data on the network range from daily wholesale prices for specific fruits and vegetables in a particular market to annual national summaries of price and shipping information for groups of commodities. Information is collected on a daily basis from across the nation and is transmitted nationally by telephone recorders, newspapers, radio, television, facsimile machines, and on-line terminals. This information ultimately is aimed at enhancing marketing decisions by shippers, buyers, and producers of agricultural products.[52]

The AMS has six market news branches: fruits and vegetables, livestock and grain, poultry, cotton, dairy, and tobacco.[53] Not all field offices collect information for all of the six categories. The information collected and disseminated by each field office is dependent on where it is located and which commodities are produced and shipped within that region. AMS field offices are usually jointly operated by the USDA and state departments of agriculture; personnel are trained during a three-month period by the USDA at the expense of the federal government.

Network architecture. The AMS network has used numerous technologies to collect and disseminate information since its inception. Since 1980 the network has used a combination of telecommunications technologies to link up the 130 field offices, including dedicated telephone lines and satellite uplinks and downlinks. The network primarily carries information from one field office to all other field offices and to some private users through a dedicated star network.

On a daily basis, nearly 300 federal and state market reporters travel to local farmers' markets and shipping points to record the prices and shipping information of a set of agricultural commodities. These reporters log this information onto a computer at the AMS office. The computer then transmits the information via modem through a dedicated telephone line to a mainframe computer, which processes the data, in the Washington, D.C., area. These data are then transmitted through a satellite uplink and downlink back to the field offices, which are equipped with receive-only VSAT dishes.

Although the satellite broadcasts a continuous flow of information compiled from all of the field offices, each office receives only information that is relevant to agricultural producers and shippers that operate within that region. Each field office is equipped with a data selector programmed to accept only a designated number of AMS reports. There is a backup system based on an electronic bulletin board should the main system go down. The only time the backup system has been used was during one 24-hour period when the satellite linkup was interrupted by an earthquake. Since most AMS offices are equipped with facsimile machines, which have increased in transmission speed, AMS administrators foresee a day when these could become integrated into the existing AMS network.[54]

Dissemination of information. The immediate target audience of AMS information is not the public at large but rather information multipliers—for example, news wire services and private information services such as PRONET and AGRICOLA. An individual with a dedicated computer can select and receive some very broad categories of information, such as all livestock or fruit and vegetable reports. On-line selection and retrieval of individual reports is not allowed, although some states are experimenting with making AMS information more user-friendly by reformatting it and making it selectively retrievable.[55] Approximately 5 to 6 percent of AMS reports are carried by another USDA computer network, the Computerized Information Delivery Service, which is directly accessible through personal computers with modems.

However, depending on the field office, AMS information is made directly accessible to users through printed reports or by recorded voice messages that can be dialed at no cost. One AMS field office representative in Texas estimated that approximately 1,500 callers per week dial the office's 800 number for its AMS recorded voice message.[56] Local media, especially country radio stations, often broadcast this information to the public.

Despite various attempts to make AMS information more accessible, AMS officials admit that their network is not in the business of disseminating information to private subscribers but rather to large information disseminators such as PRONET and the news wire services. The main goal is to disseminate information between field offices and to get AMS information to information multipliers.[57] In other words, the AMS considers itself to be a wholesaler of information, leaving it to the private sector to act as the retailer for AMS information.

Private subscribers that have a dedicated computer can receive AMS data on-line. These subscribers pay a small fee for getting AMS information, which they can reformat or distribute and resell as a value-added service. Approximately 30 individuals and organizations subscribe to the AMS service in this manner.[58]

Users. Since many of the end users of AMS information get their information through the information multipliers, users are often unaware that the original information source was the AMS. Therefore, it is difficult to assess who are the primary users of AMS information.

Small as well as large farmers, shippers, and growers receive AMS information through the broadcast as well as print media. The cost of this information to the user is extremely low or nonexistent. The most prominent recipients of on-line AMS information are the private on-line database companies. According to one study, the number of public access on-line data bases nationwide has grown from just 600 in 1980 to 3,893 in 1988.[59] The prime beneficiaries of on-line AMS information currently appear to be the large commercial agricultural producers. On the other hand, small and midsize farmers who cannot afford the private data services would appear to be the prime beneficiaries of AMS information that is put on telephone voice recorders, broadcast on radio and television, or reprinted in the press.

AMS information is not used by all states. AMS information is useful for growers and shippers in a state such as Florida since the information available through the AMS is pertinent to the large number of vegetable growers in that state. However, in Iowa many shippers and growers of grain apparently rely largely on private information data bases which track the grain futures markets from the Chicago Board of Trade.[60]

AMS officials state that farmers check AMS information for their crops on a daily basis during harvest time. Large farmers use the information and supplement it with information from private information retailers. AMS officials as well as an independent researcher claim that small farmers benefit more from AMS information than large farmers because the latter can afford to access private information services.[61]

Costs and benefits. According to AMS officials, the MNS satellite system is significantly less expensive to run than its predecessor, which was based entirely on dedicated leased telephone lines. In addition, the integration of satellite telecommunications with the computer network has reduced the amount of paperwork involved in running the MNS system and has increased its accuracy.[62]

User fees for printed copies of the daily AMS report are about $15 per month. The $600,000 collected in user fees pay for postage, supplies, and labor. States contribute $2.5 million to the system. It is difficult to place a precise economic value on this information to the end user. However, one documented case in Florida indicates that the use of electronically transmitted market information enabled watermelon growers to negotiate for higher prices, which resulted in more than $3 million in additional revenues for these growers.[63]

The Computerized Information Delivery Service

The Computerized Information Delivery Service (CIDS) acts as the central node in a computer network that links USDA agencies. The primary objective of the service is to make the data in the system available to users as soon as the data are received or at specified release dates set by the agencies. The system can be accessed through a personal computer modem and is aimed at two general communities of users: those within the federal and state governments, and information multipliers in the private sector.[64]

The system, originally called Electronic Dissemination for Information, became operational in July 1985. The main feature of the CIDS system is a comprehensive data base of agricultural statistical and narrative data issued by several USDA agencies. The information on CIDS includes some of the AMS reports, economic outlook and situation reports, foreign agricultural trade leads, export sales reports, world agricultural roundups, soil and water conservation reports, research highlights, consumer information, and press releases. All data on the system are in the public domain.[65]

During the first year of operation the quality of the system was poor. Agencies had difficulty loading, transmitting, and retrieving information. Public users complained of difficulty in accessing the network and garbled reports. The USDA responded to these complaints, and the system is currently operating according to specification.[66]

Network architecture. CIDS functions as the central storage node for on-line computer information from USDA agencies. Users can select specific reports from the network, access it when they wish, and have reports transmitted to them automatically or at specified times. CIDS can also send data to users through an automatic dial-up service.[67]

The computer network is managed by a Martin Marietta Data System mainframe computer. This network is accessible to public users as long as they have the proper equipment (a personal computer with a modem) and are willing to pay a monthly fee.

In a 1979 federal survey that compared CIDS with the Environmental Protection Agency's Toxics Release Inventory data base, both systems were deemed as comparable except that access to the EPA system was found to be more cumbersome and time consuming.[68]

CIDS users. Currently there are 11 USDA agencies that are loading data on CIDS in addition to extension services in 16 states that distribute information through CIDS.[69] Other federal agencies, besides the USDA, also use the CIDS system. Each agency determines the type and the amount of information that is loaded onto the network. In 1989, 10 state agricultural departments were listed as users of the system. In 1989, there were 13 news and information services that subscribed to the CIDS service.[70] The number of information multipliers that add value to the agricultural data received from CIDS and resell this value-added information has grown from 16 in July 1986 to about 50 in August 1989.[71]

The contract for CIDS specifies that service to public users is aimed at those who want to receive broad categories of data in large quantities and that "the targeted audience is thought to include but is not limited to commercial information retailers, publishers, agribusiness establishments, public institutions or organizations administering information dissemination systems."[72]

The USDA publishes catalogs of available agricultural data that can be obtained in hard copy, periodicals, monographs, and various electronic media. CIDS is aimed at augmenting, rather than replacing, the USDA's published reports.[73]

Costs. The CIDS system is financed in large part by user fees. Each agency is assessed a fee based on the amount of information that is loaded or downloaded from CIDS. The development of the system cost $250,000, and in 1989 the total amount of fees assessed to agencies for using the system was $166,400.[74] During fiscal year 1989, user fees ranged from $200 to $38,000 a year. The AMS was assessed the largest fee, followed by the Extension Service, the National Agricultural Statistical Service, and the Economic Research Service.[75] The public can access the information that is on the network by requesting a printed report or with a modem. Printed reports are charged per page, while on-line access costs are based on a minimum monthly charge plus additional charges based on the amount of usage.[76]

As with AMS information, it is difficult to assess the economic benefits that accrue from CIDS. A CIDS administrator estimated that the amount of information that can be placed on the CIDS network for $85,000 would cost about $46 million to print and mail. According to this administrator, CIDS can be a big money-saver for the USDA and its agencies. For example, it costs about $550 in postage and mailing costs to mail out a typical single-page press release to 2,000 people. It costs about $1.22 to send that same information to thousands more people through CIDS.[77]

The AMS originally intended to place all its reports on CIDS. When the CIDS system was being planned, AMS officials viewed the system as a potential replacement for their network. Therefore, the AMS contributed $50,000 toward the development of CIDS. Based on the estimates of the contractor, the AMS agreed to budget $1,500 a month for using the system. However, during the first three months of operating the system the actual cost for AMS usage was $10,000 per month. The AMS was unwilling to allocate more than its budgeted $1,500 per month to CIDS. As a result, the AMS reduced the amount of information it loads onto CIDS to about 6 percent of MNS reports. An AMS official claims that the information loaded onto CIDS has a higher error rate than the current MNS system run by the AMS. Nonetheless, the AMS continues to load data onto CIDS due to USDA mandate.[78]

The following three recent actions by the USDA should make CIDS more affordable and accessible to the public: (1) the minimum monthly subscription fee has been cut from $150 to $75, (2) subscribers are now permitted to access smaller segments of long USDA reports, and (3) the minimum monthly subscription fee has been waived for depository libraries and land-grant colleges that want to access CIDS.[79]

Findings

Although our findings are based on research conducted on the two USDA computer networks, they are also pertinent to similar computer networks operated by states. The findings are as follows:

1. The best-developed computer networks are those devoted to agricultural issues and information, as, from its inception, the mission of the USDA has been to assist rural areas by promoting agriculture. The USDA, through the AMS network, has perfected and fine-tuned a superb information system that contributes to the international competitiveness of U.S. agriculture. In comparison to the CIDS network, the AMS network is more successful at meeting the following five criteria in information delivery: timeliness, accuracy, efficiency, relevance, and accessibility.
2. The success of the AMS network is in part a result of a collaborative effort between federal and state governments to collect and disseminate information on a nationwide basis. The AMS is successful not only because it engages different levels of government but also because it assigns a specific role to the private sector—that of information disseminators. Within the AMS system, the public sector acts as the collector and supplier of information on a wholesale basis, while the private sector acts as the retailer of information by offering the same information in a much more useful and accessible format.
3. While there is a wealth of agricultural information on the AMS and CIDS networks, there is a relative dearth of information targeted at assisting rural nonagricultural development. A farmer in Wachula, Florida, can instantaneously track watermelon prices in Seattle, Washington, through AMS, but a businessperson or community activist in Thorton, Iowa, must wait weeks to get information through the mail on sources of venture capital for rural businesses.
4. Information that could assist rural nonagricultural development is harder to define and identify than information for agriculture. Even professionals who are attempting to promote revitalization and diversification of rural areas could not readily identify what information would assist their efforts.
5. The appropriate design and architecture of computer networks will depend upon the type of information collected and disseminated and the target audience and use. The AMS network is well designed for its purpose, but it would not be appropriate for an information network that disseminates information for nonagricultural rural development.

6. Both the AMS and CIDS networks are difficult to access and use. The AMS has attempted to address this issue by seeking new ways of formatting its information. Nonetheless, throughout our research we found that usage of these networks was hindered by the difficulty of accessing them.
7. The CIDS network and other state networks are underused by their target audiences. This appears to be in part due to the difficulty in accessing them as well as resistance to using the networks by people such as extension agents.
8. The cost of maintaining national or statewide computer networks has increased since the divestiture of AT&T in 1984. This was more of a problem for state networks than for the USDA, whose AMS network utilizes satellite uplinks and downlinks instead of dedicated leased lines. Officials who manage state computer networks also noted that since divestiture it has become more complicated to manage a statewide network because of the additional telecommunications providers.
9. Some offices in remote rural areas experience problems in accessing computer networks because of data transmission problems due to the inferior quality of telephone lines.

CONCLUSIONS

Telecommunications advances offer many applications for public service provision to rural areas. Our research on health care and distance education examined research questions on two levels. First, how have rural communities been disadvantaged by lack of public service and how can telecommunications help? Second, which networks and partnerships constitute the best catalysts for progressive change in rural communities?

The answer to our first question is complex. To begin, small populations constitute unattractive working environments for professionals in many public services, particularly health care and education. In an era of increased specialization, many teachers and medical personnel trained in highly specific fields must practice in populated areas to find large enough clienteles. Service provision in health care and education in rural areas, therefore, has been several steps behind that of more populated communities, leaving rural areas disadvantaged.

Telecommunications now makes the provision of advanced education and health care services possible by creating new economies of scale for the delivery of public service. In the field of health care, neighboring communities are linked through medical information networks. Distance learning, in similar fashion, not only links neighboring towns but also crosses state boundaries, bringing different regions of the country into one classroom. Finally, computer networks enable farmers to access global information specifying market trends, world weather reports, and state-of-the-art growing techniques.

At this time, there is no information regarding the overall effectiveness of these systems. While we know that service providers allow rural communities to access new information networks, we are unable to predict the long-term consequences.

It cannot be stressed enough, however, that new telecommunications infrastructures are essential for the construction of new economies of scale: without the various linkages allowing for information transfer and exchange, service provision in the areas of health care and education remain impaired. Similarly, farmers are unable to access agricultural information that would help them allocate resources as efficiently as possible.

The precursor to providing such networks is, of course, access to state-of-the-art communication technology. Because so many choices are now available, ranging from satellite to fiber optics, rural areas have the opportunity to be creative while planning service provision networks. One example is the Minnesota Distance Learning Network in which fiber-optic capability allows planners to promote two-way interactive video. Because all participants in classroom broadcasts can see and hear each other, the Minnesota system simulates conventional classrooms to the highest degree possible. There is also room for a great deal of creativity regarding the information services provided by the USDA. Because such large volumes of data are transmitted simultaneously, it is often difficult for users to sift out the most critical facts. Networks hypothetically could be established to route specific findings to the appropriate communities, increasing the efficiency of the entire network.

In addition, it is important to see the policy implications involved in selecting particular telecommunications applications for public-service delivery. The aptness of a given technology is an important first criterion, such as use of the switched network for interactive school applications or multiple-point satellite distribution for national or "long-haul" distribution of materials. Of course, as mentioned earlier, these technologies can complement one another. There also seems to be a growing interest on the part of telephone companies and regulators in developing local or regional educational networks. We recommend that these be carefully evaluated from a policy standpoint. It is likely that the development of interactive networks for schools will be a worthy investment for inclusion in the rate base. It will also be a key community service incentive for service providers.[80] Nevertheless, state regulatory commissions must still encourage local telephone companies as much as

possible: If rural areas require advanced telecommunications technology to remain economically solvent, the definition of universal
service will be greatly expanded. If this occurs, telcos will be chal-
lenged to maintain existing goals of universal service but with much
broader ramifications.

It is our strong conviction that, if the preceding considerations are
addressed, the distance education, health care, and information networks discussed in this chapter can be replicated in other rural communities. Clearly, these systems do not replace hospitals at close
range, teachers in the classroom, or personal experience in agricultural
industries. They do, however, provide rural communities with services they could not otherwise obtain.

NOTES

1. Ira Moscovice, "Strategies for Promoting a Viable Rural Health Care
System," *Journal of Rural Health* 5 (1989), p. 223.

2. Ibid., p. 22

3. Office of Technology Assessment, *Linking for Learning* (Washington, D.C.:
U.S. Government Printing Office, 1989), p. 22.

4. Ibid., p. 25.

5. Ibid., p. 28.

6. Ibid., p. 39.

7. Interview with Ed Lethert, Technical Consultant, SECO, Inc., Minneapolis, Minnesota, January 15, 1990.

8. Interview with Dr. John Berling, Director, Learning Resources Center, St.
Cloud State University, St. Cloud, Minnesota, January 15, 1990.

9. Interview with Lethert.

10. Ibid.

11. Ibid.

12. Ibid.

13. Minnesota Telephone Association, *Minnesota Telecom Network: A Vision to
the Future* (Minneapolis, Minn., 1989), p. 7.

14. Ibid., p. 1.

15. Interview with Paul Hoff, Manager, Park Region Mutual Telephone Company, Minneapolis, Minnesota, January 15, 1990.

16. Community College System, *Technical Feasibility Report: Statewide
Video/Audio Telecommunications Network, Higher Education Campuses of Minnesota*
(Minneapolis, Minn., May 26, 1986), p. 7.

17. Interview with Jerry Abraham, MSET Coordinator, Upsala High School,
Upsala, Minnesota, January 15, 1990.

18. Interview with Berling.

19. Interview with Abraham.

20. Interview with Jim Decker, MidTeC Coordinator, St. Cloud Technical
College, St. Cloud, Minnesota, January 15, 1990.

21. Ibid.

22. Interview with Berling.

23. Shane Hawkins, "Technical Improvements On-Going," *TI-IN Network News* 3, no. 2 (Winter 1989), p. 3.

24. Interview with Charlene Blohm, Advertising and Promotion Manager, TI-IN Network, Inc., San Antonio, Texas, December 14, 1990.

25. TI-IN Network, Inc., *The TI-IN United Star Network Fourth Quarter Progress Report* (San Antonio, Tex., July 1, 1989–September 30, 1989), p. 6.

26. Ibid.

27. Ibid.

28. Ibid.

29. Ibid.

30. Pamela S. Pease, "Strategies for Implementing Distance Learning Technologies: Why, When and How," *School Business Affairs*, October 1989, pp. 15–18.

31. Jeffrey C. Bauer and Eileen M. Weis, "Rural America and the Revolution in Health Care," *Rural Development Perspectives* 5, no. 3 (June 1989), pp. 2–6.

32. Although this has not been shown to be empirically true, many rural residents presumably would rather drive past their local community hospital to be treated in a "real" city hospital.

33. Bauer and Weis, "Rural America," p. 3.

34. Ibid.

35. Moscovice, "Strategies," pp. 216–231.

36. American Health Consultants, "The Cost of Rural Health Care," *Business and Health* 6, no. 2 (December 1988), pp. 4–6.

37. Anthony R. Kovner, "The Hospital-Based Rural Health Care Program: A Consortium Approach," *Hospital and Health Services Administration* 34, no. 3 (Fall 1989), pp. 24–30.

38. "Consortium Links Rural Hospitals," *Healthcare Marketing Report* 5, no. 12 (December 1987), pp. 1–5.

39. Dr. Harold Foss, the first chief of staff, from 1915 to 1958, brought the group practice concept with him from his training at the Mayo Clinic in Minnesota. Under this system, physicians are employed by the hospital.

40. A Level One Regional Resource Trauma Center provides 24-hour care and conducts outreach, educational, and research programs in trauma care.

41. Other Geisinger system entities include Geisinger Wyoming Valley Medical Center, a 230-bed hospital in Wilkes-Barre; Marworth, two alcohol and chemical detoxification facilities; Geisinger Medical Management Corporation, a for-profit consulting subsidiary; ISS, a for-profit clinical equipment maintenance service; and DePuy-Lenape, a for-profit entity formed to establish a primary care center in Shawnee on Delaware.

42. Interview with Markland Lloyd, Vice-President of Corporate Communication, Geisinger System Services, Danville, Pennsylvania, January 9, 1990.

43. Interview with Gary Kurtz, Director of Technical Services, Geisinger System Services, Danville, Pennsylvania, January 8, 1990.

44. Interview with Lloyd.

45. Interview with Bill Byron, Administrative Director of Operations for Geisinger Clinic, Danville, Pennsylvania, January 8, 1990.

46. Interview with Kim Edwards, Geisinger's Lifeline® Services, Danville, Pennsylvania, January 8, 1990.

47. Interview with Jay Jones, Ph.D., Associate in Laboratory Medicine, Director of Chemistry for Geisinger Clinic, Danville, Pennsylvania, January 10, 1990.

48. Ibid.

49. Don Dillman, "The Social Impacts/Information Technologies in Rural North America," *Rural Sociology* 50, no. 1 (Spring 1985), p. 9.

50. John J. VanSickle and Thomas Stevens, "Market Information Systems: An Online Agricultural Market News Retrieval System," *Florida Agricultural Experiment Station Journal Series*, no. 1001 (1989), p. 3.

51. General Accounting Office, *Status of Agriculture's Electronic Dissemination of Information System*, IMTEC-87-7ES (Washington, D.C., 1987), p. 17.

52. Interview with Bill Crocker, Chief of Fruits and Vegetables Market News Service, U.S. Department of Agriculture, Washington, D.C., December 8, 1989.

53. General Accounting Office, *Status of Agriculture's System*, p. 17.

54. Interview with Crocker.

55. Interview with Professor John VanSickle, Food and Resource Economics Department, University of Florida, Gainesville, Florida, January 5, 1990.

56. Interview with Crocker.

57. Ibid.

58. General Accounting Office, *Status of Agriculture's System*, p. 17.

59. VanSickle and Stevens, "Market Information Systems," p. 4.

60. Interview with Deb Coats, Software Director, Iowa Extension Service, Ames, Iowa, January 9, 1990.

61. Interviews with Crocker and VanSickle.

62. Telephone interview with Crocker, November 22, 1989.

63. Interview with VanSickle.

64. Martin Marietta Data Systems, *Data Administration Manual* (Greenbelt, Md., August 1, 1988), p. 1.

65. Ibid.

66. General Accounting Office, *Status of Agriculture's System*, p. 12.

67. Ibid., pp. 17–18.

68. Memorandum from U.S. Department of Agriculture, September 29, 1989.

69. U.S. Department of Agriculture, "EDI—U.S.D.A.'s Information Mover" (Washington, D.C.) (pamphlet).

70. Ibid.

71. Memorandum from U.S. Department of Agriculture.

72. General Accounting Office, *Status of Agriculture's System*, p. 15.

73. Interview with Russ Forte, Office of Information, U.S. Department of Agriculture, Washington, D.C., December 7, 1989.

74. General Accounting Office, *Status of Agriculture's System*, p. 6.

75. U.S. Department of Agriculture, "EDI—U.S.D.A.'s Information Mover."

76. General Accounting Office, *Status of Agriculture's System*, p. 14.

77. Interview with Forte.

78. Interview with Crocker.

79. Memorandum from U.S. Department of Agriculture.

80. Interview with Hoff.

4

Small Rural Telephone Companies, Cooperatives, and Regional Alliances

Harmeet S. Sawhney, Jill Ehrlich, Sangjae Hwang, Dale Phillips, and Liching Sung

INTRODUCTION

The research reported in this chapter focuses on small rural telephone companies, cooperatives, and special alliances that illustrate innovative arrangements entered into by small companies. We found that these companies were often very close to the rural development scene—as one business executive put it, "I have to answer to my customers in church every Sunday"—and in many instances revealed innovative applications for local development and public services.

Although the importance of the Bell companies and large independents in the rural scene cannot be ignored—many are included in other chapters of this report—we believe that the small independent companies are deserving of more attention than they usually receive in the examination of rural issues. Many current discussions of changes in federal and state regulation (especially relief from the Modified Final Judgment—MFJ—which produced the divestiture of AT&T) may have different consequences on the small companies than on the BOCs. In addition, any policy strategies for telecommunications and rural development would have to involve the small companies in ways just as positive as the large ones. We hope to illuminate these issues.

Research Objectives

In this chapter we attempt to profile telcos that historically have been lumped together in the category "small independents." We hope to go beyond the anonymity created by this simple categorization and, by taking a closer look at this group, to capture the individual characteristics of its membership. We examined three aspects of rural telephone company operations:

1. *Community Orientation:* an analysis of the role telcos play in their communities. This is important given the diversity of the sites we chose. For example, ownership patterns and organizational structures may affect the relationship between the telco and the community it serves.
2. *Challenges to Rural Service Provision:* Rural telcos face many challenges in providing service to their customers. These range from physical barriers to nonaccommodating regulatory policies. The various strategies selected by the telcos shed light on the diverse philosophies of independent telcos.
3. *Impact of New Technologies:* an assessment of the motivations and mechanisms that bring about deployment of new technologies in rural settings. We will also examine how investments in new technologies affect different sectors of the rural community.

Site Selection

We chose sites that reflected a diversity of company types and conditions of operation. The sites are as follows:

Cooperatives
    Eastern New Mexico Rural Telephone Cooperative (ENMR)
    Eastex Telephone Cooperative
    Mid-Rivers Telephone Cooperative
    XIT Rural Telephone Cooperative
Small Companies
    Big Bend Telephone Company
    Bretton Woods Phone Company
    Clear Lake Telephone Company
    Kerrville Telephone Company
    North Pittsburgh Telephone Company
    Taconic Telephone Corporation
Network Services
    Iowa Network Services, Inc. (INS)

PalmettoNet, Inc.
Electric Cooperative
Cotton Rural Electric Cooperative

The telephone cooperatives chosen for study are distinctive in terms of their technology and organizational format. ENMR is deploying very advanced telecommunications, including SS7 (Signaling System 7) and extensive fiber-optic networks. Eastex is the seventh largest cooperative in the United States and the largest in Texas. Mid-Rivers and XIT show how innovative strategies can bring state-of-the-art technology to sparsely populated areas. PalmettoNet and INS also demonstrate how cooperative efforts among telephone companies make it possible to bring advanced technology and service to rural areas.

The various small telcos studied offer additional examples of innovation. Big Bend's service area is characterized by rocky, mountainous terrain. This site provides a good example of how some rural telephone companies get around topographical impediments to service. Bretton Woods is a small telephone company serving a resort community. However, it is very well positioned to keep pace with the new developments within its service area. North Pittsburgh and Taconic Telephone serve bedroom communities. Clear Lake, as a participant on the INS, has demonstrated the importance of equal access in attracting new business. It has also shown how innovative service can be successfully implemented in rural areas. Kerrville provides an example of a small independent telco serving a retiree-based rural economy. Cotton Rural Electric Cooperative represents a new type of player in the telecommunications industry. It has established itself in the satellite and cable end of telecommunications and is actively pursuing other opportunities in the industry.

Critical Issues

The introduction of competition into telecommunications has raised a number of critical issues for rural telephone companies.

Universal service. Universal service means affordable access to basic local service for both rural and urban residential customers. The FCC has estimated that, by March 1988, 92.9 percent of the 91 million U.S. households had at least one telephone. Except in extremely remote and specific poverty-stricken areas of the country, telephone service has been universally available. The preservation of universal service has been one of the most perplexing issues in the newly created competitive environment.

The threat to universal service results from both deregulation and competition. Traditionally, the goal of universal service was pursued, in part, by mechanisms that helped high-cost companies to maintain low rates and encouraged uniform toll rates. Deregulation and competition both encourage basing rates on costs, a move that threatens to increase local rates everywhere, especially in high-cost areas. This issue is particularly difficult when evaluated in the context of rural America.

Even though telephone service has been universally available in the United States, universal service is still hotly debated. Debates focus on three kinds of arguments. First, a move from a rate-of-return policy to a price-cap policy may threaten universal service.[1] Second, universal service must include the opportunity for residential and business customers to choose a long-distance carrier.[2] Third, universal service should be defined by regulators and telephone industry representatives to include access to other important information services and to a specific set of essential application services such as 411, 911, and long distance.[3]

Price caps. The FCC historically has relied upon a rate-of-return policy to ensure that rates charged to customers for services were just and reasonable and that the goal of universal service was realized. Rate-of-return regulation limited rates to the revenues needed to cover costs plus a fair return on the capital investment.

Critics of rate-of-return regulation have argued that phone companies have little reason to lower capital costs when those costs provide the basis to which the rate of return is applied. As a result, capital and overhead may have been overestimated. Moreover, rate-of-return regulation has resulted in the constant increase of administrative requirements.

Among various alternatives to rate-of-return regulation is price-cap regulation, which would modify rate-of-return regulation to permit price increases only up to a maximum that is less than the rate of inflation. In other words, in order for the telephone carriers to maintain the current level of return on investment, they would have to achieve cost reductions and/or productivity gains. Such a policy shift, if implemented, would have a direct impact on the seven Regional Bell Operating companies and GTE. The shift also would have an indirect impact on rural carriers and create another challenge to which they would have to adjust. Although its effect is disputed, some fear a move to a price-cap policy would allow telephone companies to reduce investment and maintenance in order to increase their profits.[4]

Pooling. Pooling mechanisms were designed to preserve industry stability in the current evolutionary period and are of critical importance to small telephone companies. Current pooling arrangements include separate voluntary pools to recover traffic-sensitive costs and the Carrier Common Line (CCL) pool to recover non-traffic-sensitive costs.[5]

Of paramount importance to universal service are the mechanisms built into the CCL pool, which are designed to minimize the incentive for geographic toll rate averaging. The CCL pool enables high-cost companies to charge interexchange carriers averaged rates for access to their network, which, in turn, lessens pressures for bypass, preserves toll rate averaging, and encourages other long-distance companies to compete in sparsely populated areas. Small independent companies worry about whether the long-term support mechanism can fulfill its function in a price-cap environment.

Equal access. Today, equal access is one of the problems that independent telephone companies must solve in order to establish a new definition of universal service and to attract new business to their communities. Simply put, equal access is the ability of local telephone companies to provide a choice of long-distance carriers to their customers. One of the advantages of implementing equal access is the potential for increased toll minutes of use and, thus, increased revenues. Part of the increase is likely due to the toll stimulation brought by the availability of alternative, and often less expensive, interexchange services.[6] In addition, once equal access is implemented, a telephone company is able to capture more access minutes for billing.

Another major benefit of implementing equal access is that rural telephone subscribers take part in the benefits of competition. Rural customers usually are aware of competitive carriers and the equal access service available in metropolitan areas, and they welcome having similar opportunities in their own service area. The availability of equal access also can allow rural areas to compete for economic development. The lack of telecommunications services such as equal access may put rural areas at a disadvantage in attracting new businesses to their communities.

However, independent telephone companies often have not been able to provide equal access and still maintain a reasonable profit margin. Because the number of rural subscribers and their interstate calling volumes are so low, most competing long-distance carriers choose to service only the metropolitan areas. Independent companies and a few states have developed several methods to solve the problem of providing long-distance service at a low price to rural subscribers, and new methods are continually coming on line (even though some face regulatory and other obstacles).

BETRS (basic exchange telecommunication radio service). The high cost of installing and maintaining local loops in remote areas has long plagued local exchange carriers. BETRS offers rural telephone companies a radio-based alternative that may prove to be more cost-effective than traditional wire and cable in some circumstances. Moreover, the quality of telephone conversations via radio is as good as or better than those carried by cable. With radio service, capacity could increase simply and easily as the route traffic expands.

In the past, two elements impeded digital radio's migration of the local loop: lack of cost incentives (an obstacle in the introduction of all innovative technologies to rural areas) and lack of available frequencies. But these factors began to change after 1984, when the long-term effects of the AT&T divestiture began to emerge. As competition increased in the exchange industry, the local loop costs recovered from interstate rates started to shift to the state jurisdiction. Similarly, as intrastate toll competition increased at the state level, non-traffic-sensitive loop costs were recovered directly from basic local service rates. These factors pressured local exchange carriers to become more cost effective in providing local alternatives for local loop distribution.

A breakthrough in spectral efficiency was necessary before radio could become a viable option for local loop distribution. The needed breakthrough came in the form of digital time division multiplex/time division multiple access (TDM/TDMA) technology combined with state-of-the-art modems and digital voice recorders.

In 1987, the FCC provided the necessary spectrum and developed cost-recovery mechanisms for BETRS. BETRS has provided the incentive to use radio for local distribution, while major advances in spectrally efficient digital radio have offered the means.

Cellular telephone service. The new capabilities of cellular technology offer potential for bringing rural Americans the benefits of modern, advanced mobile communications via the public-switched network. For example, cellular telephone service is vastly superior to conventional mobile service, which serves only one potential antenna and a few channels and thus severely limits the number of users and the service area. Cellular service, in contrast, is capable of serving many subscribers at once because it divides rural service areas (RSAs) into cells. In spite of such advantages, a realistic assessment suggests that cellular markets will be difficult markets to develop. The RSAs typically have small populations scattered over a large geographic area. The average RSA has just over 140,000 inhabitants, with some RSA populations as low as 12,000.

Providing cellular service to RSA subscribers will require a high capital investment. Conservative estimates put the cost of engineering, installing, and testing a simple two-cell turnkey system in the range of $1 million. A switch alone costs at least $500,000 and must be operated by an experienced technician. Moreover, the working capital needed to operate such a system amounts to an additional 30 to 40 percent of total cost. Experience suggests that a cellular operator would need to spend over $1 million to build and operate just a single-cell system in a small RSA in the first years.[7]

SS7/CCS. Telecommunications networks are changing, and the development of the Signaling System 7 (SS7) version of common channel signaling (CCS) is a key to the evolution of intelligent networks and new services. These networks and services of the future may have far-reaching implications for small telephone companies.

The primary expanded function of the CCS/SS7 network is its increased ability to connect external data bases to the network. SS7 will allow for number portability for 800 subscribers because access to interchange carriers will be controlled by a data base. Upon full deployment, it will permit custom local area signaling service (CLASS), which includes caller identification (ID) capability.

Furthermore, carriers in the CCS/SS7 system will be able to design additional new services to meet customer needs such as increased information about the networks or the customer's traffic, increased control over costs and services, and so on. In the near future, both local exchange carriers (LECs) and interexchange carriers (IXCs) will be deploying CCS/SS7 networks. With the multiple networks to be developed by the various IXCs, LECs, and other parties, many services and functions could reside on more than one network.[8] Consequently, there will be competition among LECs, IXCs, and others in the marketplace.

Bypass. Bypass refers to the growing tendency of large telecommunications users (mostly business) to circumvent the telephone company's local public-switched services. New technologies and policy changes have opened additional possibilities for competition with traditional telephone company service. For certain industries and firms, fiber optics, cellular radio, satellites, and other technologies are making bypass more efficient and economically feasible. Telephone companies perceive bypass as a threat to their continuing financial health.

Two issues are central to the bypass debate. The first is the subsidy question and the need to determine whether existing pricing policies are the cause of "uneconomical" bypass. The second concerns the nature of the incentives created by the institutional environment that support the telephone companies' contention that basic local service is indeed subsidized.

The bypass issue has become a vehicle for the industry and regulators to express real and imagined threats to universal basic telephone service, as well as threats to the monopoly power of local telephone companies. The telephone industry believes that relatively low rates for basic local telephone service will enable it to prevent bypass.

SITE REPORTS: COOPERATIVES

Eastern New Mexico Rural Telephone Cooperative

Eastern New Mexico Rural Telephone Cooperative (ENMR) is one of the most technologically advanced small independent telephone service providers in the country.[9] In addition to providing all of its customers with one-party, digital, buried-cable service, it has just completed full deployment of SS7.[10] It has also expanded its trunking architecture with almost 1,000 miles of fiber-optic transmission lines. The company's success is due in large part to its general manager, Robert Harris, who provides a good example of how independent telephone companies can adapt to remain viable in the postdivestiture environment.

ENMR was founded in 1949 and provided the first dial tone in 1951 to seven exchanges. Although it initially received almost 800 applications for membership, its membership soon decreased to 600 because of out-migration resulting from changes in federal land bank payments to farmers. Its growth remained static throughout its first 25 years of operation.[11]

Harris became general manager of ENMR in 1974, and one year later the company embarked on a massive expansion program. Growth was achieved by providing service to those areas not yet receiving any phone service and by acquisitions from less profitable US West exchanges. ENMR not only extended service to 300 new subscribers but claims that it was able to provide better service to areas previously served by Bell operating companies. The company grew from 600 lines in 1974 to 9,277 lines in 17 exchanges in 1990. During the same time period, ENMR increased its net worth from approximately $1 million to over $80 million.[12]

Part of the reason that ENMR has built such an advanced network is that, as a nonprofit cooperative, alternative uses of profits are restricted. To be considered nonprofit, 85 percent of a company's revenues must be derived from its members. Because of ENMR's nonprofit status, it is exempt from paying federal income tax.[13]

ENMR's first digital switch was installed in 1979 as a way to meet new accounting methods and meet-point billing. Before the AT&T divestiture in 1984, ENMR had seven points of connection with long-distance carriers. ENMR decided to combine all seven points into one hub after divestiture as they became more difficult to pay for and to service.[14]

The nucleus of ENMR's network is a Northern Telecom DMS-200 Supernode with a Signal Transfer Point (STP), a UNISYS A12E Service Control Point (SCP) for Custom Local Access Signaling Service (CLASS), and enhanced SS7.

The cooperative's regional SS7 network will provide enhanced services not only to its own customers but to neighboring telcos. Although the entire network cost over $6 million, Harris believes that it was a sound investment and could pay for itself in three years. Because SS7 checks the availability of a phone number before a line is accessed, it can save money over the long run by increasing circuit-routing efficiency and minimizing uncompleted toll calls.[15] Harris believes that most independents can justify investments in SS7-related equipment, but ENMR is in a particularly good position to provide SS7 because it routes calls among larger neighboring cities such as Denver, Albuquerque, Dallas, Lubbock, and Amarillo. Harris reasons that any system that can concentrate calls through a central hub "should pay for itself quickly . . . and can increase system efficiency by as much as 500 percent."[16]

ENMR's regional SS7 network is fully compatible with SIGNET 7, with which Harris eventually hopes to link his regional SS7 network. Compatibility is important because it will give the company greater control over its subscriber data and the revenues that accrue from this information.[17]

Harris also believes that the services associated with SS7 will generate more subscriber revenues. According to Harris, these services are "much more useful to consumers and, thus, more desirable." In addition, the technology on which the SS7 system is based can send calls to the lowest-cost carrier, allowing ENMR customers "rate-specific, time-of-day, and local discounts" in addition to decreasing the cost of switching.[18]

Given ENMR's recent expansion and success, it is not surprising that Robert Harris is optimistic about the company's future. Most of his long-term goals for the company—deployment of SS7, Supernode, and fiber-optic lines—have been met. Now he is focusing on expanded uses for this technology.[19] Harris admits that he has had to adopt a new service philosophy since divestiture. According to him, one now needs to be "one step ahead of the game."[20] His new attitude partially explains many of ENMR's service and equipment upgrades completed in the 1980s.

Harris believes that price caps will soon be a reality. While he does not argue with the premise behind price caps, he does believe that once they are applied to small independent companies, it will be almost impossible for the companies to make significant plant upgrades. Rural consumers and businesses already have fewer services available to them than their counterparts in urban areas because of outdated telephone infrastructure. Price caps probably will create a larger urban-rural gap, but he believes technology is advancing too quickly to remain satisfied with the status quo. For these reasons, he is trying to build an advanced network before price caps are implemented.[21]

ENMR has also expanded its operation into competitive services to help pay for some of its plant upgrades. For example, ENMR now provides billing and operator services for many rural telcos in New Mexico and Texas. ENMR has also entered into an agreement with three other rural telcos to provide cellular service. Because the FCC grants only one license per LATA in the cellular lottery, the alliance enables each party to reap a quarter of the benefits accrued from the franchise.[22] The cooperative has also moved all business services "in-house." ENMR does not hire consultants. It has a graphics and public relations department, a team of accountants, and a settlements specialist. Harris has found ways to procure equipment at low or no cost by entering into special agreements with equipment suppliers. For example, when ENMR was looking for software that would create detailed maps of its service infrastructure, it convinced one computer company to donate over $1 million of computer and graphics equipment in return for mapping programs that ENMR promised to develop for the company. ENMR now uses the equipment not only for high-tech mapping but also for public relations, advertising, and video graphics.[23] The cooperative also makes substantial earnings in interest income by investing much of its capital in T-bills, treasury notes, and other short-term investments. In addition, a wholly owned subsidiary of ENMR sells typewriters, facsimile machines, telephones, and desk sets in Clovis, New Mexico.[24] ENMR also saves money by buying equipment that it anticipates will promote greater efficiency. For example, ENMR now has remote-testing ability, which saves substantially on service calls, given its expansive service area. ENMR's two-way trouble dispatch also cuts the cost of service calls through trouble analysis management.[25]

Harris is not too concerned about the potentially adverse effects of divestiture on ENMR. He says that the move toward cost-pricing is inevitable and that he has prepared for it by introducing greater efficiency into his network and by increasing usage. He believes that cross-subsidies will need to continue and that no rural company will be able to survive without them. The industry's eventual 25-percent cap on the subscriber price factor (SPF) concerns him because ENMR's SPF was 63 percent before divestiture. Despite this concern, ENMR has managed to maintain the same low rates for the past ten years.

Harris is concerned about recent state regulatory decisions. New Mexico's new settlements plan, called the Originating Responsibility Plan, requires that the originating caller's company pay for the entire phone call, from end to end. This definitely puts rural areas at a disadvantage because a larger volume of rural calls are long-distance calls. If the regulatory climate grows worse, Harris will be forced to become a reseller by setting up the company's own 800 number in Albuquerque to cut costs.[26]

The company's community economic development push is focused on distance learning. Now that fiber-optic lines have been installed, interactive distance learning seems to be one of the best ways to put them to use. Eastern Telecommunications Service Company (ETSC), a subsidiary of ENMR, has embarked on an extensive rural education development (RED) campaign ("Big RED") to sell distance learning to schools. The goal of the campaign is that ETSC enter into a working relationship with educators to furnish a means through which the institutions and schools will be able to provide higher-quality instruction to their students. The campaign is also directed at nurses, emergency medical technicians, police departments, and fire departments for accredited training. To date, three universities, 17 schools, and three vocational schools have shown interest in the idea.

ENMR has already shown its ability to deliver distance learning, but educators question the ability of a telephone company to administer an instructional program. Their concerns range from curriculum development to loss of local control.[27] Now that the technology is in place, developing the necessary partnerships with educators and community leaders will be the next big challenge for ETSC and ENMR.

Robert Harris has been the main force behind ENMR's expansion and innovation. The company is considered a "leader in bringing SS7 services to its far-flung subscribers."[28] But in an article in *Rural Telecommunications*, Harris stated that "we don't feel like we are a national leader . . . we feel like we are fighting for our survival and that SS7 is necessary to sustain our very existence."[29] In the same article Harris warned that other rural telcos "had better wake up, or they're going to lose control of their fate."[30]

Eastex Telephone Cooperative

Eastex is one of the largest telephone cooperatives in Texas. It has a total of 20,711 access lines and its service area covers 2,250 square miles. Its 21 exchanges range in size from 2,459 (Livingston) to 253 (Hudson) access lines, with an average per mile subscriber density of 4.2. Though the cooperative has its headquarters in Henderson, the town itself is served by GTE. The cooperative serves the outlying areas of Rusk, Panola, Cherokee, Shelby, Harrison, Hardin, Liberty, Tyler, San Jacinto, Polk, and Walker counties.[31]

Eastex has come a long way since its inception in June 1950. With 204 subscribers in two exchanges (Laneville and Goodsprings), it was

one of the first REA telephone borrowers in Texas. Because cooperatives tend to be essentially local affairs, it is rather unusual to have
one as large as Eastex. Servicing an area that could have supported a
number of smaller cooperatives, Eastex began to experience steady
growth when it began to incorporate a number of small telephone
companies into its service territory. Their owners, who were being
pressed to provide more and better services, were eager to get out of
the telephone business. Thus, Eastex, with REA help, acquired, rebuilt,
and interconnected a number of these systems.[32]

From its beginning, Eastex's internal efforts have been aided by the
resources made available by the REA. Over a period of years, Eastex
has benefited from more than $40 million in REA loans. At the same
time, it is one of the few cooperatives to generate sufficient internal
growth to wean itself from perpetual dependence on REA assistance.
It ended its dependence on REA loans in the late 1970s and since then
has been financing its own growth through internally generated resources.[33]

Eastex's service area previously was a cotton-growing region, but
today the region's main crops are watermelons, tomatoes, and hay to
support a rather marginal cattle and dairy industry (in this area a cattle
lot of 300 head is considered very large). Most of the agricultural
activity is undertaken by retirees who have relocated to the area or by
local farmers of retirement age.[34] Except for the Texas Utilities Company, the only businesses in the area are small country stores with only
one or two telephone lines. In spite of the modest growth environment, Eastex has more than lived up to its motto of "A Phone for Every
Farm." Sixteen of its 21 switches are digital. The remaining five are of
the step-by-step vintage and will be replaced with digital switches by
1992. Since 1978, all subscribers have been enjoying one-party service.
Since 1974 the entire network has consisted of buried cable—particularly important to an area that bears the brunt of frequent and severe
lightning.[35]

Eastex's philosophy as articulated by Allen Dorman, its general
manager, is to anticipate the future. Eastex does not have the resources
to invest in research and development (R&D), but it can stay abreast
of developments and capitalize on opportunities as they arise. For
example, Eastex recently studied the potential for SS7-based services.
After a preliminary evaluation, it concluded that its best option would
be to tie into another company's SS7 facilities. Later, if the technology
shows sufficient revenue potential, Eastex will invest in the required
hardware.

Eastex has initiated several innovative institutional affiliations even
as it has improved its physical plant and service offerings. For example, Eastex is a member of the independent telco consortium that

operates the US Intelco network, which it plans to join at a later date. It plans to start laying fiber in its interoffice trunk routes. In the case of cellular service, it has a head start over other independents because of its prior involvement as a limited partner with Centel for the Tyler and Marshall MSAs. The partnership resulted from the fact that some of the territories of these metropolitan service areas fall within Eastex's service area. For the rural service areas, Eastex has entered into a limited partnership with United Telespectrum and GTE's Mobilenet.[36]

Eastex has consistently purchased state-of-the-art equipment to upgrade its network. Some of the latest software is cheaper when purchased along with digital switches. If purchased as an add-on, the software is very expensive. For this reason, Eastex purchased the Centrex software package along with digital switches. Yet Eastex does not offer Centrex service because there is little market for it among its residential and business users, which tend to have only two or three lines at most. Similarly, though Eastex has the software for equal access, equal access service has not been implemented because no IXC has requested it. As for custom-calling features, call waiting is the most popular, but few customers buy an entire package (e.g., call forwarding, call waiting, conference calling, and so forth).[37]

Although almost all Eastex customers are one- or two-line customers, one large customer is Texas Utilities. The Texas Utilities operation within Eastex's service area consists of mining sites and a power generation facility at Tatum. The surface lignite mines, which are spread over a 30-mile area, feed as much as 40,000 tons of fuel per day to the power plant. The plant supplies power to the regional grid, which serves about one-third of Texas.[38] Texas Utilities has its own Northern Telecom SL-1 switch, which is operated and maintained by Eastex through a lease-purchase arrangement. The mining facility has 300 extensions, and the power operation has 100 extensions. The switch is also used by a power plant maintenance contractor that operates from within the company's facilities.[39] The switch serves as a large PBX for communications within the Tatum facility and between the Mountain View and Fairfield plants and the Dallas headquarters. Although Texas Utilities has had the switch since 1982, only recently has it set up its own microwave network linking all its facilities. Earlier it leased 30 dedicated lines, but now it leases only a few lines as backup for its microwave network.

Aside from reduced costs, Texas Utilities perceives greater network control to be the major advantage of having its own microwave system. The earlier dedicated lines arrangement necessitated coordination among three companies, Eastex, Southwestern Bell, and AT&T. The message path consisted of Eastex's local loop to Southwestern

Bell's microwave haul to AT&T's POP in Longview.[40] Eastex believes that providing service to Texas Utilities has been a constant learning experience. Without the presence of Texas Utilities, Eastex might never have had the incentive to keep abreast of the latest technological developments. And Texas Utilities is happy with Eastex's personalized service and positive attitude—"we cannot guarantee we will fix it, but we will be here working on it."[41] One of Eastex's employees spends almost all his time servicing Texas Utilities facilities.

For those areas in which Eastex does not have expertise, it relies on consultants or outside suppliers. For outside plant design Eastex relies on an engineering consulting firm; it uses a consulting firm to file tariffs. The other information resources on which Eastex relies include state and national industry associations. It is a member of the Texas Telephone Association (TTA), the Texas Statewide Telephone Cooperative Incorporated (TSTCI), the United States Telephone Association (USTA), and the National Telephone Cooperative Association (NTCA). Eastex also uses NTCA for employee-oriented services such as medical, pension, and savings plans. For training its employees it relies on Texas A&M University and equipment manufacturers like Northern Telecom. Its billing is currently done by an outside source. The billing supplier directly accesses Eastex's computer for toll data, processes it, and then sends laser-printed bills to Eastex. The final addressing and mailing are done within the cooperative. Eastex is in the process of buying a new computer and hopes to handle its billing in-house within the next few years.[42]

Eastex initially regarded the new, potentially competitive opportunities and threats to the cost of local service under the MFJ as a major threat, but the company has not been seriously affected by it. Although General Manager Dorman acknowledges the complexities resulting from the MFJ, he feels that they have not directly hampered Eastex. The last time Eastex appeared before the Public Utilities Commission (PUC) was in 1976 for a franchise boundary case. It was last involved in a rate case in 1974 when its REA loans boosted its rates. Since then, its local rates, depending on the exchange, have varied between $6.40 and $7.15 a month.[43] The pooling system has made it possible to keep these rates low. While other rural telcos are now facing pressures for extended area service, Eastex has long been providing such service. About 75 percent of its customers live in rural areas but work in towns such as Henderson, Longview, and Tyler; thus, in the 1950s Eastex made arrangements with the adjoining companies for extended area service.[44] (Dorman believes that the process of providing extended area service has now become very complicated; in earlier days all that was required was a mutual agreement between the concerned companies.)

In the aftermath of floods that hit east Texas in 1989, Eastex displayed a remarkable degree of community commitment. It rewired all the rehabilitated houses free of charge.[45] The company also assisted with emergency operations and arranged telecommunications links for President George Bush's tour of the afflicted area.[46]

Although Eastex has not yet been drastically affected by the MFJ and subsequent developments, it has kept up with the rapid pace of technological developments. This status has been the result of the sophistication of its management rather than pressure from its members, which have relatively simple telecommunications needs.

Mid-Rivers Telephone Cooperative

Mid-Rivers Telephone Cooperative, Inc.—serving an area marked by erosion and scanty vegetation, the so-called badlands of eastern Montana—is known as a progressive independent telephone company in the industry. The co-op, headed by an ex-REA employee, provides telephone services in a huge landmass (about the size of West Virginia) with one of the lowest customer densities in the United States. The company, however, is equipped with the most advanced switching and transmission technologies—almost fully digital switches and hundreds of miles of fiber-optic cable.

Mid-Rivers was established in 1952. The company provides telephone service to about 25,000 square miles in a 20-county area of eastern Montana and one county in North Dakota. It is the largest landmass telephone cooperative in the lower 48 states.[47] The cooperative is headquartered in Circle, Montana, a small rural town with a population of only 800. It operates 20 switches and serves approximately 5,500 customers. The company employs 63 people with an average salary of $30,000 per year (the average annual wage in the area is $10,000-$13,000). It is also the largest property taxpayer in McCone County, where its headquarters are located.[48]

Large and more congregated communities in eastern Montana—such as Glendive, a regional hub with a population of 5,500—are served by US West, one of the Baby Bell companies. Mid-Rivers serves only the extremely remote rural communities surrounding these regional centers. Traditionally, the co-op and US West have had a so-called gentlemen's agreement not to get into each other's territory. However, this agreement was put to the test in the summer of 1990, when Mid-Rivers' fiber-optic cable crossed through the city of Glendive. Because the state of Montana does not have franchise regulatory authority to protect telephone companies' territories, Mid-Rivers' fiber-optic line, which will connect two Glendive schools to its system and which has the potential to draw customers away from US West territory, will draw attention to some regulatory issues.

Mid-Rivers has been in the spotlight recently because of its proposed educational service. The co-op interested several rural schools in using its fiber-optic cable to transmit interactive television courses in the fall of 1991. It plans to expand the network to include Glendive's community college and high school. If the interactive television proposal succeeds, it will be the first distance learning system in eastern Montana and the first such system provided by a telephone co-op in the state. Its interactive television proposal was received positively by the involved communities.

Mid-Rivers is also an AT&T subcontractor and as such provides AUTOVON (Automatic Voice Network) service for a U.S. Department of Defense facility about 20 miles northeast of Glendive. It is the only co-op in the nation to support this military communication network service. A subsidiary of the cooperative, the Cable and Communications Corporation, owns five cable television systems in eastern Montana and markets television receive-only (TVRO) satellite dishes, mobile telephone equipment, telephones and accessories, facsimile (fax) machines, and telecommunications devices for the deaf (TDD) equipment. Unlike its parent company, which is a cooperative, the subsidiary is not constrained by the guidelines for nonprofit organizations.

In addition, Mid-Rivers is a limited partner in providing cellular phone service in Billings, the largest city of Montana, and a general partner in six rural service areas, including one in North Dakota. The company is interested in the cellular phone business because nonwire technology has the potential to compete with land-line service and contribute to bypass of the local loop, especially in sparsely populated areas. Mid-Rivers has involved itself in the service as a protective measure to guard its territory. Its cellular phone services in the six RSAs started in 1990.[49]

Mid-Rivers' telephone plant investment is $39.8 million, $26 million of which is from REA loans. So far the company has paid back $10 million to the REA. The cooperative's monthly basic phone service charge for residents is $12; business users pay $19. However, because free calling areas are limited, the average customer's monthly payment is $50. It is estimated by the company's managers that about 70 percent of Mid-Rivers' revenue is from toll calls.[50] It serves some of the most rural communities in the United States with the most modern technologies. The co-op's telephone plant is equipped with state-of-the-art digital switches and fiber-optic cable. All customers have single-party line service; they also enjoy advanced customer services such as call waiting, call forwarding, and three-way calling—which are not available in the city of Glendive, located in a US West service area.

Mid-Rivers is in the process of upgrading its switching and transmission systems. It began converting analog and electromechanical switches to digital in 1981. In the summer of 1990 the last four switches were replaced by digital ones, effecting a fully digitized switching system. The co-op started to lay fiber-optic cable in 1988. So far, 200 miles of fiber lines have been installed and another 200 miles are projected in the next two years. The company plans to replace all trunking cable and microwave links, which were installed at various times until 1984, with fiber optics.[51] The cooperative has provided AUTOVON services to the U.S. Department of Defense in conjunction with AT&T since 1970. The AUTOVON system also will be upgraded to digital switching and fiber optics in 1990 and 1991.[52] In the summer of 1990, the co-op built a 20-mile fiber-optic line to connect its AUTOVON site in the northeast suburb of Glendive with the digital facilities it maintains in West Glendive. This fiber-optic trunk will run through the city of Glendive and parallel part of the existing fiber-optic cable owned by US West.

Executives of Mid-Rivers maintain that to go the route of fiber optics and digital switching is the only way to provide services of the future. General Manager Gerry Anderson, who worked with a number of independent telephone companies and served a ten-year stint with the REA before becoming the head of the co-op, states: "The [modern] telecommunications infrastructure has to be there in order for other things to happen." Anderson argues that modern technologies have helped the co-op operate more cost-effectively.[53]

Bill Wade, Anderson's assistant, cited several reasons why Mid-Rivers is going with fiber optics. First, fiber-optic cable has become cheaper and more cost-effective to install in recent years as more and more fiber-optic cable is being laid. Second, the technology has improved significantly. For example, the ease of fiber splicing has made repairs quicker. As a result, fiber is now easier to install and maintain. Third, fiber-optic technology has almost unlimited capacity, which makes it possible to carry video, voice signals, and data at the same time. Although video signals can be transmitted over microwave as well, they take up so much bandwidth that there is little space left for voice. According to Wade, fiber-optic cable's high capacity makes it an ideal medium for interactive television transmission.[54] The company started to market interactive television to schools after it realized that such a service could yield some additional revenue.

In the process of laying fiber-optic cable, the company passed through four rural high schools that are 15 to 112 miles away from each other. Mid-Rivers approached these schools in the spring of 1989 with a proposal to provide interactive television courses through its fiber-optic lines. The schools are interested in the proposal because some of them are relatively small and are unable to meet a new state mandate to provide foreign language courses to junior high school students.[55] Furthermore, because of the economic recession that hit the region in the early 1980s, most communities in eastern Montana are losing population and student enrollment is declining. The interactive television proposal provides these schools a way to share resources and, more important, to keep the schools open and maintain teaching and staff positions.

As the co-op's upgrading plans grow, so does its interactive television proposal. Mid-Rivers has approached Dawson Community College and Dawson County High School in Glendive in an effort to include them in the distance learning network, which currently encompasses only four rural schools outside the Glendive area. Mid-Rivers will have to lay extra miles of fiber-optic cable to connect the two schools.[56]

Mid-Rivers has received favorable feedback from the high school and the college regarding the expansion of the fiber-optic interactive television network. Dawson County High School is interested in the project for economic reasons. In recent years the school has experienced a dramatic drop in enrollment due to the economic difficulties the region experienced in the 1980s. The school was built to accommodate 1,000 students but now has only 500. Through the distance learning system, the high school intends to become a program provider for smaller schools outside of the city in order to keep its teachers and staff members in place.[57]

Dawson Community College is one of two institutions of higher education in eastern Montana. It serves as a cultural as well as a community education center, offering adult literacy courses, for example. The college would like to enhance its role in the community through the interactive television system. Donald Kettner, the president of Dawson Community College and an advocate of distance learning, looks at the interactive television proposal as a way to market the college outside of Glendive. Plans are also being discussed to link the college through fiber-optic cable with Miles City Community College, 76 miles southwest of Glendive, so that both colleges can share courses and faculty members. The fiber-optic connection, if approved, will be provided by US West.

Mid-Rivers already has sent a formal proposal to Dawson Community College. Although the high school has not received a similar proposal, serious discussions between the phone company and school board suggest that some formal action will take place soon.[58]

The pilot project to link four remotely located schools through fiber optics has been finalized. The first interactive television course was delivered in the fall of 1990.

Two questions have been raised regarding Mid-Rivers' interactive television proposal. First, why is the co-op so actively pushing to provide educational service? Second, will Mid-Rivers violate the so-called gentlemen's agreement when it puts fiber-optic cable into Dawson Community College and Dawson County High School, which are in US West's service area?

Mid-Rivers claims that the use of fiber-optic cable for educational purposes will benefit the entire community and represents the most effective use of its resources. It argues that the interactive television service is an unexpected bonus that grew out of the company's modernization plan. Bill Wade has stated, "As we were upgrading our network, we happened to pass through these rural schools. At that time we noticed that we had a great opportunity to provide distance learning and our technology can make it cost-effective for the schools to participate in such a system."[59] Critics, however, claim that interactive television is nothing more than an excuse for the co-op to use the revenue pooling system and gives the company a justification for implementing expensive, yet not absolutely necessary, facilities.

Despite these arguments, Mid-Rivers' interactive television proposal was received positively in recent economic development workshops, which are part of a regional cooperative effort for economic revitalization. Various community leaders in the region embrace the educational service proposal because they recognize human resources as a critical factor for economic development. In addition, although the State of Montana recently passed an initiative to assess the educational application of telecommunications, the possibilities of establishing a state-run distance learning system in eastern Montana are minimal. Mid-Rivers' interactive television proposal, however, provides a viable alternative for local communities.

With regard to violating the "gentlemen's agreement" with US West, the problem is more complex. First, it will result in duplicated infrastructure. Mid-Rivers' proposed fiber-optic cable route through the city of Glendive will parallel a small part of the existing fiber-optic line built by US West to connect the two phone companies' plants.[60] Although the duplication at this time occurs for only a short distance, there will be greater infrastructure duplication in the future when the proposed US West fiber-optic cable is extended from Billings to Glendive.[61]

Second, Mid-Rivers will totally bypass the US West network to provide service to the high school and the college—both of which are in the Bell company's service area.[62] To date, US West has not taken any action against Mid-Rivers, primarily because there is no certified territory in Montana and it is legal for one telephone carrier to provide service in another's trade territory. An equally important reason is that US West does not provide a similar educational service. However, if Mid-Rivers uses its fiber-optic cable to provide phone service in Glendive, considerable friction will be generated.

Mid-Rivers has expressed little interest in taking customers away from US West. According to Gerry Anderson, the co-op's intent is to provide interactive television to the entire area. Anderson stated, "It is not our plan to get into a competitive war with US West. We have to cooperate with them in many ways and we intend to keep this cooperative relationship."[63]

To some extent Mid-Rivers' interactive television proposal highlights a long-term debate: Are subsidized telephone companies overinvesting or are they providing quality service when they install expensive modern equipment in less-populated areas? One argument against investing in equipment upgrades is that the farmers and ranchers that Mid-Rivers serves probably do not care much whether their phone calls are analog or digitally switched as long as the calls get through. Nor can they tell the difference between a phone conversation delivered by fiber-optic cable and one delivered by copper wire. Opponents thus argue that it is not necessary to provide sophisticated telephone technologies when what is needed is only a dial tone. Moreover, it is more costly to install a new system in remote rural areas because of the lack of economies of scale. Because Mid-Rivers, like other co-ops, benefits from various public policies, its investments should be well scrutinized. Critics question whether the co-op is using interactive television as a mechanism to manipulate the system and to overinvest in unnecessary equipment.

Proponents of upgrading rural telecommunications infrastructure, on the other hand, argue that telephone service is a greater necessity to people who are 30 miles away from any business or public service than it is to people who live in urban centers. Advanced telephone systems, according to them, are even more important in isolated areas because they can better overcome distance barriers. Moreover, rural people should have phone services equal in quality to those of their urban counterparts. There is no reason to deprive rural people of the right to enjoy and take advantage of advanced telecommunications technologies and, more important, the potential economic opportunities offered by these technologies.

Gerry Anderson responds strongly to the argument of overinvesting. He states that his company is upgrading only the older and fully depreciated plant. Furthermore, new technologies such as digital switches and fiber-optic cables provide cost-effective services. They require less maintenance and are capable of doing more things faster. Anderson indicates that thus far all the funds for upgrading have been generated internally. The company has not raised new debts to finance its modernization plan.[64]

XIT Rural Telephone Cooperative

XIT Rural Telephone Cooperative is in many ways a natural outgrowth of the area it serves. It would be expected that any telco that serves a segment of the expansive landscape of northern Texas would have a very low subscriber density, but it is difficult to imagine one as low as XIT's—0.7 per mile. XIT serves only about 1,050 access lines within its vast service area of 32,001 square miles. XIT is truly a rural cooperative. Even its name is derived from the branding letters of one of the oldest cattle ranches in the region.

XIT's headquarters are located in Dalhart, but the town itself is served by GTE. In a reverse case of urban-rural disparity, Dalhart still has electromechanical equipment while all seven switches in XIT's service area are digital. In 1980 XIT decided to acquire digital switches instead of expanding on the existing equipment. From the perspective of rural telephony, the digital switches have had an interesting impact on the maintenance time—important in rural areas where distances can mean a great deal of driving. Earlier the cooperative often had to send a technician 40 miles for even simple functions like customer disconnects. Now these functions can be performed remotely from the main office.[65] In general, the cooperative members are well served by the digital switches. Among other things, the cooperative members enjoy the benefits of custom call features that are not available to residents of the more urban Dalhart.

One major disadvantage faced by XIT's members is lack of equal access. Conversion had been hampered by the inability of the cooperative's commercial billing computer to do billing for equal access, but a new commercial on-site billing computer was acquired in 1990. This should position XIT to accommodate a request for equal access.

XIT tied its six outlying switches into a tandem switch at Coldwater in 1981–1982. At present the outlying switches feed into the tandem switch for a variety of reasons. The network arrangement aggregated demand at the Coldwater tandem switch to a level that made it an attractive pickup point for ten other interexchange carriers for Feature Group B and interim 800 service. The arrangement also provided XIT with the toll facility for serving interexchange calls that originate and terminate within its territory. With the present network configuration, the circuit for interexchange calls between any two points within its own territory is accomplished at the Coldwater tandem. In the past, calls went from the originating point to Amarillo and then returned to the terminating point in XIT territory. Currently, approximately 13 percent of the total toll calls by XIT's members originate and terminate within its territory. The advantage that XIT derived from developing a tandem at Coldwater included not only the toll revenue but also greater network control.[66]

XIT is one of the first cooperatives in Texas to offer cellular service, which became operational in June 1990. It is operated through a limited partnership with Southwestern Bell, in which XIT has 99-percent ownership and is the operating partner. The partnership was forged basically to increase the chances of getting the license to pro-vide cellular service in the RSA lottery process; it increased the odds of getting the license from 1:6 to 1:2. Southwestern Bell has some say in frequency management, but its input especially was required for connections with the cellular system.[67] The arrangement seems to be working very well. (Earlier XIT had rejected a proposal from some other telcos for an equal partnership arrangement among a group of companies. XIT believed that a committee approach was unlikely to work in a competitive situation.)[68] XIT now has two cells in operation, with a total of 175 customers. A cursory comparison with Amarillo's service area highlights the rurality of XIT's service area. Amarillo's and XIT's service area each has two cells, but the former's population base is about 250,000 while the latter's is only 35,000.[69] Although XIT does not expect profits for the next six or seven years, it believes that its service area holds good potential for cellular services. One source of optimism is the presence of major highways crossing its service area. It expects that in the future about 60 percent of its cellular revenue will come from the pass-through traffic.[70] XIT's cellular sys-tem is an excellent example of how rural telephony can add value to the urban networks.

XIT also expects extensive use of cellular service by the local popu-lation, given the current use of radio on farms and ranches. For example, Larry Kemp, who farms two properties, bought a cellular set as soon as the service was available in his area. Because his two medium-sized farms are 16 miles apart, a cellular phone made great sense to him. XIT expects cellular technology to have a dramatic impact on rural telephony.[71] One anticipated effect is that cellular technology will cause significant changes in the calling pattern on XIT's network. Currently, the peak traffic period on XIT's wired net-work is between 9 and 11 P.M., a time when farmers are not busy working in the fields and have an opportunity to call neighbors and suppliers. Cellular service is likely to change this pattern; farmers will have access to a phone throughout the day.[72]

The biggest problem facing XIT with its new cellular service is making the necessary commercial and regulatory arrangements. For example, eventually XIT will have to enter into a roaming agreement with each of the cellular service providers in the United States. It is now concentrating its efforts only on the wire-line companies.[73] In this matter XIT is fortunate; because of its partnership with Southwestern Bell it needs only to make amendments to Southwestern Bell's prior agreements. XIT also benefits from its prior experience with cellular operations through an earlier limited partnership for five SMSA (standard metropolitan statistical area) markets. In these partnerships Southwestern Bell has 71-percent ownership, and XIT and five other partners collectively own 29 percent. The cellular operation has induced changes in the way XIT runs its business, particularly in the area of marketing. According to J. D. Jones, assistant general manager, "cellular is dragging us into marketing."[74]

XIT Telecommunications & Technology is the subsidiary that handles all the deregulated operations. Through the activities of this subsidiary the innovativeness of the XIT approach finds its best expression. For example, XIT Telecommunications & Technology built a fiber-optic link from Coldwater to downtown Amarillo, which is served by Southwestern Bell, and it is now reselling the capacity to AT&T.[75] Southwestern Bell believed that XIT would not be able to install the link and that if it did succeed, it would not be able to operate it. The success of the fiber-optic link personifies XIT's business philosophy as articulated by Jimmy White, general manager: "XIT cannot increase the population in the area; it also cannot increase its efficiency beyond a certain limit. But it can go for AT&T and GTE dollars for some specialized markets." Coming from a 1,050-line cooperative with such low subscriber density, this is indeed a spirited stance. At the same time, XIT realizes that it can improve its own system to only a certain degree. For larger-scale efforts it sees the need for entering into partnerships with other telephone companies.[76]

Unlike many other rural telcos, XIT does not lament the rural nature of its customer base. In fact, XIT has a very positive attitude toward its rural customers. It believes that in rural areas the market potential is doubled by virtue of the fact that a farm represents a business as well as a residential customer.[77] Jerry Lobley, a resident of Texline, is an excellent example of this type of customer; he is a trader in cattle feed whose business grosses approximately $13 million annually. He operates a telecommunications-intensive business because he needs telephones to trade with a business community of about 150 buyers and 100 sellers.[78] His telephone bill for 1989 was just under $27,000; he is XIT's largest customer. But, despite his large telephone bill, at present he is basically a "plain old telephone service" (POTS) customer. He has three lines with a call rollover feature.[79] He does not as yet have a computer but feels the need for one. He also plans soon to buy a fax machine, which he thinks would be useful for exchanging weight tickets and contract copies. This capability would be particularly useful because "in this business, often the consignment is delivered before the contract itself."[80] At one time he had an answering machine, but he does not use it anymore because he feels that his acquaintances do not like answering machines. Furthermore, there is always somebody near the phone. The access problem has been further reduced by cellular phones. Of the custom-calling features, he particularly likes speed dialing. He does not think that 800 numbers would be particularly helpful in his business because, compared with the dollar amounts of his transactions, the telephone tolls are relatively insignificant. The only piece of relatively sophisticated telecommunications equipment he has is a VSAT feed that gives him the latest commodity prices.[81]

Jerry Lobley is pleased with the service he gets and does not see any major disadvantage in the fact that his telephone needs are served by a small rural cooperative. In fact, he believes that he receives more personalized service than he would if he were located in a bigger city.[82] Although he could have located his business anywhere, he chose Texline because he found it to be "peaceful." Among other things he runs about 400 head of cattle, more as a hobby than a business proposition.[83]

The fact that a person like Jerry Lobley is operating in XIT territory is a tribute to the service provided by the cooperative. To date, there has been no major disruption in service to Jerry Lobley, whose business is critically dependent on telecommunications links. Now, with cellular service, XIT can provide a backup system: "If his lines are down, we will get him cellular."[84] This attitude pervades XIT's business operations. Even though the only equipment XIT sells is telephone instruments, it helps members of the cooperative with computers, modems, and fax problems. The members appreciate this aid because in most cases the product support system of the original vendors does not extend into rural areas.[85]

XIT's sense of service has been demonstrated on other occasions. Caprock Industries, a large feedlot operation, appreciates the cost-effectiveness study that XIT conducted to evaluate 800 services for Caprock's business operations. Based on the study, Caprock Industries decided against the 800 service option.[86] In Texline, where there is no extended area service, XIT installed special coin phones in schools so that children could call home for 25 cents.[87]

That XIT is able to serve an expansive, thinly populated landmass with a level of service on par with the best is a tribute to its management. Along with efficient management of minimal resources, XIT has consistently planned for the future in a proactive way. XIT demonstrates how rural enterprises can use effective management to circumvent some of the handicaps inherent in being rural.

SITE REPORTS: SMALL COMPANIES

Big Bend Telephone Company

Big Bend Telephone Company serves 3,000 subscribers in over 17,000 square miles of the Chihuahua Desert in west Texas.[88] The service area is very sparsely populated and is characterized by forbidding mountains and rocky terrain. While Big Bend serves a few small towns, many of its subscribers are ranchers whose homes are widely scattered.[89]

The parents of the current owner, Jeff Haynes, founded Big Bend in the late 1950s. The Hayneses needed telephone service themselves and decided to establish their own telephone company. Considering the very low population in the company's initial exchange area, this was a very speculative investment. The company could install only a two-way radio patch at first. The driving force behind Big Bend Telephone Company was a $2 million loan from the REA for the company's 165 subscribers. The loan was used to invest in open-wire transmission technology.[90]

Since then, Big Bend has enjoyed steady growth, providing telephone service to areas that were not previously certified and buying other telephone companies and exchanges. As the company has grown, open-wire transmission has become prohibitively expensive to maintain and service. Ironically, the company has been experimenting with emerging radio technology in the past several years, the same basic technology with which the company began.

Approximately 80 percent of Big Bend's network is still on open wire, which poses many problems for Big Bend and its subscribers. First, open wire requires very high maintenance and therefore is very costly. It is especially vulnerable in the Big Bend area, where it attracts a lot of lightning, is prone to freeze, and often falls in heavy storms. The aerial cable in Big Bend National Park is eaten through by woodpeckers every five years. Another problem is that the equipment is so old that very few companies even make the wire and equipment necessary for its maintenance.[91] As a result, customers suffer from down time and prolonged and costly service calls.[92]

While Big Bend tries to provide state-of-the-art technology, its equipment is contingent upon the terrain, the available technology, and the service density. It basically provides whatever kind of technology works within an exchange. Big Bend was one of the first telcos to use the Motorola rural radio system (first-issue BETRS) in 1978. Although very useful in its day, it is now outdated; Motorola does not even make the system anymore.[93]

Big Bend will begin REA field trials for a new Rockwell BETRS system in very hard-to-reach service areas. As an REA trial site for the system (which must be tested by the REA in selected areas before it is "REA approved" and therefore used by REA loan recipients), the company will be one of the first to provide it. Big Bend is testing the system in the Heath Canyon exchange, but if the system is approved, the company will apply for a loan to provide BETRS in its other exchanges.[94]

Currently Big Bend is using a Canadian-manufactured radio system that is very similar to BETRS but operates on a different frequency. Although Big Bend is very happy with the system, its price has skyrocketed since it was first purchased several years ago. It has also become very expensive to do business with the company because of tariffs, taxes, and the distance to Canada. Big Bend's president, Bill Golden, sees BETRS as a very important component of the company's future infrastructure. However, both Haynes and Golden emphasized that no one technology is a panacea for Big Bend, given the varying topography of its service area. Rather, the company must rely upon a "concert of technologies" for service provision.[95]

Most of Big Bend's upgrades are occurring in its more concentrated service areas. Many of the more populated exchanges already have buried cable. But, because of the terrain, each exchange is a little different and requires different technology. For example, cable cannot be buried in rock and over mountains.[96] Currently, only 4 of its 14 exchanges have digital switching. Yet the Texas Public Utilities Commission's (PUC) depreciation schedules have hindered many necessary plant upgrades in the past. The company has little financial incentive to make new investments; although it is still paying off its original loan, because the equipment is so out of date, Big Bend is forced to retire its plant long before its debt.[97]

Although Big Bend is not able to provide the most advanced services for all of its customers, it does seem to have improved upon the quality of service in areas formerly served by other independents or BOCs. For example, all of Big Bend's exchanges are connected by digital microwave, which is very useful for the long distances that the company must cover.[98]

Two of Big Bend's larger exchanges, Sanderson and Presidio, were formerly served by Southwestern Bell. One Presidio resident criticized Southwestern Bell because workers had to drive long distances to make service calls. It was this customer's feeling that Southwestern Bell had no ties to the community and therefore did not care about the lack of quality service in the area.[99] Indeed, Jeff Haynes admitted that he is very conscientious about the level of service he provides to his customers, who are also his friends. When asked why he pays so much attention to his customers' needs, he replies—only halfway joking— "They know where we live."[100]

Big Bend's current goal is to upgrade all of its plants to one-party service. Although the company would like to achieve this in five years, it realistically predicts that it will take ten. The company is also under pressure to provide more advanced services than before. It hopes that the Rockwell BETRS will soon make what was once impossible a reality.[101]

The company's biggest problems in the past dealt primarily with the logistics of getting service to its customers; today the problem is one of cost. Rarely before divestiture was technology developed for rural uses. Today, many new technologies are available from different suppliers to facilitate service in rural areas, but paying for this technology is the problem. It is difficult for companies with such low user density to make enough profit to invest in newer technology. Stringent REA guidelines and lengthy depreciation schedules also make it difficult to obtain loans and upgrade plants. Big Bend hopes that the Texas PUC and the REA will begin to look at the benefits of shorter depreciation schedules, as the newer equipment would require less maintenance and thus be less costly in the long run.

Given that its cost for providing service is approximately $12,000 per subscriber, the company is also very concerned about the fate of pooling. No company would be able to provide service to this area without traditional pooling or some other mechanism to subsidize operating costs. Although Big Bend has explored many ways to rely less heavily upon traditional industrywide subsidies, it defends these "tooth and nail" out of basic survival instinct. Jeff Haynes criticizes companies that take advantage of the pooling system by overinvesting in their infrastructure, accusing them of fueling the Bell companies' arguments for instituting voluntary pooling.

Both Haynes and Golden feel that costing in Texas is also a mounting problem. The PUC commissioners refuse to increase local rates by attributing more costs to the local exchange. The resulting high cost of toll calls is steadily increasing the amount of bypass. They attribute this problem to pressure from consumer groups. If the commissioners do not act, Haynes and Golden believe that more and more large users will leave the public network and the problem will reach crisis proportions.

Presidio is Big Bend's fastest-growing exchange. As a result of increasing government and business activity in the town, cable was buried there in 1987, vastly improving the quality of service. The U.S. Customs Office in Presidio operates a TECS II computer that facilitates border enforcement by enabling the border patrol to input all incoming license plates and commercial cargo. The system formerly experienced significant service interruptions due to thunderstorms, thus hampering enforcement efforts. Today the system experiences far fewer blackouts of much shorter duration. Yet service interruption due to power failure is still a problem in the area. Lack of sufficient lightning protection on its wires causes many brownouts and blackouts.

Several years ago, many large companies were interested in building twin plants—as maquiladora projects—in Presidio and its sister city across the Mexican border, Ojinaga. Maquiladoras are twin plants located with operations on both sides of the American-Mexican border. Labor-intensive work, such as assembly, is done on the Mexican side to take advantage of lower wages, while the corporate functions are performed on the U.S. side. At that time Ojinaga had crank-type telephones and operators manually switched calls, and Presidio had analog switches and open wires. The companies found that their computers would not communicate across the international border with such poor infrastructure. Even plants that were solely interested in setting up manufacturing operations in Presidio complained of too much static and interference on the lines to transmit data and facsimiles. Presidio's underground cable has alleviated these problems, and the president of the local chamber of commerce, Robert Bryson, is pleased with the town's new service.

Big Bend serves the most physically challenging area of all of our sites. It also has one of the highest costs per subscriber in the country. While the company has benefited from divestiture in terms of new technology and service possibilities, it stands the most to lose if traditional mechanisms for universal service are frozen or phased out. As a result, the company is actively defending the policies that have ensured its survival in the past. At the same time, the company is dedicated to bringing the best service and technology to its subscribers. It has pursued several avenues to realize this goal and is constantly assessing technological and financial opportunities as they arise. The owner of the company, as an active member of the Texas Telephone Association, is in a position to assess other trends in the telephone industry.

Bretton Woods Phone Company

Several factors led us to include Bretton Woods Phone Company in our study of rural telephone companies and rural economic development. Bretton Woods is the only site in our sample completely dependent on tourism and resort traffic for its revenue base. Bretton Woods is very innovative in adopting new technologies compared with other telephone companies similar in size, number of access lines, and type of exchange area. Another unique feature of the site is that there are few residential customers; most lines are for rental properties. The success of Bretton Woods Phone Company depends on a combination of several factors: the scheduling of meetings and conferences in the town; the ski season and weather conditions, and planned development by real-estate developers. Bretton Woods is also heavily reliant on trade associations and larger telephone companies for sharing information on new technologies.

The history of Bretton Woods Phone Company, located in Bretton Woods, New Hampshire, began with the operation of the Mount Washington Hotel.[102] The company's operations were centered around the hotel and its grounds, with its switchboard and office located in the hotel itself.[103] The hotel business required phone service, but New England Telephone was reluctant to service the area because it did not believe its costs could be recovered in such a remote area, in spite of the business offered by the hotel. This situation led to the formation of the Bretton Woods Phone Company.

An exchange map filed with the New Hampshire Public Utilities Commission (PUC) on February 1, 1940, shows the boundaries within which Bretton Woods was allowed to operate.[104] The map was the first notification to the PUC that Bretton Woods Phone Company was in operation. The company filed its first annual financial report in 1947.[105] It also filed its first tariff on June 15 of the same year, which meant it could legally operate as a public utility.[106] However, the telephone company was run in a highly departmentalized manner rather than as an individual public utility. For example, it did not have its own set of books.[107] The PUC allowed this idiosyncracy because there were no outside customers. The Bretton Woods Phone Company's "existence" as an entity wholly separate, physical and otherwise, from the hotel began on July 1, 1988.

Even though Bretton Woods is small, the company has the ability to provide innovative custom-calling services such as call waiting, call forwarding, and three-way calling. It has replaced virtually the entire outside plant in the past five years with all new cable.[108] A DS-10 digital switch was installed in anticipation of growth in the area.[109] Before the digital switch, the company used a CX-1000 central office step switch.[110] The plant manager describes the upgrade this way: "Before the old switch was replaced by the DS-10, most of the plant technician's time was spent in the trailer just keeping it going. Now he has the time to do engineering and to help advise the company on how it should position itself for expansion."[111]

Bretton Woods does not offer a true emergency phone service.[112] However, if someone does dial 911, the call is directed to the state police barracks and a trained dispatcher handles the call. Even with its limitations, Bretton Woods is technologically far ahead of many of the surrounding communities, which are still rotary-dial and are serviced by New England Telephone. Bretton Woods has installed fiber-optic cable.

1+ dialing is available to areas surrounding Bretton Woods and is considered a long-distance call, but no toll charge is generated. This is not a concern as most people in Bretton Woods are vacationers and do most of their calling outside of the Bretton Woods exchange.[113]

Though there is some evidence that small telephone companies like Bretton Woods sometimes face difficulties in anticipating the level of services for customers, especially larger ones, Bretton Woods has managed to offer choices to satisfy the needs of its largest customer, the Mount Washington Hotel. Bretton Woods is negotiating with the hotel on the use of either a Centrex or a PBX system within the hotel. Although large telephone companies generally can estimate more predictable continuous trends in costs and demand than small companies, it is reassuring to know that a small company like Bretton Woods can meet the standards set by larger carriers.

Bretton Woods is unique in how it deals with phone service for rental properties. Tourism is an integral part of the Bretton Woods area and, as such, most condominiums (condos) here are rented out and managed by private rental companies. The first condos were built in 1974. There are few residential customers in Bretton Woods. Therefore, most phone service is restrictive in that guests must use the phone in a certain way to generate phone bills as a part of their room charges.[114] Phone service for rental property is billed at the business rate of $20.60 per month instead of the residential rate of $10.80.

Because most customers are vacationers, there is no demonstrable need for link-up services for low-income residents. With the area's strong tourist industry, the need for a link-up program probably will never arise even though the PUC has designated participation in such a program as compulsory.[115] The State of New Hampshire approved a link-up program at the end of 1988. Some independent telephone companies voiced opposition to the program because of the burden of identifying eligible participants and assigning administrative responsibility for the program. Another practical problem cited by the independent telephone companies is getting eligible participants to come forward once they have been identified.

Small telephone companies in remote areas sometimes have trouble getting relevant information in the rapidly changing telecommunications environment. In this regard, the network of OPASTCO (Organization for the Protection and Advancement of Small Telephone Companies, a professional association) is a vital communications link for small independents like Bretton Woods. Through OPASTCO a great deal of sharing of knowledge of technological issues takes places. According to the Bretton Woods plant manager, "We ask them, 'We are interested in doing this. Do you know anybody doing this?' Or they ask us, 'I hear you are doing this, can you tell me about it?' "[116] (Bretton Woods originally became involved with OPASTCO to take advantage of the network's group health insurance offering.)

Bretton Woods does not offer equal access and is not obligated to provide it, but customers can access other carriers through an 800 service. Bretton Woods believes that providing equal access, along with the conversion necessary to accomplish the process, is not feasible for some independents. Bretton Woods also wants to avoid the "problems, steps, and procedures involved in providing equal access."[117] As a member of OPASTCO and USTA (United States Telephone Association), it sees the hesitancy of some of the larger telephone independents in moving to equal access and believes that it must be cautious as well. According to the plant manager at Bretton Woods, "If we are going to spend $20,000 on software for our central office to provide equal access, we must ask: Where is the gain?"[118] Put simply, Bretton Woods does not believe that in its present situation the costs of providing equal access in an area like Bretton Woods can be recovered. Moreover, as most of its customers are tourists, there is little need for equal access in terms of customer demand.

For a small company like Bretton Woods, "everything is hinged on something else: the ski area is hinged on the weather; the hotel is hinged on securing meetings and conferences; the development is hinged on the real-estate market."[119] The plant manager describes the uncertainties this way:

> We are in a constantly fluctuating situation because of the changeable nature of the rental business in resort communities. For example, a developer working in town who had planned on putting in 200 units a year for the next few years has put in approximately 70. They [developers] are guided by sales and our progress is tied to their progress as well. That [planned development] was the reason for filing the rate case and getting everything going and then we found out we did not have to rush, unfortunately.[120]

The acquisition company that owns Bretton Woods Phone Company has purchased some tracts of land in the area.[121] Growth is proceeding but not at the rate originally hoped for.

In terms of the future, Bretton Woods operates in a forward-thinking manner. The company's general manager sums up the Bretton Woods philosophy this way:

> Our aim was to be up and ready and have everything in place and fine-tuned. We desperately wanted to be ready for expansion of the hotel and the growth of the development and to be able to continually add to what we have. Everything is in place. As the industry changes with SS7, etc., we will go with that. That is one of the real nice things about having a digital switch. It grows. As the software changes, you update your software and the hardware stays good. We anticipate going with the mainstream in this respect. We are well positioned; we have laid the groundwork for the future.[122]

Clear Lake Telephone Company

Clear Lake Telephone Company is located in Clear Lake, Iowa.[123] Founded in 1895 and incorporated in 1899, the company transmitted the first long-distance call in the State of Iowa.[124] For a number of years, Clear Lake was affiliated with Northwestern Bell and shared engineering personnel. The company is family owned and operated; Jan Lovell, the great-granddaughter of the founder and now the company's assistant manager, represents the fourth generation of her family to work at the phone company.

The company has always tried to keep up to date on technological changes. It was among the first telephone companies in Iowa to install a dial system and among the first independents to install a digital switch (in 1982). The company is now considering a possible upgrade.[125] This pressure to change is due in part to the competitive pressures catalyzed by AT&T's divestiture. As Lovell explained, "One advantage of smaller telcos had been that we could take care of all their [customers'] problems and answer all their questions and there was no second-guessing. Now it's more complicated with different carriers."[126] Tourists from larger cities, used to advanced phone services, pressured Clear Lake for the same level of service they were used to at home.[127]

Clear Lake has adapted to new technology-based innovation in several ways. To facilitate equal access, Clear Lake decided to participate in Iowa Network Services (discussed later in the chapter). Lovell commented, "We saw what was happening in the cities with equal access and we were not hearing anything from the carriers. Here was little old Clear Lake all by itself and trying to get carriers interested (because we want to be on par with what the cities are doing), but no one was coming to our doorstep because of the expense involved in building the network."[128] Another innovation is the availability of custom calling features. However, they have not sold particularly well. There is no cellular service in the region yet, but like other small companies, the telco is in a partnership and is awaiting FCC approval of its license. Clear Lake is not involved in cable television; because the population of Clear Lake was above the limit set for telco-cable cross-ownership (over 2,500 people), the company did not qualify. However, it is very interested in the issue of cross-ownership and how it may change in the future."[129] Encouraging people to use these services is an educational process, though new residents (from more urban areas) seem to demand them right away. Surprisingly, local farmers have adopted one new technology, mobile phones, very quickly. According to Lovell, "We foresee farmers as good users of cellular phones, especially portables."[130]

Clear Lake has no REA funding. It purchased its digital switch with industrial revenue bonds provided by the city, a method of funding that seems to be rapidly disappearing. But the bond funding is emblematic of the company's relationship to the locality. Clear Lake Telephone Company has always tried to be a progressive part of the community. It was instrumental in bringing a telemarketer and subsequent jobs to town and believes it was "a direct result of having equal access."[131] The company has found that what is good for the community of Clear Lake is often good for the phone company. The largest employer in town, UNISYS, depends on the company even though UNISYS has its own network; Clear Lake's immediate service is a real benefit to it.

Representatives of Clear Lake believe that the relationship between the Iowa Utilities Board and small telcos is excellent: "They seem to have an understanding of how we relate with our communities in that we really are different from the Bell companies because we are especially close to small customers. Their philosophy, at this time, is very cooperative. More can be accomplished, at the state level, when everyone is working together."[132]

Lovell summarizes the challenges facing the Clear Lake Telephone Company this way: "As the role of the phone evolves, so does the definition of universal service. The traditional definition of universal service has been basic telephone service so you can communicate with the rest of the world. As our definition of how to communicate evolves, I think our definition of universal service will change, too."[133]

Lovell's assessment of these challenges describes the position of many small rural telcos:

> We are really in a balancing act when it comes to looking at adopting new services as a means of generating revenue. We want to provide quality basic phone service at the lowest possible cost for our customers. But we also have to worry about the other side of the spectrum, that is, customers like UNISYS, which demands very sophisticated technology. So it is a continuous balancing act.[134]

Kerrville Telephone Company

Kerrville Telephone Company serves mainly retired people who relocate from metropolitan areas such as Houston, Dallas, Chicago, Cleveland, and other parts of the Midwest. The area has a few mobile home communities, but the vast majority of the retirees in Kerrville are permanent residents. The retirees tend to come from the 50–65 age group and are educated, fairly affluent professionals. They are drawn to Kerrville because of the quality of life it offers, particularly the climate. In addition, Kerrville has three major hospitals, and the medical centers of San Antonio are close by. The retirees form a sophisticated customer base for Kerrville Telephone because they are aware of the services available in metropolitan areas and expect quality service at a reasonable price.

Kerrville's natural charms also attract tourists to the region, creating a major industry in tourism. Closely related to Kerrville's tourism industry has been Kerrville's growth as a conference center.

The area is served by a telephone company that grew out of the community itself. Kerrville Telephone is a closely held company owned by descendants of two families who founded it in 1896, one family providing the capital and the other expertise.[135] The company was incorporated in 1906. From these small beginnings, it has grown to 15,000 access lines with four central offices, all of which are digital. At present Kerrville Telephone has no fiber, but it believes the economics are already there, and in the next two years it plans to install fiber in the main trunk routes between the central offices.[136] Kerrville Telephone's customers feel that the company is very responsive, with a fee structure better than that in most places.[137]

As is the case for other rural telcos, a major factor in the existence of Kerrville Telephone is its proximity to an urban center, San Antonio. At the time of divestiture, when LATA boundaries were being drawn, Kerrville Telephone could have opted not to be in the San Antonio

LATA. But, because San Antonio was within the "community of interest" of Kerrville, the company agreed to be placed in the San Antonio LATA.[138] There is no extended area service (EAS) between Kerrville and San Antonio, but there seems to be little consumer pressure for EAS because customers perceive that the 60–70 miles to San Antonio is a distance sufficient to warrant a toll charge. Nonetheless, customers would prefer lower rates.[139] The intrastate toll rates in Texas are exceedingly high; at times it costs twice as much to call within the state as it does to call New York. Despite the high rates, lack of EAS facilities may actually be beneficial for local businesses. The Kerrville Area Chamber of Commerce, which is promoting shopping at home, does not find the possibility of EAS particularly attractive.[140]

Until recently, some outlying areas within the company's service territory were levied mileage charges. But these have been phased out. The company has been making use of carrier technology and remote concentrators to serve its outlying areas. It is also evaluating the use of digital microwave for local loop applications.[141] Kerrville Telephone does not offer equal access because of the lack of interest among other interexchange carriers; it believes that if exchange carriers were interested, it would have received an order. Currently there are about 21 or 22 interexchange carriers serving the area; they are accessed by their individual dialing codes. The resellers take the principal amount of traffic.[142] In Kerrville Telephone's service area the ratio of 800 calls to all long-distance calls is very high. The originating side revenue for 800 service is particularly remunerative for the telco. For the 800 service needs of its large customers—such as James Avery, which has remote retail outlets and multipoint dealer networks—Kerrville Telephone provides dedicated circuits to IXC's POPs in San Antonio.[143]

Bypass activities have hurt Kerrville Telephone to the extent that some of its larger customers, like Mooney Aircraft, lease dedicated lines instead of using the switched network. Kerrville Telephone does not often get an opportunity to provide an alternative to large customers because large companies, like Wal-Mart, McDonald's, or JC Penney, have their own networks. In a recent case of this nature, a Kerrville hospital was linked directly with a Chicago medical facility for diagnostic services. Kerrville Telephone accepts the inevitability of these bypass activities so long as rates do not reflect costs; it also recognizes that the small LECs cannot be everything to everybody. It sees itself as a local telecommunications resource that its clients can turn to for the majority of their communication requirements.[144]

In order to stay abreast of technological developments, Kerrville Telephone has made significant investments in SS7 technology. For one, it has the SS7 supernode capabilities. Although its custom-calling offerings have not yielded significant revenue, it foresees a long-term migration to SS7. It also sees much revenue potential in the database services made possible by SS7 capabilities. The original impetus for its SS7 investment was the expectation that the FCC would mandate equal access for 800 services. Kerrville Telephone believed that the resultant "800 number portability" would open revenue generation potential. But the 800 decision has been stalled in the regulatory process, and an early resolution is unlikely. Kerrville Telephone now has set its sights on the opportunities that will arise after the 1992 expiration of the database agreements entered at the time of MFJ between AT&T and the regional BOCs. Kerrville Telephone has SS7 capabilities at the tandem level. It is presently evaluating its options for joining an SS7 network and is inclined toward joining the US Intelco network via a VSAT hookup. The main reason for this preference is that US Intelco is operated by a consortium of small independent telephone companies. Though Kerrville Telephone has the supernode capabilities, it does not see itself as developing into a regional hub for the SS7 network. But, at the same time, it believes that neighboring LECs may access its facilities for SS7 capability. At one time Kerrville Telephone cosponsored a feasibility study for a regional network, but the economics were not attractive. Although Kerrville Telephone has not yet used the supernode in any major way, it believes that the costs of acquiring it were reasonable and that it has given the company time to familiarize itself with the technology.[145]

On the transmission side, Kerrville Telephone believes that fiber optics will revolutionize rural areas. But in order to encourage investments in fiber optics, some of the regulatory restrictions need to be removed. At the same time, it does not see any particular need to lift the MFJ restrictions on cable and other information-related services. The telephone companies could continue to be common carriers that offer transmission capacities to parties interested in providing cable or any other information service. Even if all the cable-telco restrictions were removed overnight, Kerrville Telephone would be very cautious about entering into the cable business. It believes that at this stage fiber-optic cable services may not be very economical compared with coaxial technology. Kerrville Telephone regards entry in the cable business as a difficult decision and would prefer to wait until its options are clearer.[146]

Kerrville Telephone's philosophical orientation makes it particularly well poised for capitalizing on the business opportunities that technological developments open up. It has gracefully accepted the inevitability of technologically driven change. The company also has a balanced understanding of those issues likely to undermine seriously its position. This spirit is reflected in the attitude that "competition is good; it makes people feel good about their telephone company."[147] In spite of its relatively small size, Kerrville Telephone sees its competitive advantage over gigantic regional BOCs and IXCs in the following areas: (1) closer relations with customers and the community, (2) greater flexibility and quicker response time because of fewer organizational layers, and (3) fewer regulatory constraints, making it a "one-stop" shop.[148]

Kerrville Telephone believes that further technological developments will reduce artificial boundaries like LATAs. Although it may not want competition with Southwestern Bell and other larger telcos, it believes that at some point such competition is likely to occur. It sees the importance of good relations with Southwestern Bell and anticipates situations that will require both competition and cooperation. Even with the further erosion of local franchises, Kerrville Telephone does not think that Southwestern Bell will ever raid its territory to pick up one or two customers. Kerrville Telephone does visualize an increasing number of joint services with larger LECs and IXCs, the complementary 800 services being just one example. Already in the process of building a cellular service, it has been working closely with Southwestern Bell. It is not particularly worried about the lifting of the MFJ restriction in the areas of manufacturing and information services provision by the BOCs.[149]

The company holds that rate-of-return regulation belongs to the past and tends to induce unwise use of economic resources. It sees a definite need for another type of incentive structure. At the same time, it perceives a dark side to these market-oriented initiatives. Even though it is a net payer into the state pool, it believes that subsidization mechanisms are required for sustaining telephone services in thinly populated areas. In its opinion, a small company like Big Bend, which serves a territory larger than New Jersey, can never survive without external support because of operating conditions.[150]

The president of Kerrville Telephone believes that most of his customers have not felt much impact of the MFJ. Kerrville Telephone still leases consumer premises equipment to 70 percent of its customers and believes that, not unlike a banker, a telephone company must understand the customer's business. Telcos should also go beyond merely deploying state-of-the-art technology to actually developing customer-oriented applications. At the same time, Kerrville Telephone takes pains to familiarize itself with the newer technologies before selling them to its customers. For example, it is currently experimenting internally with out voice mail. Similarly, Kerrville Telephone is studying potential applications for the Centrex feature of its switches. It feels possible clients may include schools, hospitals, and state agencies.[151]

North Pittsburgh Telephone Company

North Pittsburgh Telephone Company is an example of an earlier rural company now serving suburban customers.[152] It was established in 1906 by a group of farmers because Central District Printing and Telegraph Company had refused to provide service to their region. North Pittsburgh later expanded and acquired Saxonburg and Freeport Telegraph and Telephone Company. REA financing played a significant role in North Pittsburgh's growth and modernization. The company services approximately 42,000 access lines. It has approximately 8,600 business subscribers (eight party lines remaining) and 33,000 residential subscribers (650 party lines remaining). It operates eight exchanges, of which three serve bedroom communities in suburban areas and the other five serve rural areas characterized by agriculture and mining. North Pittsburgh has been experiencing major growth in its suburban areas because of the in-migration from metropolitan Pittsburgh. The demand for telecommunications is growing as urban development reaches the area. The company offers almost all of the presently available advanced services, such as call forwarding, call waiting, and three-way calling. It also provides equal access to 13 long-distance carriers and resellers, including its affiliated, nonregulated company.[153]

In 1985 the business was organized into a holding company.[154] North Pittsburgh Systems, Inc., became the parent company of North Pittsburgh Telephone Company and Penn Telecom, Inc. North Pittsburgh Systems itself has no operational functions. North Pittsburgh Telephone Company provides local exchange services and other regulated businesses. Its service area comprises 287 square miles north of Pittsburgh covering portions of four southwestern Pennsylvania counties.[155] Penn Telecom's operations are in five divisions. The Supply Division distributes the products of over 100 companies to telephone companies and to other users of communication equipment and material. It provides engineering and installation of remote line concentrators and fiber-optic cable. The Sales (interconnect) Division furnishes and installs PBX, voice mail, facsimile, and key telephone systems, along with telephone sets of all varieties, to customers both inside and outside of North Pittsburgh's operating area. The Cellular Division, at one time active in the retailing of mobile telephone sets, currently operates installation and maintenance centers for Bell Atlantic Mobile Systems, Inc. The Resale Division offers North Pittsburgh Telephone Company long distance service to customers within North Pittsburgh's area and provides direct interLATA service at reduced rates to other customers. The Qwest Division offers special inner-city service facilities to various large communication users both inside and outside of North Pittsburgh's operating area.[156]

North Pittsburgh is at the forefront of technological development. The new growth within its service area has provided North Pittsburgh with opportunities to put in place state-of-the-art equipment. In 1989, North Pittsburgh Telephone had a construction plan of $8 million per year. Of this, about $4 million was for central office equipment to meet growth as well as to provide an interface with the new nationwide signaling system that was seen as an opportunity for future revenues. Another $3 million was for outside plant, mostly new access lines.[157] North Pittsburgh Telephone is evaluating a 1,200-home upscale development project as an opportunity for bringing fiber optics to residences. For newer developments North Pittsburgh has been considering leaving conduit space for the future installation of a video drop to the home.[158]

In addition to expenditures on equipment, North Pittsburgh spends $140,000 per year on tuition for the continuing education of its employees. Extremely low employee turnover has made this expenditure a long-term investment. The company prides itself on the quality of services it provides. North Pittsburgh believes that its service is as good as any, including that of the Bell companies, and is offered at an extremely low cost. The base rate for residential services is only $6.45 per month.

The biggest factor in the existence of North Pittsburgh as a business entity is its proximity to Pittsburgh. Its service area is geographically, economically, and socially integrated into the Pittsburgh metropolitan area. Businesses in Pittsburgh have branch offices in North Pittsburgh Telephone territory. The area is also attracting many of the high-tech firms from Pittsburgh. Much of its growth is fueled by people who commute to Pittsburgh and use the service area as a bedroom community (the area's hilly terrain is more suitable for housing than agricultural purposes). In 1988 telephone-switched access lines grew by 5.1 percent and the number of billed toll calls increased by 6.4 percent, up 1.3 percent from the previous year. The Crider Corners, Cranberry, and Wexford exchanges grew between 11 and 14 percent.[159] The construction of the new highway I-279 (a bypass of I-79) has been a catalyst for further growth and has generated pressures for extended area service.[160]

EAS is an issue all over Pennsylvania because of the recent growth of bedroom communities either from the state's own metropolitan areas or from New York.[161] EAS is not particularly popular among the telephone companies because it reduces their toll earnings.[162] But through EAS they have a stable source of revenue. Actual earnings depend on the level at which rates are set. Some companies in Pennsylvania have been using EAS as a way of reducing their excess earnings and at the same time pleasing their customers. In some cases the terminating costs are 125 percent of the total revenue generated by a particular call.[163] It is natural that AT&T opposes such services, especially interLATA EAS. AT&T argues that access charges should be reduced before any of the revenue is diverted to services like EAS. At present, AT&T pays independent telephone companies twice the access rates it pays Bell of Pennsylvania.[164]

The Pennsylvania PUC began an investigation into EAS in 1982. The investigation continued longer than anticipated because of the difficulty of developing standards that would be acceptable to all of the affected parties.[165] Finally a consensus was forged. As might be expected, the standards are inherently arbitrary. The commission notes that "the proposed regulations were the product of negotiations among those with different perspectives and that compromises were made to achieve a workable result."[166] The commission has established two thresholds. When calls reach a level of 2.0 calls per access line from one exchange to another and where at least 25 percent of the access lines in the calling exchange have been used for 1.0 or more calls per month to the receiving exchange, the telephone companies will have to offer discount plans. When the corresponding figures are 5.5 calls per access line and 50 percent of access lines used for 1.0 or more calls, the telephone company is obligated to poll for EAS.[167] The commission has thus articulated its EAS philosophy: "Overall, the Commission has looked to whether the boundaries of the local calling areas create artificial and inequitable economic boundaries within an otherwise cohesive community. It is the community, not the individual, need which has been our overriding concern. EAS should not be viewed as merely an alternative to interexchange toll rates."[168]

North Pittsburgh Telephone is particularly impacted by these deliberations as most of its area is contiguous with the Pittsburgh metropolitan area. Because of the intricate linkages, both social and economic, there is much pressure for EAS service. At present the company offers the Circle Calling Plan as an optional service. Under this plan, for a flat monthly charge of $25 customers are allowed to make unlimited calls within a radius of 16 miles. The Circle Calling Plan to a degree mitigates pressures for EAS.[169]

One of the biggest concerns of North Pittsburgh Telephone has been network diversity, particularly for routes into Pittsburgh. Earlier there was only one route into Pittsburgh—along Route 8. North Pittsburgh Telephone for many years pressed Bell of Pennsylvania for alternate routes into Pittsburgh. The BOC's response was that even its own exchanges of comparable size did not have the kind of diversity sought by North Pittsburgh Telephone. North Pittsburgh Telephone took the position that such a policy was Bell of Pennsylvania's internal matter and was not a valid argument against its request for alternative routing.[170] What finally brought about a change was a lumber company fire that destroyed 13,000 wire pairs.[171] Now there are three routes into Pittsburgh. One is a microwave link provided by Qwest that links North Pittsburgh Telephone to AT&T's POP in Pittsburgh. The other two are fiber links that were created through the interconnection of North Pittsburgh Telephone's own fiber and circuits leased from Bell of Pennsylvania. North Pittsburgh Telephone has also built a high degree of reliability into its own network. All of the exchanges have been interconnected with fiber, and there are at least two routes out of each exchange.[172]

North Pittsburgh Telephone is actively evaluating its options for acquiring SS7 capabilities. Because of its service area integration into the Pittsburgh metropolitan area, it would prefer to align itself with Bell of Pennsylvania. In general, the independents in Pennsylvania have an excellent relationship with Bell of Pennsylvania.[173] They use the United States Telephone Association and Pennsylvania Telephone Association (PTA) as forums for joint action.[174] This relationship mitigated to a great degree the fears of "loss of control" surrounding SS7 issues. In the case of North Pittsburgh Telephone Company, the relationship is particularly good because of close personal ties between the senior executives of both companies.[175]

North Pittsburgh Telephone believes that it does not make sense to go to another vendor because it would simply mean introducing an intermediary between itself and Pittsburgh. Hence, options such as US Intelco do not hold much attraction. Moreover, under such an arrangement the data base would be unnecessarily remote. Nor does North Pittsburgh Telephone perceive any "loss of control" threat in the contracts it may sign with Bell of Pennsylvania. It will retain control over the subscriber data. North Pittsburgh Telephone believes that some of the vendors are using the "loss of control" issue as a marketing argument to draw unsure independents into their fold. North Pittsburgh Telephone has been discussing SS7 arrangements with Bell of Pennsylvania but believes that Bell of Pennsylvania is being overcautious and has not been moving fast enough.[176] Bell of Pennsylvania, on the other hand, is concerned about the MFJ restrictions for interLATA traffic. For calling-card validation Bell of Pennsylvania will have to send the query data across LATA boundaries. North Pittsburgh's president gave testimony before the FCC for a waiver in February 1990.[177] If an arrangement cannot be made with Bell of Pennsylvania, North Pittsburgh Telephone also has an option provided by AT&T.[178]

One of the factors holding up implementation of SS7 is cost-allocation information. The Pennsylvania Telephone Association is organizing a seminar on the various aspects of costing SS7 services. The vendors also will be invited to give presentations on the options they offer.[179] Another inhibiting factor is the privacy debate about caller ID, or Automatic Number Identification (ANI). The consumer lobby, which is very strong in Pennsylvania, has taken a particularly strong stand against ANI, believing it is a threat to privacy.[180] As a compromise, Bell of Pennsylvania is willing to provide selective blocking of critical numbers, but the consumer groups insist on optional blocking. This is not acceptable to the BOC because it feels this stipulation will reduce the market for intelligent services.[181] The Pennsylvania PUC has approved the provision of services based on caller ID by a 3 to 1 vote, but the consumer groups have secured a court injunction. The legal issue is whether caller ID services violate the Pennsylvania wiretap law.[182] A development that may aid SS7 implementation is the state initiative on 911 service. A bill is pending that would make it mandatory for all counties in Pennsylvania to implement 911 service. The question is how to finance it. The options being considered are a telephone surcharge or a tax.[183] The plan works on a county-by-county basis. Perhaps tying the 911 service to the network concept will help facilitate SS7 implementation. Furthermore, the county-based plan has raised the peculiar problem of exchange boundaries that cross county lines. Bell of Pennsylvania is planning a central computer for monitoring 911 service for all the areas it serves.[184]

North Pittsburgh is well poised for technological innovations. First, its location within a high-growth area provides for new investment opportunities. The more affluent upscale developments allow for experimentation with more expensive services. Second, it has the vision and technical resources to exploit the opportunities. Frank Reese, North Pittsburgh's president, was earlier the president of GTE Automatic Electric Laboratories. The company also has been steadily working toward enhancement of its human capital through various training programs. The national and state telephone associations have been very helpful in this regard. North Pittsburgh Telephone takes an active part in the activities of the PTA and USTA. For example, North Pittsburgh Telephone's president is the secretary of PTA's Rates Theories Committee as well as USTA's Operations and Engineering Committee. He is also a member of the board of directors of each association.[185]

Taconic Telephone Corporation

Taconic Telephone Corporation was formed in 1971 through the merger of the Copake Telephone Company and the Columbia-Rensselaer Telephone Corporation.[186] The history of both these companies goes back to the early days of telephony when local business leaders formed independent telephone companies to bring telephone service to the rural areas of the Hudson Valley.[187]

Taconic Telephone serves 21,313 customers in portions of Rensselaer, Columbia, and Dutchess counties of New York and part of Berkshire County, Massachusetts.[188] Its name comes from the "beautiful mountain range that hugs the New York State line from Southern Vermont to Northern Connecticut, much like the company's service area."[189] Taconic Telephone's service territory covers about 600 square miles.[190]

The company considers itself to be in the communications business and not just in telephony.[191] It views itself as a "regional telecommunications business offering quality communications services to a diverse base of customers throughout the Hudson Valley and Western New England."[192] Though it is constantly seeking to diversify into other telecommunications areas, it considers telephony to be the mainstay of its business. The biggest concern of Taconic Telephone is the perceived threat to its franchise through technologies that may permit alternative dial tone within its territory.[193] Its proximity to the New York City metropolitan area plays no little role in generating the unease. Taconic Telephone has taken a leading role in forums that seek to protect the franchise of independent telephone companies.[194]

The parent company, Taconic Telephone Corporation, has three subsidiaries. Taconic Technology Corporation sells and leases telephone equipment as a regulated company in and out of the telephone company's service area. Taconic Long Distance Service provides long-distance services throughout the Capital District and Hudson Valley. Taconic Cellular Corporation is involved in cellular projects.[195]

Taconic Telephone also offers cable television. Through its subsidiary Taconic Technology, it entered the cable business in 1983 when it was awarded franchises for the towns of Chatham, Canaan, and Ghent. As in many cases of cable-telco cross-ownership, Taconic Telephone maintains two separate plants for cable and telephone. The company estimates that it would cost $2 million to convert the non-switched cable network.[196] In 1987 its cable television subscribers totaled 1,670, 60 percent of the potential market.[197] In 1988 the figure rose to 1,800.[198] The company is planning to put in an addressable system so that programming requests can be changed at the central office via software. At present descrambler chips are being used.[199]

Taconic Telephone is well abreast of technological developments. It has ambitious plans and is often characterized as a "small company with big ideas."[200] Though it has "big ideas," its implementation plans are on the cautious side. Taconic Telephone does not take the plunge in order to "catch the bus"; it believes the destination is more important than the bus.[201]

In 1987 Taconic joined in a limited partnership to provide cellular telephone communications in Dutchess and Orange counties. Similarly, through a partnership, it participated in a subsequent RSA lottery process. It has entered the cellular business not so much for immediate revenue potential but for experience with nonwire technologies.[202] It has avoided the paging business because of the hilly terrain within its service area. At the same time, it is evaluating BETRS technology as a means of reducing the cost of stringing copper to serve new customers. Because of the terrain and the associated pattern of residential settlement, houses are not concentrated in clusters but are widely dispersed.[203] On average it costs as much as $1,000 to run copper to a home.[204] A preliminary evaluation indicates that it will take only three BETRS towers to cover the entire territory. To the final customer the technology is transparent; at the same time it will reduce the costs of providing service.[205]

Taconic Telephone is one of the very few independent telephone companies that provides its own operator-assisted services. Taconic Telephone provides operator-assisted service not because it generates immediate revenue but because in many ways it creates a foothold for marketing futuristic intelligent services. The company envisions an integrated database access system with a "live intercept," the operator, that will play a key role in the provision of information services. Taconic Telephone's conceptual enthusiasm and cautious implementation are perhaps best reflected in its response to SS7.[206] It believes that, though the technology holds much promise, its actual applications and consequent benefits need to be better defined. It believes that SS7 primarily is a technology that was developed for generating network efficiencies. Therefore, its primary benefit would be geared toward carriers of high volume. Taconic exercises great care in analyzing both the primary and secondary (intelligent services) benefits of SS7 in light of investment costs. It also believes that vendors have generated a sense of urgency as a marketing ploy and intends to develop a better grip on the issues involved before it makes substantial investments. In order to study the technology, Taconic Telephone has formed an SS7 committee comprised of personnel from a number of departments: (1) central office, (2) outside plant, (3) customer service, (4) service, and (5) marketing.[207]

The company prides itself on being marketing oriented. It has a vice-president specifically in charge of marketing and customer service. The marketing orientation extends beyond periodic surveys to a general attitude within the company. For instance, the company has regular employee focus groups. It also has a drive-up payment window, which not only is convenient for customers but also facilitates customer contact.[208] In addition, the company has instituted an action line for customer complaints. These consumer-oriented efforts have started to have a visible impact. For example, consumer input helped in the redesign of the billing system; knowledge of consumer preferences led to the addition of channels over the cable system; and consumer demand prompted the creation of a direct-dial facility for international calls. In the case of the direct-dial facility, the switch capacity already existed and the company only had to reprogram the switches. The direct-dial facility was implemented within six months.[209]

The deployment of SS7 and other technologies in rural areas raises the question of whether the demand will justify the investment. To deploy SS7, Taconic, with its 21,313 access lines, would need an investment of approximately $4.5 million.[210] In order to assess the demand and, in general, to ascertain consumer needs more effectively, the company has initiated programs that seek to generate closer consumer contact. Taconic Telephone periodically conducts consumer surveys for the following reasons: (1) to gain a better understanding of the types of customers served by the company; (2) to identify wants and needs of the customers served; (3) to establish a channel of customer input and feedback to the company; and (4) to measure the customer perception of Taconic Telephone—the services and information it provides, the image the company projects, and the capability of all levels of personnel to serve and satisfy the customer.[211]

In June 1988, Taconic Telephone mailed survey questionnaires to 20,019 customers with their monthly bill statements; the company asked the customers to return the survey questionnaires with their payments. Although no premium was offered for returning the questionnaires, more than 14 percent of the customers responded. The survey revealed that Taconic Telephone's customer base is broadly comprised of two segments: natives and move-ins.[212]

At present, natives comprise 55–60 percent of the population, but their proportion is rapidly shrinking with the in-migration from urban areas. The traditional economy is based on agriculture—dairy farming is the main industry. Natives are by and large satisfied with POTS.[213] Move-ins are of two types: (1) wealthy individuals from New York, which is about two and one-half hours from Chatham, and (2) residents working in the Albany area, which is 30 minutes from Chatham. Move-ins in the first category tend to have a home that they use for weekends and summers. They usually buy an old farmhouse and a substantial amount of land. This group presently comprises approximately 25 percent of the population. A typical demand profile is as follows: first line—normal usage; second line—children; third line—fax, modem, or personal computer.[214] Move-ins in the second category tend to work with either the government or industry in and around the Albany area. They tend to have an average or better house with one or two acres of land. This category consists of professionals in their forties seeking a rural environment. They comprise approximately 20 percent of the population. Their top telecommunications priority is cable television. It is even more important than a telephone. If they have personal computers and modems at home, they tend to use the single-voice line.[215]

The survey also revealed the differing perceptions of the natives and the move-ins. The long-time customers were appreciative of the service provided by Taconic Telephone; the move-ins tended to be less appreciative.[216] The less-positive attitude of the move-ins probably has more to do with their exposure to advanced facilities in urban areas than to the quality of service provided by Taconic Telephone. Much to the chagrin of Taconic Telephone personnel, move-ins often comment that they do not have similar trouble with New York Telephone. The company feels that such a view is not a function of the actual quality of service provided but the perception that a small company is unsophisticated in comparison to a large corporation.

The survey also attempted to gauge the potential for advanced services within the service area. The analysis revealed that in addition to the 29.3 percent of respondents who had the push-button feature, 26.9 percent more indicated an interest in having it if available. This was particularly important information to Taconic Telephone because with its existing facilities it can offer push-button dialing through all of its exchanges. Thus the obvious marketing task is to develop awareness campaigns to alert customers that push-button dialing is available. The response for custom-calling features was very low. Only 2.2 percent had call waiting (with only 5.1 percent expressing interest in having it if available); only 0.4 percent had call forwarding (with only 0.6 percent expressing interest); none had three-way calling (with only 0.8 percent expressing interest); and 0.8 percent had speed dialing (with only 1.6 percent expressing interest).[217] The company believes that the lack of interest in custom-calling features may reflect the lack of awareness and understanding of their possible applications and potential benefits.[218]

The communities served by Taconic Telephone have been designated as growth areas throughout the 1990s by the magazine *American Demographics*. Taconic Telephone's service territory is witnessing an interesting change in population patterns due to in-migration from the New York metropolitan area.[219] In fact, the residential patterns are not unlike Peter Goldmark's concept of the "new rural society," one in which urban dwellers bring new values and practices to rural areas. The company expects continued growth in its customer base. The growth rate in 1990 was 4 percent and is predicted to continue at 4 to 6 percent annually until 1995. The customer base is expected to reach 25,000 in just five years.[220] This growth offers opportunities for introducing new services. For example, Taconic Technology has actively promoted a line of security alarm systems for residential and commercial operations. It has taken advantage of the local housing boom and is cooperating with developers and home buyers to wire security systems into homes and businesses as they are built.

Taconic Telephone is very interestingly positioned because telecommunications is an important factor for many of the developments within its service territory. It is telecommunications technology that has facilitated the phenomenon of move-ins.[221] Many of the second-home move-ins often do their work at home. The ability to work from a rural setting has been made possible by telecommunications technology. Aside from the number of modem and fax lines, this is reflected in the increased number of international calls from the Taconic Telephone region. It is possible that some home offices may expand into full-fledged business activities.[222] R. T. Blass, president of a New York City-based advertising agency, provides a concrete example. Blass had a second home in the Taconic Telephone service area and often spent his weekends there. The fact that he could run his business from the pleasant environment of his second home without serious disadvantages induced him to shift an entire 300-employee unit to the area.[223] This example is in keeping with similar trends documented in our other case studies. The combination of an inviting locale and a responsive telecommunications service provider is likely to generate much economic activity within the Taconic region.

SITE REPORTS: NETWORK SERVICES

Iowa Network Services, Inc.

Iowa Network Services, Inc. (INS), located in West Des Moines, Iowa, is unique not only in its development of a new way to handle equal access but also in its emergence as a new type of telephone company. Determined to give rural Iowans a choice of long-distance telephone companies after the breakup of the Bell system, 125 small-town telephone companies joined together in early 1987 as INS in order to build a telecommunications network that would entice AT&T's rivals to compete for business in rural and small-town Iowa.

For the project, the towns raised $7 million and borrowed another $20.8 million from the Rural Telephone Finance Cooperative. When the idea of INS was first discussed, many people doubted whether the network could be established smoothly. But by 1990, some three years later, 152,000 business and residential customers in 275 Iowa towns were able to choose from several long-distance providers—AT&T, US

Sprint, MCI, and Telecom USA—which pay an access fee to INS. In addition, INS itself has entered the long-distance business, giving rural Iowans five options when earlier they had only one.

INS is composed of two separate operating divisions: the Iowa Network Access Division and the Iowa Network Interexchange Carrier Division. Through the Iowa Network Access Division, the company offers (1) interconnection to all interLATA interexchange carriers equal in type and quality to the interconnect with AT&T; (2) presubscription, whereby individual subscribers of participating companies will be given an opportunity to select the interLATA long-distance carrier of their choice; and (3) access to all interLATA interexchange carriers via a minimum number of digits. Through the Iowa Network Interexchange Carrier Division, the company constructed a fiber-optic telephone transmission network between toll center locations (the participating companies' central office) and Central Access Tandem in Des Moines. The Interexchange Carrier Division, which constructed the network and the switch and which is also the owner, leases use of the network to the Access Division.[224]

The intended benefits of the company's centralized equal access service are (1) making equal access and long-distance competition available to subscribers of the participating companies sooner than do most individual conversions; (2) making service to the rural areas served by independent telephone companies more attractive to competitive long-distance carriers, with a likely increase in the number of carriers available to most consumers; and (3) reducing the need for interexchange carriers to invest in or acquire transmission facilities to serve the rural exchange of the participating independent telephone companies.

INS has a voice-mail service and 830 miles of fiber network. The fiber network assures that rural Iowa will have a network in place to deliver information services to its 152,000 business and residential customers in 275 Iowa towns. As a strong player in Iowa, the company has forged alliances with other companies, the Iowa PUC, and state economic development agencies.

INS has a six-member board of directors. All telephone companies participating in INS are voting members of the corporation with shares of Class A common stock. The number of shares per company is determined by three factors: one-third of the stock is divided equally among the participants, one-third is divided according to the number of access lines the company has, and one-third is divided according to the amount of traffic the company brings to the network.

When the idea of INS was discussed initially, proponents argued that long-distance competition would help spur economic development. According to Governor Terry Branstad, "That kind of capability will make a small community more attractive to other types of business and industry, as well as improving the competitive position of the businesses that are already there."[225] Although INS has been operating only since May 1989, Panora and Clear Lake, two of the companies participating in INS, claim they have been able to attract telemarketing firms to their towns because of it.[226] By joining together under INS, the small phone companies can afford the equipment and technology necessary to provide sophisticated telecommunications services to businesses.

Bob Sherlock, the director of engineering services at INS, states:

Having a choice of carriers seems to make it easier to attract business to the area. When people are shopping around for a place to locate, they just like to have the flexibility. They may wind up with AT&T anyhow, but at least they have the choice. While we do not presently provide service to people in Des Moines, having another fiber-optic network available in the state tends to promote competition and lower the costs.[227]

INS is enthusiastic about its voice-mail program and its ability to enhance communications between INS and member companies. Telco staff members who have questions about service or billing can follow up with telephone inquiries or voice-mail messages to INS. System managers believe that voice-mail will speed up the exchange of information.[228] One example of an enthusiastic member company is the Amana Society Service Company. The Amana Society Service Company is an investor-owned utility providing telephone, electric, and water service to the seven villages that make up the Amana Colonies. Although the villages, with their brick shops and quaint restaurants, have an old-world feel, the people who live there want state-of-the-art services. The company plans to implement voice-mail service for Amana Society management, which involves 25 to 30 people.[229]

INS may look into a 976 number that provides sports updates, soap opera updates, and several other categories of information.

According to Sherlock,

By the [PUC] board's order, when they set their rates for centralized equal access, they stated that they did not expect that we would over a long period of time support INS solely from centralized equal access. We would generate enough revenue so that the centralized equal access rate will at least come close to going away. As it is right now, we support the whole network basically on a little over a penny a minute.[230]

One of the main problems for INS was the frequent difficulty in obtaining the necessary regulatory approvals, particularly because of opposition from other parties (especially US West, which brought suit against INS from the outset). Much of the criticism leveled at the INS proposal by other telephone companies was based on the claim that the existing networks were capable of providing all of the services that INS would provide. The argument regarding duplication of facilities can be leveled against almost any new entrant to an existing market. But the PUC board concluded that, in the increasingly competitive telecommunications business, the argument does not carry much weight. One of the intended purposes of the PUC board's telephone rules is "to allow fair competition in the public interest while assuring the availability of safe and adequate communications service to the public."[231] The board believes that competition in most types of business involves inevitable duplication of facilities and services. Any duplication resulting from the creation of the INS network does not provide a basis for the board to refuse to approve the INS tariff.

One of the issues raised by the parties is to identify the nature of the centralized equal access services that INS provides. These services, if provided by a local exchange company, would have been considered intrastate access services under the previous definition of intrastate access services in board rules. The board has concluded that the centralized equal access services to be provided by INS, even though INS is not a local exchange company, are access services that must be provided pursuant to an approved access tariff.

It is appropriate to note at this point that board rules generally provide for mirroring interstate access tariffs in a telephone utility's intrastate access tariffs unless otherwise ordered by the board. INS has filed intrastate tariffs for board approval during a stage in its development when it does not yet have an interstate tariff to mirror. For its voice mail services at one time, the Iowa PUC wanted INS to file a tariff, but INS did not believe it should have to because it does not view voice mail as a tariffed service. There are other companies selling voice-mail that are not on a tariff (such as Teleconnect). INS sells the services to a participating company, which then resells them to its customers (for whatever price it wishes) if it views the services as worthy.

The board believes that by concentrating toll traffic INS will provide tangible benefits to the rural local exchange companies and their customers, to the interexchange carriers who choose to serve them, and to the general public in Iowa. The board has attempted to devise means by which those receiving the benefits of the network will share in paying the costs.

The concentration of toll traffic provides a benefit to the interexchange companies that will serve rural customers. The history of 1985–1990 in Iowa has shown clearly that service to these customers by interexchange carriers other than Northwestern Bell and AT&T was not economically attractive. Concentration of the traffic will alter the economics of serving these customers, making it less expensive to serve them. The concentration is also beneficial to the rural end users who receive equal access and gain the capability of obtaining modern information services as they become available. The board claims, moreover, that the concentration will benefit the general public in Iowa by assuring that a substantial portion of rural Iowa will have a network in place to deliver information services. The board also believes that a network like INS provides the means to assure timely access to information services in rural Iowa.

In terms of rates, the board believes it is appropriate that the expense of INS rates be shared by interexchange carriers, participating telephone company end users, and Iowa telephone customers generally, because the benefits of the system will be enjoyed by these groups. Therefore, during the start-up period of INS, before it receives substantial revenues from services other than centralized equal access, interexchange companies will be permitted to recover a portion of the INS originating and terminating rates through a surcharge to their toll customers on all calls carried by INS.

In the world of deregulation and accompanying uncertainty, the small phone companies that have joined together under INS can provide the latest telecommunications services to their rural customers. With a strong spirit of cooperation among the independents in the state, INS is well on its way to achieving its goal of ensuring that equal access service is available to rural subscribers. The benefits resulting from providing equal access and fiber optics in Iowa's rural areas outweigh the concern of keeping local rates low. Iowa takes a proactive position in the dilemma between the modernization of technology and rate increases.

PalmettoNet, Inc.

PalmettoNet is an integrated network consisting of 600 miles of fiber backbone running through South Carolina. As a "carrier's carrier," PalmettoNet leases transmission capacity to other telecommunications service providers. Interexchange carriers are by far its largest customers. PalmettoNet is perhaps the first regional network created through collaboration among independent telcos.[232] The way it has been put together is particularly innovative. It was created through a collaborative arrangement among the telcos along the fiber route. Each of the participating telcos owns and operates the network segment within its territory. But to PalmettoNet's customers, which get transmission capacity on an integrated network, the arrangement is undetectable; there are no extra costs or strange bills. PalmettoNet is not a patchwork of pieces of fiber infrastructure that were already in place. Following a master plan, each individual telco built the segment of fiber network within its territory especially for PalmettoNet according to its specifications. The only portion of the network that PalmettoNet itself built is that where a section of the network crosses BOC territory.

PalmettoNet then leases capacity from telcos and thus integrates the individually owned segments into a network. The participating telcos maintain their particular segments of the network. PalmettoNet maintains a remote network control center. The control center monitors key network parameters as well as building and security alarms. When a problem arises, the equipment sounds an alarm by making an off-network connection to the Network Control Center.[233]

The collaborating LECs derive a number of benefits from such an arrangement. First, as in all business investments, they get a return on their investment. Second, economies of scale are generated. For example, if PalmettoNet requires four fibers and the independent telco needs six fibers for its own use, the costs of the ten fibers are shared in a proportionate manner.[234]

The ultimate tribute to the ingenuity of this arrangement is that the entire business is managed by only two people—Jim Carlson, the general manager, and Roseanne Meyers, the network operations director. The major portion of the network segments is owned and maintained by the participating telcos. PalmettoNet's accounting, engineering, and regulatory matters are, in part, contracted through its member companies. To the customer these elaborate arrangements, both business and technical, are also transparent. PalmettoNet provides an excellent example of how the complementarity of contiguous local exchange companies can be harnessed to create state-of-the-art networks in rural areas.[235]

One of the biggest threats to fiber-optic networks is service interruption that results when fiber is cut. Much of PalmettoNet's network follows rights-of-way along highways where digging by highway maintenance crews can cause serious damage. A similar threat is generated by the state government's attempts to bring water to rural areas. To ward off such threats, PalmettoNet uses locating services that monitor digging permits. If any such activity is scheduled to take place

near the network, PalmettoNet sends a representative to the site to
ensure that there are no accidents. The costs of repairing a severed
cable range from $5,000 to $10,000. The service interruption carries a
relatively higher cost. PalmettoNet has also developed a strategy,
through presentations and other means, for educating people living
along the route about the potential for damage. The company hopes
that people will report any threatening activity. The people who are
particularly helpful are those whose work involves frequent travel on
the highways, such as telco employees, plumbers, contractors, and
police. All of this activity supplements regularly scheduled bimonthly
patrolling.[236]

PalmettoNet is planning a fiber link from Rock Hill to Clemson,
the home of Clemson University. With a link to Clemson, PalmettoNet would then serve all the university towns in South Carolina;
it therefore would be a natural candidate for linking together all of
the university towns under the Super Computer Project, which
proposes to link all the state's universities with an electronic network.

At present PalmettoNet has no plans to go beyond being a "carrier's
carrier," primarily because of the regulatory complications any such
plans would create. Currently PalmettoNet does not file tariffs. It files
its contracts, but these are kept under seal. Furthermore, it does not
want to get into a competitive situation with its customers. For the
time being, PalmettoNet does not feel the need to go beyond South
Carolina into other states.[237]

After the MFJ, the independent telcos in South Carolina recognized a need for collaborative activity and PalmettoNet was a viable
option. Hence, the PalmettoNet partnership was created not to
exploit a market opportunity, but to get the telcos into a collaborative mode. Today the concept has become a $4 million business and
is growing rapidly. Success with PalmettoNet has encouraged
further collaborative activity among the independents. The coordinated action for an RSA lottery for cellular phones is one such
example. PalmettoNet has also been a model for ValleyNet in
Virginia.[238]

As a "carrier of carriers," PalmettoNet serves customers that are
other telecommunications providers. What does the final customer
gain? First, through PalmettoNet, customers in remote areas gain
access to state-of-the-art technology. Second, costs are reduced, although the degree of cost savings depends on how much of the savings
the telecommunications providers are willing to pass on to the final
consumers. Third, PalmettoNet aids equal access. Carriers like MCI
have used PalmettoNet to access remote areas of South Carolina that
they might otherwise not have.

SITE REPORT: ELECTRIC COOPERATIVE

Cotton Rural Electric Cooperative

One of our research sites was not a telephone company but a rural electric cooperative in Walters, Oklahoma. Our reasoning for studying a power cooperative was to see which rural groups, if any, were looking at ways to enter into the telecommunications and information markets. Headquartered in Walters, Oklahoma, the co-op serves portions of eight counties that surround the larger communities of Lawton and Duncan.

The Cotton Rural Electric Cooperative became involved in the telecommunications industry through expanding services in the community it served. The school system in Walters, like school systems in many small U.S. communities, had difficulties in offering its students advanced courses because it could not attract teachers to the area. One severe deficiency was in the area of foreign languages. Because of state educational curricular requirements, the school system faced the transfer of students and state aid to other school systems offering language courses. The Cotton Co-op offered to provide satellite dishes to each of the 23 high schools in the eight counties it served. The satellite network is operated under the auspices of Oklahoma State University in Stillwater.

Classes by satellite are now available at all 23 high schools in Cotton Rural Electric Co-op's service area in southwestern Oklahoma, thanks to the co-op's contribution of the satellite dishes. At Indiahoma High, limited resources forced a choice between buying some computers or a satellite antenna; thus, the offer from the co-op was extremely helpful. Tyler also boasts that the local high school can now offer three foreign languages. In addition, approximately 100 co-op members—comprised of communities, schools, and businesses—take advantage of the cable programming offered through the co-op.

According to Larry Manning, a rate analyst with the Oklahoma PUC, there are areas in telecommunications in which the PUC is making changes. For example, Oklahoma has reduced mileage charges for Southwestern Bell service. Southwestern Bell has a base rate for each of its exchanges, and outside this area charges are based on mileage to the customer's location. In Oklahoma the customer traditionally was allowed the first one-quarter mile free and then was charged 77 cents per quarter mile beyond that. This figure has been cut in half, and over a three-year period the maximum mileage charges will be $3.85 per call, no matter how far away the calling destination is from the base-rate area. Because this rate system goes into effect one mile outside of the base-rate area, there is no charge for the first mile. This measure was part of a state tax reform act.[239]

Initially, when cellular radio became popular and two-way service was already in use in Oklahoma, the PUC wanted to keep a "regulated eye" on the interested parties.[240] The first four companies that were certified in Oklahoma were regulated, but in 1986, House Bill 1171 deregulated all radio common carrier services: two-way, paging, and cellular. Even the telcos that had their own cellular and two-way services now had to operate these as "arms-length" unregulated services.

The Oklahoma PUC has developed an innovative way to save taxpayers money on rate cases. A telephone company can, without having to go through the time and expense of a rate case, raise local rates two dollars every 12-month period. It must, however, notify customers 60 days before it implements the rate hike. If 15 percent of the customer base files a complaint, the commission will hear it as a general rate case. The commission can audit the company's records within the 60-day period, but after this time the rate cannot be changed.[241] Oklahoma is also looking at price-cap regulation.

The State of Oklahoma is in the process of implementing the Link-Up America program. In this program, the state government cooperates with the federal government plan to reimburse the local exchange companies for hooking up customers. Half of the installation fees are paid out of federal funds. This measure is only awaiting an official order from the commission for implementation.[242] Income verification is a problem with programs of this type in many states; Oklahoma is proceeding with a solution that might serve as a model to other states wrestling with the problem of accurately identifying qualified Link-Up participants.

Manning explains how potential participants will be identified:

> The way the program is stylized is that each participant must be prequalified by the Department of Human Services [DHS] through participation in some sort of other 'help' program sponsored by the state. The only people who can provide that information are DHS, and they are in full cooperation with the telephone companies and have set up the facility to do so.[243]

Manning recognizes the problems that other states might be having in adopting and implementing Link-Up programs:

> It helps to have statewide human services. There are a lot of states which do not; they provide many human services at a county-wide level. But implementing such services by county may cause problems. In Oklahoma we also have county welfare agencies, and they are fully cooperating with the program. Nevertheless,

everything filters through DHS. Applications received by county welfare offices are then forwarded through the state Department of Human Services.[244]

The phone companies have also been supporting the Link-Up program. Manning explains:

> It is to the benefit of the phone companies to do this [program] because it increases their customer load, plus it gives them the opportunity to make back some of that money and not tap the customer for it. So they were motivated to get the program up and running.[245]

The Cotton Rural Electric Co-op is a very active force in marketing itself and its services and works hard for its members. It is one of the few rural electric co-ops in the country with a full-time marketing director.[246] It is visibly concerned with the economic development of its community. By setting up cooperative arrangements with schools and by using the new satellite dishes, it has helped to enhance the education of every young person in Walters. Helping rural schools stay competitive is an example of how telecommunications providers can continually apply their imagination, creativity, and organizational skills to today's concerns while making an investment in the future. At this point, however, the Cotton Co-op has made few additional inroads in the telecommunications arena other than as a reseller of cable television programming and as a provider of satellite dishes to each of the 23 high schools in its eight-county service area.[247]

In regard to telecommunications in Oklahoma, Manning believes that "without a doubt the smaller companies are better positioned for the future than the larger companies because most are digital now and are ready to go with the flow. Where they will be hurting is the toll-relief interstate and intrastate because, if [the PUC] eliminate[s] pools, they eliminate their subsidies. They are going to have to pick up that revenue from somewhere. But [Oklahoma PUC is] working with them if this contingency arises."[248]

OBSERVATIONS

Certain observations were made for all types of sites, and these observations were taken as important generalizations about the status of small companies in rural environments. Following these generalizations, policy implications are considered. The present observations fall into three areas: community orientation, challenges to rural service provision, and the impact of new technologies.

Community Orientation

Small, locally owned telephone companies appear to have a special symbiotic relationship with the local community; several factors contribute to this relationship. First, because locally owned telcos are established indigenously, they seem especially aware of their community's service needs. Second, they typically wish to maximize the business potential of the communities they serve because these are usually the only markets that they can access. Unlike telcos that also serve high-density populations, they do not have the buffer that is provided by higher revenue-yielding areas from which they can subsidize rural operations. Therefore, they also may be more inclined to cultivate economic growth. Third, realizing their mutual interdependence, communities often take a special interest in the well-being of their telephone companies. For example, Clear Lake Telephone Company purchased its two NEC NEX 61 digital switches through industrial bonds issued by the city.

In this section we discuss the issue of local ownership. Next, we highlight examples from our case studies that illustrate the special relationship between locally owned telcos and the communities they serve. Finally, we attempt to understand further the motivations that generate the locally owned telcos' community orientation.

Sparse populations in rural areas are not attractive to larger service providers. The presence of independent telcos today is a direct result of the failure of larger providers to offer rural services. According to one analyst, "The failure to service small towns and rural areas created a reservoir of unsatisfied demand."[249] The frustrations generated by this lack of service led to the creation of indigenous telephone companies and cooperatives. Our sites provide examples of both. Big Bend, Bretton Woods, Clear Lake, Kerrville, North Pittsburgh, and Taconic are all examples of local initiatives that took the shape of private enterprises, whereas ENMR, Eastex, Mid-Rivers, and XIT were established as subscriber-owned cooperatives. INS was specifically established in response to the lack of interest in rural areas from large service providers.

Because of local ownership, these service providers are especially responsive to local conditions. For example, Big Bend makes special arrangements to provide service to some of the more distant ranchers in its service territory. Bretton Woods has established its headquarters within Mount Washington Hotel, the most significant economic entity in its service area. One of Eastex's employees spends almost all of his time serving the needs of Texas Utilities, the cooperative's largest customer. In Texline, where there is no extended area service, XIT installed special coin phones in the school so that children could make calls for 25 cents. Kerrville Telephone is very sensitive to the needs of its retiree population, which has relocated from metropolitan areas. Because small telcos frequently rely upon the health of the local community for their well-being, they are often actively involved in community affairs. Most of the companies at our sites have taken a leading role in economic development activity. Telco employees are encouraged to join local associations such as the chamber of commerce, the Lions' and Rotary clubs, and school boards. Mid-Rivers and ENMR both have taken the initiative to create interactive distance learning facilities for local schools in their service territory.

The very presence of a small telco—through both intentional and unintentional acts—has a ripple effect on the communities that it serves. Invariably, most small telcos are major employers within rural communities or areas. Not only do they provide jobs in the community, but also through their in-house training activities they can enhance the community's human capital. These telcos tend to groom talent from within. Many responsible positions within these companies are staffed by "mustang engineers," those who have worked their way up through the company without the benefit of a formal technical degree. For example, North Pittsburgh spends approximately $140,000 a year in tuition for employee training.[250] On a regular basis, Eastex sends its employees to training programs at Texas A&M University. Within 12 years, Big Bend's vice-president of plant operations worked his way up through the company from his initial position as an auto mechanic.[251] These companies can afford to invest in their human capital because rural communities tend to have much lower turnover rates than urban areas, and it is difficult for them to attract talent from outside the community. Hence, in many ways, they have no other choice but to train their own employees.

Some small telcos are community oriented because they can "afford" to be as a result of access to external sources of financial support. For example, the REA has played a large role in financing plant upgrades in rural areas. It enabled ENMR to invest in SS7 and in its extensive fiber network. Through similar assistance, Big Bend was able to bury cable in exchanges previously served by a BOC. The REA is also providing technical assistance to Big Bend in its experimentation with BETRS. Over the years, Eastex has benefited from more than $40 million in REA loans. INS has received $20 million in loans from the Rural Telephone Finance Cooperative (RTFC). The policy implications of these findings will be discussed in the final section of this chapter.

From a policy standpoint it is important to understand what factors contribute to a small telco's sensitivity to local conditions. This orientation does not necessarily stem from an altruistic inclination, but may be a direct result of the parameters within which a locally owned telco operates. We believe that there are three general motivating factors: (1) the future of the local telco depends upon the health of the local economy, (2) locally owned telcos have more social ties to the community, and (3) the small telco has access to financing in the form of low-interest loans and subsidies.

Challenges to Rural Service Provision

Rural telcos face many challenges in providing service to their customers. These result from factors as diverse as implementing appropriate technology, nonaccommodating regulatory policies, and scarce human resources.

Appropriate technology. Isolation is the main impediment to the development of telecommunications infrastructure in rural areas. Whereas distance is an element inherent in the term "rural," a wide diversity in topographic factors can result in extreme isolation. Telcos that serve these isolated areas previously have found it difficult to find technology that works under these conditions. Only recently have advancements in BETRS and other nonwire technologies made it possible to service hard-to-reach areas. Big Bend Telephone Company has had a difficult time reaching many of its customers in the past because of the mountainous and rocky terrain that characterizes its service area. Although viable technological alternatives exist, telcos like Big Bend must now find ways to finance their deployment. At the same time, nonwire technologies such as BETRS, toll microwave, and cellular can be more cost-effective. For example, it is very expensive for Taconic to take copper wire to homes that are widely scattered throughout the hills in its service area; the company has evaluated a BETRS system that would provide a less-expensive alternative to copper. But radio technology is not always appropriate for hilly terrain. For example, cellular applications require a larger number of cells in hilly areas. The consequent higher investments that are required, combined with low population densities, make cellular service commercially impractical in these areas. North Pittsburgh and Bretton Woods provide examples of this problem.

The regulatory climate. Our studies revealed specific examples of the consequences of larger regulatory issues on small telcos. For example, although technology is increasing Big Bend's options for providing service to remote areas, financing the acquisition of these systems has become problematic, particularly as the traditional sources of revenue and financing are becoming increasingly undependable. Even though better, less costly technological alternatives exist, Big Bend's vice-president of plant operations fears that the company will not be able to replace much of its outdated equipment because of long depreciation schedules. Big Bend is also concerned about the plight of the pooling process. While some rural areas will be able to survive the consequences of reduced revenues, the very existence of other rural telcos depends upon the pooling process. According to Big Bend's president, Jeff Haynes, the company would not survive six months without pooling.[252]

ENMR is being placed at a disadvantage by the Originating Responsibility Plan, a new separations arrangement for intrastate long-distance calls that was recently instituted by the New Mexico PUC. Divestiture has given the states a much larger role in regulatory decision making. Because of the complexities created by intra- and interLATA divisions as well as intrastate divisions, the earlier system of cost allocations had to be replaced by newer plans. In the case of intrastate issues, the earlier integrated mechanisms had to be replaced by state-specific arrangements. In some cases, these newer arrangements have had a negative impact on rural telcos. In the New Mexico plan, all originating telcos are responsible for paying for the entire cost of each intrastate long-distance call, from point to point. This requirement puts ENMR at a disadvantage because more of its long-distance calls originate from the ENMR service area than from other service areas. The net effect is that ENMR pays a disproportionate amount of the actual costs incurred by the calls originating within its territory.

Although the development of the North Pittsburgh service area as a bedroom community has fueled the growth of the company, it has also led to pressures such as EAS that tend to cut into its revenue base. Another way in which regulation affects North Pittsburgh Telephone is its plans for implementing SS7 technology. It has the technical expertise and the resources, but deployment is being delayed by a peculiar regulatory problem. Because of its geographic, economic, and social proximity to Pittsburgh, it would prefer to align itself with Bell of Pennsylvania's SS7 network. The problem is that, because of MFJ restrictions, it is unclear whether Bell of Pennsylvania is permitted to transport the database query across LATA lines. The matter is presently under review by the FCC. In contrast, developments triggered by the MFJ may open opportunities for electric cooperatives like Cotton Rural Electric Co-op to get into the telephone business. But even in this case, regulatory uncertainty has stalled any substantive move in that direction.

Human resources. One of the biggest problems small telcos face is to attract people of requisite caliber who can deal with the present-day complexities—both regulatory and technical—of telecommunications. One fortunate resource has been retirees from larger companies, for example, AT&T, the BOCs, and GTE. These retirees have the opportunity to enjoy a rural lifestyle while using their knowledge, expertise, and insight, which benefits the local telcos as well. For example, a former US West employee taught a course at a local community college in Des Moines, Iowa. His efforts resulted in a pool of qualified graduates that INS has readily tapped. Otherwise, the small independent telcos are too dependent upon external sources of information and advice from, for example, consultants. One encouraging development has been the increasing role of telephone associations, both at the federal and state levels, for services traditionally provided by consultants.

Impact of New Technologies

We chose our sites because of their innovative approaches to providing rural telephone service. In this section we explore the motivations, the enabling factors, and the implementation strategies and processes of bringing these innovations to rural areas. Although the full impact of the various investments made at our sites will not be fully visible for several years to come, we did recognize some early benefits stemming from these investments.

Economic benefits. Even the most basic technological upgrades have made tangible impacts on the communities. The president of the Presidio Chamber of Commerce, part of Big Bend's service area, noted significant improvements in economic development activity once Big Bend moved from open wire to buried cable in the Presidio exchange. Before this investment was made, businesses complained that the telephone facilities would not support their potential communication needs. Now the Presidio area is able to capitalize on its geographic location on the Mexican border by attracting the attention of companies interested in maquiladora operations.

One hundred and twenty-eight companies formed Iowa Network Services (INS) to get equal access to rural areas. Residential consumers have benefited from the alternatives available to them for their long-distance calls. One of the INS partners, Clear Lake Telephone Company, provides a visible example of the importance of equal access for business location decisions. The company was instrumental in attracting a telemarketing business to town. Equal access seems to have played a significant role in the location decision.

XIT's cellular project holds much promise because of the presence of major highways crossing its service area. It expects that in the future about 60 percent of its cellular revenue will come from the pass-through traffic. XIT's cellular system is an excellent example of how rural telephony adds value to the urban network.

Extended reach. The availability of new technologies has greatly increased the reach of rural telcos. Both Big Bend and ENMR have successfully deployed nonwire technology to serve hard-to-reach areas.

Internal efficiencies. Aside from the external economic development benefits, technological investments can improve the internal efficiencies of the telephone network. According to ENMR's evaluation, the cost savings that will accrue in network operations will itself justify the investment in SS7. According to ENMR's general manager, Robert Harris, "Our system could pay for itself in as little as three years by minimizing uncompleted toll calls, increasing circuit-routing efficiency, and reducing long-distance access charges."[253] Unlike other rural telcos, ENMR has high traffic concentration due to its location on the "golden highway." ENMR routes calls to and from metropolitan areas such as Denver, Albuquerque, Dallas, Lubbock, and Amarillo.

Generating demand. Aside from cutting costs and creating future revenue potential, there are other underlying motivations for investing in new technologies. ENMR wanted to make capital investments before the anticipated implementation of price-cap regulation. ENMR believes that price caps will make it difficult for rural telcos to make such large investments because rates will be determined by the cost of the service and not the sunk investment. Thus, ENMR in some cases has made investments where there is no apparent demand. These lead to a situation in which the presence of technology could influence demand. The small telephone company can play an active role in suggesting applications for the technology. Fiber-optic investments provide interesting examples of this phenomenon in the cases of ENMR and Mid-Rivers Telephone Cooperative. ENMR has launched a rural education development campaign to promote interactive distance learning in the schools. This application would justify its extensive fiber-optic network. Mid-Rivers is also promoting interactive distance learning over its fiber-optic network. When the investment decisions were made, distance learning was not a consideration, but now that the technology exists, ENMR and Mid-Rivers are extensively promoting this application to generate revenues.

Partnerships. INS is a direct example of how a partnership arrangement can bring equal access to rural areas. PalmettoNet indirectly facilitates equal access in South Carolina. For example, through radio links, MCI interconnects with PalmettoNet's fiber-optic network to access regions it would not have otherwise served. PalmettoNet was the first regional network created through partnership among independent telephone companies. Its successful experience already has led to other cooperative activities in South Carolina. PalmettoNet is an excellent example of how cooperative arrangements can capitalize on the limited resources of small telcos to create a sophisticated infrastructure across their service areas.

Kerrville Telephone foresees future situations that would require both competition and cooperation with larger telcos. On the one hand, even with the further erosion of local franchises, Kerrville Telephone does not think that a BOC will raid its territory to pick up one or two customers. On the other hand, Kerrville Telephone visualizes an increasing number of joint projects with LECs and IXCs. The complementary 800 services are just one example.

In general, several types of partnerships have been shown to be beneficial and, in some cases, necessary to rural telephony. It is only through partnerships that many rural telcos will be able to make necessary investments in new technology.

POLICY IMPLICATIONS AND RECOMMENDATIONS

The foregoing generalizations, based on site observations as well as current literature on small telcos, suggest the following policy implications and recommendations.

A State of Change: Postdivestiture Trajectories

A fundamental observation in any consideration of rural telcos is that most are almost literally under a state of siege; change is the name of the game. In fact, companies can be differentiated in terms of their responses to this pressure. Before the MFJ was issued, independent telcos were operating in a stable and predictable environment. But with the change in the regulatory scene, many small independents were forced to adopt different strategies to adapt to the highly uncertain conditions of the postdivestiture environment. We have generalized these responses to change as occurring along the following four postdivestiture trajectories: (1) fight for status quo, (2) self-sufficiency, (3) regional alliances, and (4) alert.

Fight for status quo. The introduction of competition has disrupted the support mechanisms that sustained many small telephone companies. Whereas some companies could find new ways to survive in the postdivestiture environment, others had no choice but to fight for the status quo. These companies are fighting change not because they are passive or unprogressive but because they are trying to survive.

Self-sufficiency. In order to survive, some companies move toward becoming self-sufficient and thus less reliant upon increasingly undependable sources of assistance. These companies either had their own internally generated resources or had access to other external sources of financing. Many of them developed in-house expertise in areas traditionally provided by external sources, such as billing and operator services, accounting and separations specialists, and graphics. Creating in-house facilities cuts costs and opens the possibilities of selling services to other small independent companies. Not only have these companies survived, they have capitalized on the opportunities ushered in by divestiture.

Regional alliances. While some companies have struck out alone, others have chosen to form regional alliances to deal better with the postdivestiture environment. As LECs, independents within the same region do not compete with one another; thus, this situation affords opportunities for collaboration. One type is an alliance that makes investments viable through aggregating demand via centralizing technologies (for example, centralized equal access). Regional fiber-optic networks provide an excellent example of this type of alliance. Another type is a regional alliance that capitalizes on complementary relationships. As in the case of PalmettoNet, individual telcos build segments of the network within their territory and then come together, creating a separate organization that manages the separate segments as a network.

Alert. Some companies are not so threatened that they must take immediate action. These companies choose to wait and assess the opportunities that are available to them. By taking a more cautious stance, they hope to make informed investments and strategic moves. In this case, lack of action does not necessarily mean lack of activity. These companies have put up their antennae and are constantly monitoring their environment.

Directional Forces

The trajectories on which telcos embark are not necessarily due to the same directional forces. Each trajectory results from a varying combination of forces. Therefore, two telcos may have traveled down the same trajectory as the result of a different set of directional forces. These forces can be conceptualized along five different dimensions: human, economic, topographic, political, and proximal.

The human dimension. The telecommunications industry is driven by different types of human factors. Small companies tend to be very individually driven. Often the company's strengths and weaknesses are those of the individual in charge. At the same time, the small-company environment allows a "champion" to undertake and execute innovative strategies. The choices made after divestiture have frequently been colored by the personal visions of these individuals.

The economic dimension. Economics determines to a large extent the possibilities open to small telcos. Some companies have access to resources that make it possible to expand their operations or to become more self-sufficient. Other companies find it necessary to create economies of scale by joining with other telcos to provide services. Still others find that their costs are so high that they can rely only upon the traditional mechanisms in the industry that have ensured universal service.

The topographic dimension. Often the physical terrain further compounds the difficulty of providing service to isolated population groups in rural areas. Since the MFJ, there have been significant developments in technology for surmounting these challenges. Now, although the technology is available, the problem of securing financing remains. One way independents have been able to circumvent the financial burden is through collaborative regional networks. But willing telcos cannot enter into these partnerships if their service areas are not contiguous with one another's.

The political dimension. In the uncertain and changing policy environment created by the MFJ, telcos are increasingly affected by political considerations at the state and national level. Often at the state level, the independents carry a disproportionate amount of political clout, usually because these telcos are run by influential individuals or families. States also may take a more favorable stance toward local companies than toward larger corporations whose headquarters are not in-state. At the federal level, independents are more distant from the policy arena and work through organizations like the Organization for the Protection and Advancement of Small Telephone Companies, the National Telephone Cooperative Association, and the National Rural Telecommunications Cooperative or through their congressional representatives.

The proximal dimension. One of the biggest strategic considerations for a small telco is the influence of other players in its proximity. This may be the collective activity of other small telcos or of a larger player such as a BOC.

Policy Aspects

The innovative actions of successful small rural telephone companies can be viewed as experiments from which policymakers can gain insight to develop appropriate policies for rural telecommunications. Large-scale initiatives could be modeled after the desirable aspects of these innovations. At the same time, policymakers have the benefit of knowing the problems that these telcos faced in implementing their innovations.

We view our sites as reflecting a diversity of telecommunications innovations in rural America. Building on our analysis in the findings and generalizations section, we now identify several critical policy areas within which policymakers could provide a more facilitative environment for developing a more advanced telecommunications infrastructure in rural areas.

Telco heterogeneity. Telcos tend to be grouped into the following categories: BOCs, AT&T, Other Common Carriers (OCCs), and large and small independents. GTE, an independent, is larger than some of the BOCs, while another independent is a very small company serving as few as 29 customers. Small independents are diverse not only in the number of subscribers they serve but also in the conditions under which they operate. Policymakers and other large players tend to lose sight of the diversity. In our research, we consistently found that policy literature rarely provided specific information concerning a particular independent; the literature grouped all independents, large and small, into a single category. We found this method both at the state and federal level. In order to create policy that benefits both small and large independents, policymakers and regulators must understand the diversity of the small independent telcos. It is in profiling the diversity of various rural telcos that our study perhaps makes its largest contribution.

Information deficiency. In the pre-MFJ environment, small rural telcos had the benefit of "free advice" from Ma Bell. Today, in the rapidly changing telecommunications environment, there are few dependable sources of information for small telcos. State and national telecommunications associations play a critical role in providing services and information, yet there are areas in which greater access to information would greatly benefit rural telcos. Information is especially crucial today as technology and regulatory considerations are constantly changing.

Small independent telcos and economic development. In our studies we have found that telecommunications is a necessary but not sufficient condition for economic development. Benefits to rural areas are especially visible given the distance barriers that rural businesses and citizens must overcome. It is important that state and community policymakers understand the role of telecommunications to economic development. Beyond this, it may be useful for state PUCs to work with state and local economic development agencies to coordinate strategies.

Competition and economies of scale. One of the strongest arguments against competition in telecommunications is the duplication of infrastructure. Although the enhanced efficiencies generated from competition in urban areas may more than compensate for the costs of duplication, the same cannot be said for rural areas. In fact, in rural areas competitive activity may counter the need for economies of scale through demand aggregation. For example, rural utilities want to take advantage of the opportunities to enter the telecommunications business to create internal operating efficiencies and to expand their service offerings—as do telephone companies that want to increase their service offerings by providing cable television. This competitive activity tends to fragment utilization of the infrastructure, making it more expensive for service providers and customers.

Alliances with IXCs. One way that rural telcos have been able to cope with the changing times is to strike alliances with other rural telcos. These have taken the shape of regional networks. We did not notice many incidences of partnerships with IXCs. Such partnership would generate more synergies through complementary relationships. For example, telcos have entered into agreements with IXCs for the provision of 800 services.

Human resources. Before divestiture, providing telecommunications service was mostly a stable and routine undertaking. The complexities and changes brought about by divestiture have created uncertainties; they have also opened opportunities for the more astute telcos. A high level of expertise is required to deal with complexities created by greater choices in technology, an increased number of equipment suppliers, the possibilities of striking partnerships and alliances, and greater opportunities to diversify within and outside of the telecommunications industry. Some of the telcos we studied have cultivated this expertise by training their employees and recruiting retirees from larger telcos. The associations have also assisted rural telcos by providing training and technical assistance. These efforts should be further enhanced by formulating policies (perhaps through the REA or PUCs) that provide more resources—both financial and technical—for training. Policymakers also could push local educational institutions toward providing training courses relevant to rural telecommunications service delivery.

Pace of network upgrade. With so much talk about the intelligent network and the coming of the information age, rural telcos feel pressured to make large investment decisions hastily. They believe that, if they do not make network upgrades right away, they will "miss the bus." It may be worth pondering whether a given investment is the "last bus" for the intended destination. Because of their limited resources, rural telcos do not have a large margin for error. Rural telcos are likely to rely on just one equipment supplier. An investment decision made in haste would reduce their future options. SS7 provides a good example of this quandary. It may be more prudent for rural telcos to wait and see which technologies have greater staying power or are more successful.

Transition costs. Regulatory agencies need to undertake studies that analyze the various costs, both social and economic, associated with different rates of network upgrade. Given the imbedded plant and the large amount of investment that is required, telephone network upgrades are phased in over a number of years. Because of the economics of service provision, network investments generally are first made in urban areas. The question is how fast rural areas should follow. There is no accepted criterion since economics cannot be the sole consideration. A balance needs to be struck between economic and social considerations. At one extreme, although a hypothetical situation, would be an instantaneous upgrade of the entire network. Here the danger is that bad investments would have long-term consequences. At the other extreme, an unduly slow pace of investment may lead to expensive transition costs. These costs may be associated with the interfacing equipment required and with the socioeconomic costs of areas long deprived of modern technology. The pace of investment is one factor that regulators can perhaps influence the most; hence, it is critical that they understand the implications of the pace of transition.

Incentives for large telco collaboration. Often rural telcos cannot collaborate because their service areas are not contiguous. Large telcos frequently fill the gaps between small rural telcos. Collaborative activity can be possible only if large telcos cooperate. They often do not. It would not be too difficult for regulators to provide incentives to nudge them in the cooperative direction.

Aggregation of demand. The biggest problem in providing telecommunications to rural areas is insufficient demand due to low population density. The only way of creating a self-sustaining infrastructure in rural areas is to aggregate demand to the greatest extent possible. Increasingly, technological capabilities are opening opportunities for innovative arrangements that aggregate demand. Aggregation of demand could be generated by the following strategies: multiple users, centralizing technologies, "piggyback" arrangements, and partnerships. We discussed the first strategy under the "Competition and Economies of Scale" subsection. Centralized equal access provides a good example of the second strategy. Cabella's and EMRG (discussed in Chapter 2, "Doing Business in Rural America") are good examples of "piggyback" arrangements for network access. PalmettoNet is an example of how telcos within partnerships can use their complementary positions to create a sophisticated network. Regulators should study and facilitate these types of activities.

Facilitating regional networks. In the early days of rural telephony, the reluctance of Ma Bell to serve rural areas forced rural communities to create their own telecommunications networks. These usually took the organizational form of cooperatives. Now that most rural areas have basic telephone service, the next challenge is to upgrade their networks and service offerings toward the intelligent network. The cooperative spirit now manifests itself in the form of regional networks designed to meet the challenge of new possibilities. Just as earlier policy facilitated the creation of cooperatives, primarily through the REA, a similar approach needs to be developed to bolster regional networks.

Study of organization and incentives. In our study we found that the structure of telcos influenced their ability to provide advanced telecommunications services. For example, cooperatives seem to have greater incentive to invest in the local plant; as nonprofit companies they are restricted in their use of profits and, consequently, tend to invest more than they might otherwise. More in-depth analysis needs to be made of organizational structure because it directly impacts the development of infrastructure in rural areas.

In considering telecommunications and rural development in the United States, it is critical to understand the roles served by small independent telephone companies and cooperatives. These companies have already provided a basic telecommunications infrastructure to rural America and in many cases have acquired advanced telecommunications capabilities for their customers. Rural America will continue to benefit from telecommunications only if these companies remain healthy and progressive. Given the rapid pace of technological advances and the changing regulatory and policy environment, to keep these companies healthy and progressive will take a concerted effort.

The policy options discussed above will facilitate the growth and well-being of small independents. In general, policymakers must take care to include these companies in larger debates concerning the future roles of AT&T and the BOCs, as their decisions will have lasting effects on small independent telcos.

NOTES

1. U.S. Congress, House Committee on Energy and Commerce, *FCC Telephone Price Caps: Hearings*, 101st Cong., 2d sess., February 28, 1989, p. 286.

2. J. Gillan, "Universal Service and Competition: The Rural Science," *Public Utilities Fortnightly*, May 15, 1986, pp. 22–26.

3. National Telecommunications and Information Administration, Telecom 2000, NTIA Special Publication 88-21 (Washington, D.C., 1988), p. 96; Pacific Bell, "Pacific Bell's Response to the Intelligent Network Task Force Report" (San Francisco, 1987).

4. U.S. Congress, House Committee on Energy and Commerce, *FCC Telephone Price Caps*, p. 213.

5. U.S. Congress, House Committee on Energy and Commerce, *FCC Telephone Price Caps Proposal: Hearings*, 100th Cong., 1st sess., November 10, 1987, p. 308.

6. Ellen S. Deutsch and Andrew G. Mulitz, "Equal Access: More Than Just a Switch," *Roundtable,* Summer 1988, p. 17.

7. U.S. Congress, Committee on Commerce, Science, and Transportation, *Rural Cellular Non-wiring Licensing: Hearings,* 100th Cong., 2d sess., January 27, 1988, p. 40.

8. J. Rose, "Understanding the Intelligent Network," *Roundtable,* Fall 1989, pp. 15–17.

9. Pertinent facts about Eastern New Mexico Rural Telephone Cooperative include the following: *address:* Clovis, New Mexico 88101; *service area:* eastern New Mexico; *gross revenues:* $1,242,069; *switch:* digital; *network:* fiber, microwave; *miles of lines:* 7,286; *miles of network:* 612; *data and long-distance alternative:* no equal access; *enhanced service and technology:* all custom-calling features, high-speed data lines, cellular, BETRS; *trade associations:* National Telephone Cooperative Association, Texas Telephone Association, Western Rural Telecommunications Association, Rocky Mountain Telephone Association; *assistance programs:* New Mexico and Texas Lifeline; *funding source:* REA.

10. SS7 is a key to the evolution of intelligent networks. Its primary feature is its increased ability to connect external data bases to the network. An SS7 system also gives increased information about the network's or the customer's traffic by sending the calling party's number to the terminating number before the call. The resulting network efficiency significantly reduces costs.

11. Interview with Robert Harris, General Manager, Eastern New Mexico Rural Telephone Cooperative, Clovis, New Mexico, January 8, 1990.

12. Ibid.

13. Ibid.

14. Ibid.

15. Robert Harris, "The Regional SS7 Network: An Intelligent Application for Rural Telcos," *Rural Telecommunications,* Summer 1989, p. 12.

16. Ibid.

17. Ibid., p. 13.

18. Ibid.

19. Interview with Harris.

20. Ibid.

21. Ibid.

22. Ibid.

23. Interview with Sandy Vandevender, Data Processing Supervisor, Eastern New Mexico Rural Telephone Cooperative, Clovis, New Mexico, January 8, 1990.

24. Interview with Harris.

25. Ibid.

26. Ibid.

27. Interview with Charles W. Ward, School Superintendent, Santa Rosa Schools, Santa Rosa, New Mexico, January 9, 1990.

28. Harris, "The Regional SS7 Network," p. 12.

29. Ibid., p. 12.

30. Ibid., p. 12.

31. Interview with Allen Dorman, General Manager, Eastex Telephone Cooperative, Henderson, Texas, August 3, 1990.

32. "Big and Getting Bigger," *Rural Lines*, May 1961, p. 15.

33. Interview with Dorman.

34. Interview with Rusty Dorman, Assistant General Manager, Eastex Telephone Cooperative, Henderson, Texas, August 3, 1990.

35. Interview with Allen Dorman.

36. Ibid.

37. Ibid.

38. Interview with Ken Parks, Mine Administrative Superintendent, Texas Utilities Mining Company, Tatum, Texas, August 3, 1990.

39. Ibid.

40. Ibid.

41. Interview with Rusty Dorman.

42. Ibid.

43. Ibid.

44. Ibid.

45. Ibid.

46. Interview with Allen Dorman.

47. Mid-Rivers Telephone Cooperative, internal data sheet, no date.

48. Interview with Gerry Anderson, General Manager, Mid-Rivers Telephone Cooperative, and Bill Wade, Assistant General Manager, Mid-Rivers Telephone Cooperative, West Glendive, Montana, January 5, 1990.

49. Ibid.; telephone interview with Anderson, March 26, 1990.

50. Interviews with Anderson and Wade, January 5, 1990.

51. Ibid.

52. Interview with Anderson, March 26, 1990.

53. Interviews with Anderson and Wade, January 5, 1990.

54. Interview with Wade, January 6, 1990.

55. Interview with Gary Tuggle, School Superintendent, Ekalaka, Montana, January 8, 1990.

56. Interview with Glendive community leaders, Glendive, Montana, March 17, 1990; telephone interview with Wade, March 22, 1990.

57. Interview with Hilary Hopfauf, Dawson County High School, Glendive, Montana, March 16, 1990.

58. Telephone interview with Gary Kirkpatrick, School Board Member, Dawson County High School, and Community Affairs Manager, US West, Glendive, Montana, March 23, 1990.

59. Interview with Wade, January 6, 1990.

60. Telephone interview with Wade, March 22, 1990; interview with Kirkpatrick.

61. Interview with Kirkpatrick.

62. Ibid.

63. Interview with Anderson, March 26, 1990.

64. Ibid.

65. Interview with J. D. Jones, Assistant General Manager, XIT Rural Telephone Cooperative, Dalhart, Texas, July 19, 1990.

66. Interview with Jimmy White, General Manager, XIT Rural Telephone Cooperative, Dalhart, Texas, July 19, 1990.

67. Ibid.

68. Ibid.

69. Interview with Jones.

70. Ibid.

71. Interview with Larry Kemp, Farmer, Dalhart, Texas, July 19, 1990.

72. Interview with White.

73. Interview with Jones.

74. Ibid.

75. Interview with White.

76. Ibid.

77. Ibid.

78. Interview with Jerry Lobley, Cattle Feed Trader, Texline, Texas, July 19, 1990.

79. Interview with White.

80. Interview with Lobley.

81. Ibid.

82. Ibid.

83. Ibid.

84. Interview with Jones.

85. Interview with White.

86. Interview with Mary Perkins, Office Administrator, Caprock Industries, Dalhart, Texas, July 19, 1990.

87. Interview with Jones.

88. Pertinent facts about Big Bend Telephone Company include the following: *switch:* digital; *network:* T1, toll microwaves; *lines:* 2,641; *data and long-distance alternative:* no equal access; *enhanced service and technology:* call forwarding, radio paging; *assistance program:* Texas Lifeline; *trade associations:* Texas Telephone Association, Organization for the Protection and Advancement of Small Telephone Companies, National Telephone Cooperative Association, United States Telephone Association; *funding source:* REA.

89. Interview with Bruce Wood, Vice-President, Plant Operations, Big Bend Telephone Company, Alpine, Texas, January 11, 1990.

90. Interview with Jeff Haynes, Owner, Big Bend Telephone Company, Alpine, Texas, January 11, 1990.

91. Interview with Wood.

92. Telephone interview with Dale Short, Director, Port of Entry Presidio, U.S. Customs Office, Presidio, Texas, January 17, 1990.

93. Interview with Wood.

94. Ibid.

95. Interview with Haynes; interview with Bill Golden, President and General Manager, Big Bend Telephone Company, Austin, Texas, February 19, 1990.

96. Interview with Wood.

97. Interview with Haynes.

98. Interview with Wood.

99. Interview with Robert Bryson, President, Presidio Chamber of Commerce, Presidio, Texas, January 17, 1990.

100. Interview with Haynes.

101. Interview with Wood.

102. Joel Daniels, "History of the Bretton Woods Phone Company" (Bretton Woods, New Hampshire, 1975), p. 1, internal brochure.

103. Ibid.

104. Ibid., p. 5.

105. Ibid., p. 1.

106. Ibid.

107. Ibid., p. 2.

108. Interview with Ollie Cole, Plant Manager, Bretton Woods Phone Company, Bretton Woods, New Hampshire, January 5, 1990.

109. Interview with Nanci Hubert, General Manager, Bretton Woods Phone Company, Bretton Woods, New Hampshire, January 5, 1990.

110. Interview with Cole.

111. Ibid.

112. Ibid.

113. Ibid.

114. Interview with Hubert.

115. Interview with Les Stachow, Rate Analyst, New Hampshire Public Utilities Commission, Concord, New Hampshire, January 6, 1990.

116. Interview with Cole.

117. Interview with Hubert.

118. Interview with Cole.

119. Ibid.

120. Interview with Hubert.

121. Ibid.

122. Ibid.

123. Pertinent facts about Clear Lake Telephone Company include the following: *address:* 107 North 4th Street, Clear Lake, Iowa 50428; *service area:* Iowa does not have certificated agreements; this is an issue that the Iowa Utilities Board is currently working on; there are written agreements that exist between affected telephone companies; *gross revenues:* $3,748,515; *switches:* two NEC NEX 61 digital; *network:* fiber (part of INS); *special carrier:* 13 T spans with a total of 35 data circuits; *lines:* 5,837; *miles of lines:* 30,860; *data and long-distance alternatives:* AT&T, MCI, US Sprint, Telecom USA, INS; *enhanced service and technology:* call forwarding, paging; *trade associations:* Organization for the Protection and Advancement of Small Telephone Companies, Iowa Telephone Association; *assistance program:* Link-Up America; *funding source:* industrial development bonds.

124. Interview with Jan Lovell, Assistant Manager, Clear Lake Telephone Company, Clear Lake, Iowa, January 9, 1990.

125. Ibid.

126. Ibid.

127. Ibid.

128. Ibid.

129. Ibid.

130. Ibid.

131. Ibid.

132. Ibid.

133. Ibid.

134. Ibid.

135. Interview with C. R. Weinheimer, President, Kerrville Telephone Company, Kerrville, Texas, June 18, 1990.

136. Ibid.

137. Interviews with Phil Neighbors, President, Kerrville Area Chamber of Commerce; Charles Manade, Director of Engineering and Maintenance, Sid Peterson Memorial Hospital; and Charlotte Thompson, General Manager, Inn of the Hills, Kerrville, Texas, June 18, 1990.

138. Interview with Weinheimer.

139. Ibid.

140. Interview with Neighbors.

141. Interview with Weinheimer.

142. Ibid.

143. Ibid.

144. Ibid.

145. Ibid.

146. Ibid.

147. Ibid.

148. Ibid.

149. Ibid.

150. Ibid.

151. Ibid.

152. Pertinent facts about North Pittsburgh Telephone Company include the following: *address:* 4008 Gibsonia Road, Gibsonia, Pennsylvania; *service area:* 287 square miles; *operating revenues:* $37,270,000 (1988); *switches:* eight (all digital); *fiber:* all trunk routes (between exchanges); *lines:* 42,000; *data and long-distance alternatives:* equal access to 13 carriers; *enhanced service and technology:* call forwarding, call waiting, three-way calling, talking yellow pages, cellular, paging; *trade associations:* United States Telephone Association, Pennsylvania Telephone Association; *funding source:* REA.

153. Telephone interview with Frank Reese, President, North Pittsburgh Telephone Company, Gibsonia, Pennsylvania, October 10, 1989.

154. Interview with Reese, January 8, 1990.

155. North Pittsburgh Systems, Inc., *Annual Report 1988* (Gibsonia, Pennsylvania, 1989), p. 1.

156. Letter to authors from Frank Reese, President, North Pittsburgh Telephone Company, Gibsonia, Pennsylvania, May 4, 1990.

157. North Pittsburgh Systems, *Annual Report 1988*, p. 4.

158. Interview with Reese, January 8, 1990.

159. North Pittsburgh Systems, *Annual Report 1988*, p. 3.

160. Interview with Reese, January 8, 1990.

161. Interview with David Riles, Director of External Affairs, Bell of Pennsylvania, Pittsburgh, Pennsylvania, January 8, 1990.

162. Telephone interview with Dave Scholl, Assistant Vice-President, Pennsylvania Regulatory Affairs, AT&T, Harrisburg, Pennsylvania, December 20, 1989.

163. Interview with Caroll Smith, Manager, Telecommunications Division, Pennsylvania Public Utilities Commission, Harrisburg, Pennsylvania, January 9, 1990.

164. Interview with Scholl; interview with Larry Bowers, Manager, State Government Affairs, AT&T, Harrisburg, Pennsylvania, January 9, 1990.

165. Interview with Francis Mangan, President, Pennsylvania Telephone Association, Harrisburg, Pennsylvania, January 9, 1990.

166. Pennsylvania Public Utilities Commission, "The EAS Decision," *Pennsylvania Bulletin* 19, no. 11 (March 18, 1989), p. 1179.

167. Interview with Smith.

168. Pennsylvania Public Utilities Commission, "The EAS Decision," p. 1181.

169. Interview with Reese, January 8, 1990.

170. Ibid.

171. Interview with Riles.

172. Interview with Reese, January 8, 1990.

173. Ibid.

174. Interview with Mangan.

175. Interview with Riles.

176. Interview with Reese, January 8, 1990.

177. Interview with Riles.

178. Interview with Reese, January 8, 1990.

179. Interview with Mangan.

180. Ibid.

181. Interview with Riles.

182. Interview with Smith.

183. Interview with Mangan.

184. Interview with Riles.

185. Interview with Mangan.

186. Pertinent facts about Taconic Telephone Corporation include the following: *address:* Taconic Place, Chatham, New York 12037; *service area:* 600 square mile; *switches:* all digital; *lines:* 21,313; *enhanced service and technology:* call waiting, call forwarding, three-way calling, speed dialing, cellular; *trade associations:* Organization for the Protection and Advancement of Small Telephone Companies, United States Telephone Association, New York State Telephone Association; *funding support:* REA.

187. New York State Telephone Association, *The History of the New York State Telephone Association* (Albany, N.Y., 1987), p. 102.

188. Interview with Todd Rielly, Vice-President, Taconic Telephone Corporation, Chatham, New York, January 10, 1990.

189. New York State Telephone Association, *History,* p. 102.

190. Interview with Irene Waldorf, Manager, Customer Service, Taconic Telephone Corporation, Chatham, New York, January 10, 1990.

191. Interview with Rielly.

192. Taconic Telephone Corporation, *Annual Report 1987* (Chatham, N.Y., 1988), p. 2.

193. Interview with Rielly.

194. Interview with Eileen Mahoney, Director, Government Relations, New York State Telephone Association, Albany, New York, January 10, 1990.

195. Interview with Rielly.

196. Telephone interview with Rielly, August 10, 1989.

197. Taconic Telephone Corporation, *Annual Report 1987*, p. 3.

198. Taconic Telephone Corporation, *Annual Report 1988* (Chatham, N.Y., 1989), p. 4.

199. Interview with Rielly, August 10, 1989.

200. Interviews with Paula Adams, Associate Communications Rates Analyst; Angello Rella, Principal Valuations Engineer; and Gregory Ptattenade, Senior Systems Analyst, New York Public Utilities Commission, Albany, New York, January 11, 1990.

201. Interview with Rielly, January 10, 1990.

202. Ibid.

203. Ibid.

204. Interview with Mark Lippford, Director, Network Operations, Taconic Telephone Corporation, Chatham, New York, January 10, 1990.

205. Interview with Rielly, January 10, 1990.

206. Interview with Waldorf.

207. Interview with Rielly, January 10, 1990.

208. Interview with Waldorf.

209. Interview with Rielly, January 10, 1990.

210. Interview with Rielly, August 10, 1989.

211. Taconic Telephone Corporation, "Taconic Telephone Consumer Survey" (Chatham, N.Y., June 1988), p. 7.

212. "Taconic Questions Customers," *Roundtable*, Summer 1989, p. 17.

213. Interview with Rielly, August 10, 1989.

214. Ibid.

215. Ibid.

216. "Taconic Telephone Consumer Survey."

217. Ibid.

218. Interview with Rielly, January 10, 1990.

219. Interview with James Calvin, Columbia County Chamber of Commerce, Hudson, New York, January 11, 1990.

220. Taconic Telephone Corporation, *Annual Report 1988*, p. 7.

221. Interview with Calvin.

222. Ibid.

223. Interview with Rielly, January 10, 1990.

224. Jan Lovell, "Network of Iowa Carriers Works Towards Equal Access," *Roundtable*, Summer 1989, pp. 22-23.

225. Press Eldridge, "Phone Network to Aid Customers," *Iowa*, January 18, 1989.

226. "Joint Phone Network Creates 'New World' for Rural Iowans," *Des Moines Register*, December 31, 1989, p. A-1.

227. Interview with Bob Sherlock, Director of Engineering Services, Iowa Network Services, West Des Moines, Iowa, January 8, 1990.

228. Ibid.

229. Ibid.

230. Ibid.

231. Docket No. RPU-88-2, State of Iowa, Department of Commerce, Utilities Division, p. 4.

232. Telephone interview with Joseph Webster, General Manager, ValleyNet Partnership, Inc., Roanoke, Virginia, November 17, 1989.

233. Interview with Jim Carlson, General Manager, PalmettoNet, Inc., Rock Hill, South Carolina, January 4, 1990.

234. Ibid.

235. Ibid.

236. Ibid.

237. Ibid.

238. Interviews with Jack Holladay, Director of External Affairs; Glenn Mc-Fadden, Director of Marketing; and Henry M. Miller, Jr., Chief Engineer, Rock Hill Telephone Company, Rock Hill, South Carolina, January 4, 1990.

239. Interview with Larry Manning, Rate Analyst, Oklahoma Public Utilities Commission, Oklahoma City, Oklahoma, January 12, 1990.

240. Ibid.

241. Ibid.

242. Ibid.

243. Ibid.

244. Ibid.

245. Ibid.

246. Interview with Jay Clark, Marketing Director, Cotton Rural Electric Cooperative, Walters, Oklahoma, January 12, 1990.

247. Ibid.

248. Interview with Manning.

249. G. Brock, *The Telecommunications Industry: The Dynamics of Market Structure* (Cambridge, Mass.: Harvard University Press, 1981).

250. Interview with Reese, January 8, 1990.

251. Interview with Wood.

252. Interview with Haynes, January 11, 1990.

253. Interview with Harris.

5

Telecommunications and Community Development

Lane Darnell Bahl, Oswaldo M. Coelho, Richard Cutler, Julia A. Marsh, and Robert Stephens

INTRODUCTION

Rural Communities in Change

Structural changes in rural economies have resulted in slow job growth, reduced population, and underdeveloped human resources. In addition, communities lose their spirit and functional identity as farming, manufacturing, or extractive industries die out. Income leaks out without benefiting the community when goods and service providers move to urban areas. Towns find themselves swamped in crises and frequently suffer from a lack of adequate leadership.

Policy Development

Community development is clearly more than jobs and income. It is a process of mobilizing people, developing human resources, and reaching for outside guidance in order to improve physical and support services for the entire community. The result should be a sense of place, conducive to growth yet not threatening to the quality of life treasured by rural inhabitants.

Specific federal recommendations for rural policy attempt to improve the functioning of markets by providing interested parties with information on production technology and prices—rather than subsidies[1]—and encourage of rural communities to take "the major responsibility for identifying opportunities for local economic development and mobilizing resources to deal with structural change."[2] Federal policy in the 1980s had been to leave new initiatives to state governments, which would choose solutions for each community environment. In a period when taxation and revenue bases have been hit by economic recession and federal cutbacks, states need to be able to promote collaboration among neighboring towns or regions in order to take advantage of economies of scale.[3] Telecommunications has the ability to provide rapid and intensive flows of information over great distances between any number of people. Therefore, the inadequacy of telecommunications infrastructures in rural areas may be a real constraint to facilitating job creation through support of service-sector growth.[4]

Telecommunications in Rural Communities

Telecommunications may be understood to extend vertically to and from outside sources of information or horizontally across the community and to adjacent areas. For example, businesses need upward access to state, national, and global market information. Within and between communities horizontal communication is indispensable for establishing cooperative agreements on development objectives, implementation of strategic plans, and adaptation to forces that threaten to change the communities.

The ability to bridge distances is perhaps the most important feature of telecommunications for rural communities. Information travels via telecommunications instantaneously. People living far from urban areas can regain the competitive advantage of support services that urban dwellers enjoy. Data bases supply information for investment decisions, sources of support, and development opportunities. Expert guidance and training is often essential for ranking the priority of needs in an environment of reduced funding, as is practical guidance on alternative strategies for action. A community needs access to human resource development programs that train or retrain its members for the professional and service occupations that affect the quality of life for the whole community.

Making development choices tailored to a locale involves myriad of information needs and requires increased communication within and between communities. Coordination and integration of services using telecommunications to achieve economies of scale may be an essential component of community development in an era of reduced funding.

To achieve unity of direction and community goals, much face-to-face, institution-to-individual, or phone-to-phone communication is needed to make agreements, set up meetings, discuss ideas, notify participants, rally support, and conduct training. Even though population densities may be low, telephone service areas in rural America are often small, having been established by independent telcos and cooperatives. Thus, when community members seek to cooperate, they frequently pay toll charges to cross service areas. Resolving issues of intraLATA, extended area service, and equal access to competitive long-distance services is a crucial need.

Research Questions

We investigated three aspects of telecommunications and community development by conducting case studies in six rural communities. In each of the communities under study, we determined the telecommunications system's status and identified recent improvements to the system. We found that in all communities the communication system had been upgraded and various innovations adopted. We wanted to know how these improvements had affected the local communities, what further telecommunications developments were deemed desirable, and to what extent the improvements had aided the communities with respect to their economic development goals.

We also tried to identify the source of the telecommunications innovation—was it driven by the community's institutions or by people with vision? This tack was taken to identify the origins of local initiatives and leaders. Geographic isolation and political neglect—or just inertia—can often cripple local initiative in a rural community and we wished to determine why innovative behavior occurred in these communities.

Finally, we investigated the extent to which a viable, modern communications system is vital to the improvement of the community's quality of life and economic standing. We wanted to know whether the potential contribution of telecommunications systems is even recognized and whether the demand for upgrade comes from businesses serving local markets or from business serving national markets.

Overview of Sites

Six nonurban research sites were selected for their blend of telecommunications activity, planning innovation, and business growth.

Dahlonega, Georgia. Historic site of the nation's first major gold rush, Dahlonega is 70 miles from Atlanta by four-lane highway. After businesses moved away in the 1970s, restoration of the downtown district and promotion of outdoor recreational activities established tourism as a major industry by 1985. We selected this location for study because city, county, college, and business leaders have successfully cooperated and attracted industrial and business investment to Lumpkin County. The local telephone company, Standard Telephone, installed a fiber-optic system and digital switch that adds to the potential for business and service-sector development with Atlanta and beyond.

Hailey, Idaho. Severe economic decline in extractive industries and agriculture in the 1980s hit Hailey with high unemployment and general economic deterioration—as it did many other areas in western states, particularly around the Rocky Mountains. Our interest in this site centers around its up-to-date digital switches and a fiber trunk that stretches throughout Idaho. Nonpolluting, information-intensive businesses have been attracted to the area. Like Dahlonega, Hailey is an attractive location, but here the chambers of commerce in the Wood River Valley cooperate to promote the low population density and recreational attractions of the area. An infrastructure problem, lack of a full-service airport, acts as a restraint on development.

Ottumwa, Iowa. Iowa can be characterized as a state of small towns, each a small distance apart. Ottumwa, Iowa, in Wapello County, is larger than most and has been the subject of many "typical American town" studies since World War II. The general economic slump in agriculture and related industries, such as meat packing and farm equipment manufacturing, in the 1980s left Ottumwa with high unemployment. In Ottumwa, we observed the impact of community leadership training and business development and support information delivered through satellite and electronic networks. But unified development has been hampered by the fact that the chamber of commerce and a separate economic development corporation have different development goals.

Thornton, Iowa. With guidance from an Iowa Extension Service community development specialist, a resident of Thornton began working with seven towns within a 36-square-mile area to create the Area Community Commonwealth (ACC). The purpose of the cluster of communities is to maintain quality schooling, retain medical services, preserve local retailers, share economic advantages, and muster legislative clout for the surrounding region. ACC is an example of small towns aggregating their resources to become sufficiently competitive to sustain their population. Here the proliferation of small telcos, each of which extracts a long-distance toll charge for calls between the clustered towns, restrains the widening community. In ACC, some leadership training was delivered via satellite.

Kearney, Nebraska. Kearney is one of the seven largest towns in Nebraska. Moving from an economy reliant on agriculture and tourism, the town now has a balanced economy with significant employment in manufacturing, medical services, retail and wholesale trade, education, and government, in addition to its traditional sectors. Diversification in the economy occurred as a result of a viable, well-directed economic planning effort. Kearney is notable as a site where a ready labor pool of part-time working college students attracted a telecommunications-intensive catalog business and with it a digital switch that serves other telemarketing businesses. It is also a unique site where small-business success has been built upon bypassing the local telco.

Eagle Pass, Texas. Poised on the threshold of rapid change from an agricultural and Mexican trade-based economy, after being ravaged by peso devaluations and a collapsing oil economy, Eagle Pass falls under the sway of its giant neighbor across the Rio Grande, Piedras Negras. By international agreement a free-trade zone has spawned flourishing industries whose prosperity trickles over the border to tiny Eagle Pass; however, real exploitation of the Mexican industrial explosion awaits an integrated, sophisticated communication system to overcome cross-border telecommunications and postdivestiture barriers. Amid proliferating broadband alternatives, state and telco guidance is necessary to foster a succession of cooperative development strategies in order to link Eagle Pass with other cities in the middle Rio Grande region.

In the following sections, a brief case study is presented for each of these sites. The chapter concludes with a discussion of the themes that emerge from these cases and of the research findings.

DAHLONEGA, GEORGIA

Lumpkin County, with a population of 15,000, is situated in the Appalachian Mountains just 70 miles northeast of Atlanta. Nearly one-third of the county falls within the Chattahoochee National Forest, with the Appalachian Trail passing along its northern border. Dahlonega, with a population of 3,200, is the only incorporated city in the county. Historically, Lumpkin County has been isolated and inaccessible, with low per capita income and educational attainment.[5] Yet, as the site of the first major gold rush in the United States, it has capitalized on its history and the scenic beauty of its mountainous terrain. As a result, quality-of-life factors have been a driving force in economic development efforts in Dahlonega–Lumpkin County. Some other factors that have affected economic growth include strategic alliances and accessibility in terms of physical and telecommunications infrastructure.

Quality of Life

Quality of life has been a driving force in Dahlonega's revitalization efforts, which gained an impetus in the late 1960s when businesses began to shut down or move away. Based on a study conducted by the University of Georgia to determine how best to preserve and promote Dahlonega, the downtown area was established as a historic district. Downtown Dahlonega was carefully restored; the restoration included the conversion of the 1836 county courthouse into a gold museum, which depicts the history of gold mining and the Dahlonega gold rush. Other local attractions include North Georgia College, a four-year military, liberal arts unit of the University of Georgia system; the Smith House, a dining room and hotel; and several state parks and recreation areas.

Tourism has become a major industry in Dahlonega and Lumpkin County. In 1987 alone, tourists spent over $18 million in the area.[6] Other industries employing 10 percent or more of the local work force include manufacturing (30.1 percent), services (23.3 percent), and retail trade (17.8 percent).[7] Since the revitalization efforts began, per capita income has increased from 54 percent of the average U.S. per capita income in 1970 to 89 percent in 1987.

Strategic Alliances

In the 1950s, the citizens and local governments of Dahlonega and Lumpkin County pooled limited resources to purchase land for a manufacturing operation to locate in Dahlonega and provide jobs for local residents. Their willingness to communicate and cooperate is integral to economic development efforts. The consolidation and coordination of resources and services between city and county has been essential in attracting industrial and business investment to the area.

The most visible shared service between Dahlonega and Lumpkin County has been law enforcement. As described by a chamber of commerce official, "A three-way agreement among the city, county, and sheriff provides comprehensive law enforcement services by the sheriff's department to the city and unincorporated area, including traffic patrol and enforcement of city ordinances."[8] Other shared services include the jail, municipal court, volunteer fire department, welcome center, public transportation, and taxation. The goal of such intergovernmental contracts is to achieve efficiency through elimination of duplicate services and to achieve economies of scale through a larger geographic service area.[9] The resulting synergism benefits everyone in the community.

In 1985, the city and county governments joined forces with the Dahlonega–Lumpkin County Chamber of Commerce, the Development Authority of Lumpkin County, and the University of Georgia Cooperative Extension Service in a countywide economic planning effort. They identified goals in several areas, including industrial recruitment and expansion, commercial and downtown development, tourism, agribusiness, and education.[10] As a result of this strategic planning process, Dahlonega–Lumpkin County received the Governor's All Georgia Community Award in 1986. They have been an annual recipient of this award every year since.

Two programs that came out of this planning process were the Business-Education Partnership and the Leadership Development Program. In addition to the establishment of these programs, recruiting efforts have brought several new businesses to the area, including the Bedcoverings/Window Treatment Division manufacturing plant for Ethan Allen, Inc., in 1988.

The Business-Education Partnership was established to get local educators talking with local employers. Though off to a slow start, this program is gaining momentum. The school board has appointed a teacher to coordinate PALS (Partners Assuring Lumpkin's Success). The objective of PALS is to enhance the quality of education by matching school needs with community resources. Resources could include books, surplus supplies and equipment, tutors, clerical help, or transportation to special programs or exhibits. By involving the citizens on a voluntary basis, the community leaders hope to improve the schools without new taxes. The PALS program is still growing and getting organized; therefore, it is too early to know whether it will be successful.

The Leadership Development Program has undergone some changes since its inception in 1985. Originally, the program focused on familiarizing participants with local issues, such as health and human services, education, economic development, and land use. However, following an evaluation of the program in 1988, the chamber of commerce, county commissioner, and extension service decided the program needed to focus more on the development of leadership skills. As a result, they have joined forces to develop a leadership training class employing faculty from the University of Georgia system and county agents from the extension service. The first 14-week class was completed in May 1990.

Physical Infrastructure

In 1981, a major four-lane highway, Georgia State Highway 400, was completed, connecting Atlanta and Lumpkin County. With Atlanta just an hour away, traffic patterns have changed dramatically. Not only has tourist traffic to northeast Georgia increased but commuter patterns have changed. Of the 45 percent of the people who commute, a little more than half commute to nearby Gainesville, Georgia; the rest commute to Atlanta.[11]

For Bill Halderson, owner of Halderson Executive Search Firm, accessibility to Atlanta and an international airport was a major consideration in his decision to relocate his firm from Chicago to rural Georgia. As he put it, "An executive search firm can be run from anywhere. The only inconvenience is having to travel to do candidate and client interviewing."[12]

Yet accessibility is not always positive. As Atlanta industry moves north up the Highway 400 corridor, citizens of Dahlonega and Lumpkin County have been forced to consider its impact on their community. The possibility of becoming a bedroom community is not well received. Like so many rural communities, economic growth presents a real dilemma—they want to strengthen and diversify the economic base, yet they do not want to become so accessible that the precarious balance between quality of life and growth is disturbed.

Telecommunications Infrastructure

Local telecommunications service in Lumpkin County is provided by one of Georgia's most progressive independent telephone companies, Standard Telephone Company, with headquarters in Cornelia, Georgia. According to December 31, 1988, statistics of the United States Telephone Association, Standard is ranked thirty-fifth among the 150 largest U.S. telephone companies with approximately $30 million in gross operating revenues and 40,500 access lines.[13] With the phenomenal growth that has occurred in northeast Georgia in recent years, Standard has experienced a 44-percent growth rate since it celebrated its 80th anniversary in 1984.[14]

Standard's service area covers 1,571 square miles of northeast Georgia, including Lumpkin, Dawson, Union, Towns, Habersham, and White counties with some service in Banks and Rabun counties. According to a Standard Telephone executive, "The major goal of Standard is to provide telecommunications to northeast Georgia via fiber-optic transmission facilities utilizing digital switching with a full complement of custom-calling features to [its] customer base and to provide single-party service availability to everyone within [the] service area."[15] This goal is representative of Standard's long history of concern for its subscribers. Investments in advanced equipment, which require substantially less labor to maintain and operate, will help reduce costs and increase efficiency. In addition, many of the new value-added services, such as custom calling and voice messaging, are dependent upon digital technology.

To this end, the company converted the last of its switches to digital in 1989, becoming one of the first telephone companies in the United States to be 100 percent digital. In addition, the company has 120 miles of fiber-optic cable in service. Currently, all of Standard's lines are single-party in Lumpkin County, and the company plans to replace all remaining two- and four-party lines with single-party lines by 1991. With the 1988 installation of an access tandem switch, Standard has the facilities to offer equal access to competing long-distance companies and enhanced 911 (E911) services. It began offering equal access on October 1, 1989, with AT&T, MCI, US Sprint, Telecom USA, and ATC (Advanced Telecommunications Corporation) competing for customers. Standard is currently working with all of the counties in its service area to establish E911 services. Current plans are to have this service in place in 1992.

Though Standard offers its customers the latest in technology, it must deal with problems related to the large number of local exchange companies and their boundaries in Georgia. According to the Association of County Commissioners of Georgia (ACCG), "Thirty-six separate telephone companies serve the state. As many as five companies with seven exchanges and two Local Access Transport Areas (LATAs) operate in a single county."[16] The Lumpkin County area[17] is served by two telephone companies, Standard Telephone in the Cleveland, Dawsonville, Suches, and Dahlonega exchanges and Southern Bell in Gainesville, the socioeconomic center for the northeast Georgia region. When members of the ACCG sit down with telephone industry representatives to discuss why a person has to call long-distance to reach other parts of the county, they are always told that each phone company can speak only for its own service area.[18]

Extended area service is available between Dahlonega and Suches, a small community in Union County, and between Dahlonega and Dawsonville, 15 miles southwest. Suches, originally a part of the Dahlonega exchange, was given its own exchange in 1962. Because residents were accustomed to calling Dahlonega toll free, Standard offered EAS with the installation of the new exchange. Later, in 1969, Standard offered EAS to the residents of Dawsonville because many of them lived in nearby Lumpkin County. Today, however, the greatest needs are to extend the toll-free area south and southeast toward Gainesville and Atlanta. In 1990, legislation was passed by the Georgia legislature to allow countywide toll-free calling. Previously, J. B. Jones, the county commissioner of Lumpkin County, had to make a toll call from his home to the courthouse in Dahlonega.[19]

For the small-business owner or professional, the limited size of the toll-free calling area can be a competitive disadvantage. A long-distance call to reach clients, suppliers, and information services in Atlanta becomes an added cost that competitors in the metro area do not have. Likewise, companies prefer to locate where the free local dialing area is extensive. According to the ACCG, extensive toll charges add to the cost of doing business and, therefore, discourage companies from choosing such a site.[20]

Despite the availability of digital technology, telecommunications remains, for the most part, confined to telephone and facsimile use. Yet, even with limited use, a good telecommunications system is expected. According to Cullen Larson, vice-president of the Dahlonega–Lumpkin County Chamber of Commerce, "Industrial prospects will normally not consider a community competing for their investment unless it has the necessary sites, roads, water and other infrastructure."[21] Simply put, telecommunications is necessary, but not sufficient, to further community development. However, community leaders acknowledge that telecommunications is becoming increasingly important and will play a larger role in future recruiting efforts.

Summary

Responding to the rapid regional growth and the threat of urban encroachment from Atlanta, local leaders in government, business, and the community at large developed a countywide strategic plan. Through the process of communication and cooperation they have achieved economic growth and recognition. By consolidating services and resources and eliminating duplicate services, they have increased efficiency and reduced costs.

Though telecommunications has not been a leading element, neither has it been a limiting element in the success of Dahlonega–Lumpkin County development efforts to date. This can be attributed to the progressive stance of Standard Telephone. Because telecommunications facilitates the exchange of information and ideas, it is an important element in facilitating cooperative community efforts. In Lumpkin County, it is also evident that access to outside information, in order to compete in a global marketplace, is increasingly important. However, that access can be constrained by the size of the toll-free calling area with the added cost of long-distance charges.

Though alliances and accessibility to physical and telecommunications infrastructure are necessary, other factors were frequently cited as essential to successful community development efforts. Quality of life and availability of low-cost skilled labor were mentioned most often as important factors in business location decisions.

HAILEY, IDAHO

Hailey, a town that suffered ten years ago from unemployment and general economic decline typical of many small towns, has grown rapidly in recent years. The town's and state's excellent telecommunications systems have significantly contributed to this growth. In Idaho, as in many western states, the main industries of agriculture, logging, and mineral extraction have grown slowly, if not deteriorated, in the past 20 years. A public utility commissioner stated that things had become so bad that any type of development was welcome.[22] Hailey does have a special advantage, however; it is situated in a beautiful region of the Rocky Mountains, 15 minutes by car from the Sun Valley ski resort. Quality-of-life considerations are affecting specialized, clean-industry growth from New Mexico to the northwest and east to Montana.

Hailey is located in the Wood River Valley, a fast-growing area of the state, and has a population of 3,083 (an 1988 estimate), up from 2,109 in 1980. Unemployment has decreased from 5.9 percent in 1985-86 to 4.5 percent in 1988-89.[23] The Wood River Valley is the unit used to promote development in Hailey and the neighboring towns of Sun Valley, Ketchum, Bellevue, and Carey.

Telecommunications Infrastructure and the Economy

In telecommunications, Hailey and the whole of Idaho are far ahead of most rural regions and the showcase of US West. The foresight of the Idaho Public Utilities Commission is responsible for adopting measures that distinguish Idaho. In 1981, the PUC negotiated with AT&T for universal one-party service. In 1990, many other states (even those in US West territory) did not have this capability, and it is becoming increasingly expensive to implement universal service today. In doing away with party lines, Idaho was "ahead of the curve."

In 1987, the PUC determined that the BOC, now US West, was vastly overearning, and it encouraged US West to install digital switches throughout southern Idaho as the appropriate remedy. This alternative was chosen rather than returning to US West customers what would amount to "six-pack"[24] money. Hailey had earlier acquired the first digital switch in Idaho, and digital switches will be installed systemwide before 1992. After another round of overearning negotiations, US West was persuaded to install a fiber-optic tollway across the state. US West added an enhanced 911 capability, which generates the caller's name, address, and phone number on a dispatcher's screen seconds after a call is answered. These capacities, unusual for rural areas, are a selling point in attracting industries to relocate to Idaho and provide better than average rural services for the people of the state.

Since much of Hailey's economy is based on tourism and clean industry, quick access to the outside world is essential. Thus there is great demand to upgrade the airport, which is located in Hailey. The Federal Aviation Administration has approved the testing of new technology at the Hailey airport, called the Microwave Landing System (MLS). MLS in an application of microwave communications technology that can better guide incoming planes when the visibility is poor. However, MLS is an expensive initial investment and has a long test period, making it infeasible in most rural areas.

Power Engineers, Inc., is an excellent example of a technical firm adapting to its rural location. A consulting firm, Power Engineers provides a wide range of engineering services for clients nationally and abroad. Easy and quick access, in terms of air travel and telecommunications, were critical to the company, given the nature of the industry. Power Engineers, however, has the economies of scale to charter its own air transportation.

Members of the Hailey community have expressed concern about being "too accessible." Sun Valley, the ski resort at the top of the valley, has the potential to become an Aspen or Vail, but this possibility is not viewed positively by the area's inhabitants.

While the entire state enjoys a good infrastructure, Hailey's telecommunications system does not benefit from many substantive innovations. The area's lava bedrock is too difficult to blast for underground cable, so US West must carry the signal out of the valley on a series of digital microwave dishes down to Twin Falls. At the airport, a different application of microwave is utilized. Cellular radio is not available in the Wood River Valley because it has been found to be infeasible. An old radio phone system still operates out of Sun Valley. Some businesses maintain such a device, but the quality is quite poor. Sun Valley Company, a subsidiary of Sinclair Oil that runs the ski resort, had a micro-multiplex system installed by US West on the slopes for the racing circuits.

Sources of Innovation

Who and what were behind the innovations that allowed the revitalization of Hailey? The strong leadership role of the PUC, in generating an above-average public telecommunications network, was a critical factor. Commissioner Perry Swisher had a long-term vision of the state's needs and pursued the measures described above. The telecommunications network created one part of the context in which a local strategy could be pursued. On the local level, visionary Idahoans and nonnatives in Hailey have created a climate that favors selected business development and controlled growth. The community is served by dynamic citizen leadership. The Sun Valley/Ketchum Chamber of Commerce is well funded and has provided a comprehensive plan with sophisticated long-term goals. It coordinates with the Bellevue and Hailey chambers of commerce and has helped the lesser-developed areas to plan and coordinate better. Together with the Wood Valley Economic Development Council, this area represents itself well and has demonstrated impressive local initiative.

The two founders of Power Engineers decided to relocate to Hailey after their first building burned down in Pocatello, the second largest city in Idaho. They placed their company of consultant engineers in a rural area, aware that the telecommunications capacity was sufficient to support their company's operations. Tasks such as drafting are computerized, and modems allow the employees to work in their homes with an enhanced personal computer. Now the thirty-second largest consulting engineering firm in the country, Power Engineers is able to reach the world, soliciting work in China, Spain, Guatemala, and Alaska. The general manager, Pete Van Der Meulen, says, "Most companies who do what we do are on the East Coast. Quality of life and the recreational opportunities were no longer limited by the necessity to commute to work in an urban area. They look at us and say, 'How do they do it from *there*?!'"[25]

Business Needs

How crucial is telecommunications for local business operations? Van Der Meulen of Power Engineers has witnessed the increasing dependence on telecommunications. With 95 percent of its business outside the state, Power Engineers depends heavily on communications. Present technologies, however, will not suffice for long. According to Van Der Meulen, there is demand for videoconferencing and therefore for fiber. Dick Fenton of McCann-Daech-Fenton Realty, in Sun Valley, has expressed the desire for interactive fax. He believes the fax machine itself has revolutionized his business, with many prospective buyers exchanging information using facsimile technology. The realty company is also linked to a data base in southern California for members of a board of realtors.

Several businesses discussed their relationship with US West regarding the responsiveness and innovativeness of the telephone company. In a recently passed intrastate deregulation bill, Idaho has taken the unusual step of removing the PUC's oversight on all toll calls. US West is now faced with heightened competition from what used to be considered its exclusive jurisdiction, and a number of companies are considering bypass.[26] The ski resort Sun Valley Company is one. In addition, Peak Media, Inc., will migrate to satellite.[27]

Clarence Stilwill of Peak Media, Inc., a firm that produces the magazine *Oh Idaho!*, is optimistic about the future of telecommunications-intensive industries in regions like Hailey. The Peak Media, Inc., innovative telephone books offer "Talk Lines," a list of numbers that consumers can call for recorded information on various subjects— from horoscopes to local events. Stilwill stated that every six months an innovation in telecommunications comes along that his company can use in its expanded publishing business. The "Talk Lines" will soon migrate from dedicated fax lines to Twin Falls (a major trade locus) to satellite. The company also plans to launch a new national magazine in the near future, further expanding the need for access to national markets.

Jim Dutcher of Dutcher Film Productions produces nature films for National Geographic, PBS, and ABC. Dutcher says, "You can take care of menial things like banking quickly and get on with the creative things, and focus on your work. With phone, fax, and Federal Express daily errands don't take any more time than if I had to send something across town."[28]

Summary

Optimism abounds in Hailey. The successful businesspeople of the town are creative and forward looking. They have already capitalized on the potential of telecommunications technology. Further innovations such as interactive two-way videoconferencing are planned and will save high-tech service companies much in transportation costs. We had expected to find the high-technology firms in Hailey making better use of new technology. What we found was a dichotomy of local leadership, exogenous and endogenous leaders with correspondingly different aims. Stilwill and Van Der Meulen, both native Idahoans, have utilized technology as well or better than the exogenous lead firms we interviewed. An anomaly is the initial, critical economic boost brought to the area by Sun Valley Company that is not available to most rural communities. Many communities have difficulties launching revitalization programs. As areas like Sun Valley/Ketchum expand, new areas in the West noted for their quality of life will most likely be the breeding ground for revitalization of this nature. Tele-communications is the gateway for an active community to attract desirable firms and reclaim some of its natives lost to the urban enclave.

OTTUMWA, IOWA

Iowa is a state of small towns. There are more towns of less than 500 people in Iowa than in any other state in the continental United States. More people are employed in government (225,000) than in agriculture (190,000), and only 9 percent of the income is from agriculture.[29]

The state is going through a period of change. According to Don Murray, network coordinator at the Iowa Department of Economic Development (IDED), "Regional development is persuading people to merge to survive. Cities without a niche can't compete in manufacturing, and service industries need lots of education."[30] The IDED has established 15 regional area economic development offices, called "satellite centers," as the Iowa Economic Development Network (IEDN). Each regional office has an area strategic plan and serves many counties. The Region XV Area Economic Development Office (AEDO), located in Ottumwa, performs an outreach function for the IDED, but it determines locally what will best meet local needs.[31] The Ottumwa Area Economic Development Corporation (OAEDC), a group composed of business and community leaders, utilizes the AEDO to create presentation packages to encourage the relocation of industries to Wapello County. The OAEDC is concerned with developing Ottumwa into a variety of economic and community areas. Through a pilot program administered by faculty from the Iowa State University (ISU) Cooperative Extension Service (CES), the OAEDC was trained to develop and implement strategic planning.

Ottumwa is an example of a city whose citizens understand the value of quality of life as a resource for community development.

There is adequate physical infrastructure; a variety of telecommunications systems are in operation; the community college is the host for a regional economic development office and other development services; and the director of the CES has a long history of being a catalyst in community development. In Ottumwa, we observed the impact of community leadership training and business development information delivered through satellite and electronic networks. Another distinctive factor in Ottumwa is the division of development effort between the chamber of commerce and a separate economic development corporation.

The Community

Wapello County, located in southeastern Iowa, covers 432 square miles and had a 1987 population of 37,300. The county boasts of its excellent educational system and cultural opportunities and describes itself in typical rural terms as "a fine place to raise a family."[32]

Ottumwa, the county seat of Wapello County, has a population of about 25,000, larger than most of Iowa's 935 municipalities. Ottumwa has been the subject of many "typical American town" studies since World War II. The general economic slump in agriculture and manufacturing that hit the rest of rural America in the 1980s left Ottumwa with high unemployment.[33] About 10,000 jobs were lost.[34] According to Mayor Carl Radosevich, "Before we had a strategic plan, there were too many plans."[35] Developing the strategic plan was a community-wide effort consisting of tallying resources, ranking needs, and developing action plans.

The Ottumwa economy appears to be turning around. Major employers in Ottumwa are industry (3,074 employees), education (799), and the Ottumwa Regional Health Center (790).[36] A Cargill facility—a major grain handler located 15 miles away—is expanding, as are Excel—a meat packer—and John Deere—a manufacturer. In nearby Fairfield, expansion by Rockwell International and Maharishi International University has nudged up housing prices in Ottumwa. Without being a part of any local development plans, a shopping center that includes a Wal-Mart has gone up on the edge of town. The county has about $22 million in retail sales "leakage."[37]

Infrastructure

Ottumwa appears to have an adequate physical infrastructure to either attract new industries, retain established businesses, accommodate the expansion of existing firms, or provide support services for new local ventures. There are 800 acres of fully developed industrial parks, including utilities, paved roads, and railroad spurs. In addition to touting the "lowest gas and utility rates in the state,"[38] the Iowa-Illinois Gas and Electric Company has been active in community development by providing district manager Chris Swanson as OAEDC president and supplying a company plane for development promotion efforts.[39] Ottumwa claims an industrial airport that can handle corporate jets, charter flights, and daily commercial air service to Des Moines and Minneapolis/St. Paul.

Broadband communications are provided by four broadcast radio stations and two television stations. In addition to a cable operator, satellite downlinks for business and educational uses are located at the CES office, at the AEDO office, and on the Indian Hills Community College campus.[40] The local newspaper is the *Ottumwa Courier*, the cornerstone of a family-owned communications business that includes several other dailies as well as radio, television, and cable holdings in the eastern Iowa region.[41]

Local-switched (telephone) exchange services are provided by US West Communications, the carrier for EXNET, an on-line agricultural data and electronic mail service that goes to every Iowa CES county agent's office. Another on-line information and data source, Iowa Data Network Service (IDNS), electronically links the AEDO with the other regional offices.

All that Ottumwa seems to lack in physical infrastructure is a four-lane highway to link up with the nearest interstate highway, which is 60 minutes away.[42]

Telecommunications

US West is not perceived as being involved in the development of the community even though the local manager, Roger Williams, has been a member of the OAEDC Board of Trustees.[43] When the 1950s-vintage switch was replaced in 1988, residential bills went up 11 percent and business bills 15 percent. Businesspeople do not see how the upgrade helped them, and the increased rates add to the cost of doing business. Furthermore, with the new switch, local service offices were closed, and service calls are now routed to Des Moines. According to the president of the OAEDC, the extent of US West's involvement in the strategic plan has been to underwrite the wages and room and board for a professional crew to shoot two promotional videos: one on Ottumwa's industrial opportunities and one on its quality of life. The LEC was reimbursed by the OAEDC. By contrast, the Iowa-Illinois Gas and Electric Company supplied a company plane for the production crew to help reduce costs. The videos are given by the chamber of commerce to businesses interested in locating in Wapello County.

Satellite Training and the Cooperative Extension Service

The real telecommunications tale in Ottumwa is one of the interaction between external agents of change and community alliances. Satellite teleconferences were used to rally initial interest in strategic planning and then to conduct some classes. Leadership training and strategic plan development were facilitated locally by telephone conferencing and information support on electronic networks.

The story begins with the efforts of Dale Uehling, district director of ISU's Cooperative Extension Service office in Wapello County. With 32 years of experience as an agriculture extension agent, Uehling recognized his role expanding beyond agricultural concerns to include community development.[44] In 1987, he mustered enough citizens and leaders to participate in an interactive teleconference program originating at ISU. Using Wapello County's CES office, the OAEDC held an interactive teleconference with extension economists at ISU in Ames to decide whether or not to try a new strategic development program.[45] The OAEDC decided to try the pilot program, and about 80 to 90 citizens from across the community stayed fairly active during the entire strategic planning process.[46] The state CES integrated cooperation between its land grant extension staff in Ames, the local extension director in Ottumwa, and the area community resource specialist (who serves a 16-county area). Telecommunications helped bridge the distance between ISU and Ottumwa. In addition, audio teleconferencing proved useful for conducting business management meetings scheduled by the OAEDC Board of Trustees. Travel time was saved and everyone got information first-hand.[47]

Iowa Economic Development Network

Whereas the Iowa Cooperative Extension Service aims to provide communities with organizing assistance through leadership training and planning programs directed from the ISU campus in Ames, the AEDO tailors programs for start-up businesses. While not strictly part of Ottumwa's strategic plan, the following examples illustrate the extent to which telecommunications infrastructure is available to implement any plans for development. The AEDO helped establish the OAEDC. It also prepares community leaders to make presentations to prospective businesses. Outreach specialists, such as Laura Mosena, help local businesses expand by garnering government contracts. Additional telecommunications services for economic development are available to support the strategic plan through on-line and facsimile services located at the AEDO. Each of the state's 15 regional economic development offices has a computer, printer, and software to tie it to the IEDN. A data base of Iowa manufacturers and export trade leads was created in order to generate lists of vendors and potential customers who might buy Iowa products and services.[48] In 1989, for example, Iowa-based Rubbermaid Corporation teamed up with a local video production company to do training videos instead of hiring a company from out of state. Information from the network is faxed to businesses and banks in the county for immediate action. Lists of potential suppliers help businesses new to the area. The AEDO relies on the public-switched network for its on-line connections. Mosena dislikes using TELENET, the teleconferencing network available through the community college, because of its poor reception quality, but conducting monthly meetings by teleconference saves driving, especially in bad weather. She might use TELENET more if the reception were better.[49] Poor line quality is a very common reason for not using on-line services, according to Deborah Coates, ISU EXNET manager and software specialist.[50]

Community Colleges, Development, and Telecommunications

Community colleges in Iowa have a mandate to be involved in community development.[51] Most important, Indian Hills Community College provides housekeeping services and infrastructure, such as phone lines, for the AEDO and several other development-related services such as Job Partnership Training Act (JPTA) programs. The community college has its own satellite receiving dish and hosts the AEDO, which has on-line data bases, a satellite dish, and TELENET teleconferencing. The CES has used the campus downlink for large audiences or when a scheduling conflict has its own tied up. Having telecommunications technologies on campus for community development encourages the community college to hold audio teleconferences with instructional directors. TELENET teleconference meetings of fiscal officers at other campus locations are held to discuss programs and problems, contract negotiations, and auditing.[52] In addition to hosting the AEDO office, the local community college will soon be one of 15 hub sites for a statewide fiber-optic/microwave/Instructional Television Fixed Service (ITFS) distance learning network, which will also serve the county's administrative needs.

Strategic Alliances

The main strategy taught to Iowans by the Cooperative Extension Service and the Iowa Department of Economic Development staff is that each town needs to find its niche. This strategy points to the establishment or expansion of small business entrepreneurship and the training and organizing of dedicated people who will collaborate to maximize their personal and community resources.[53]

Ottumwa is characterized by many groups involved in development, notably the chamber of commerce with its emphasis on downtown business and the OAEDC, which concentrates on an overall strategic plan to develop many sectors of the community. In the strategic planning process, committees worked to identify and measure specific community resources. A major outcome of the process was that citizens formed informal interpersonal networks across institutions in a town fragmented by many development efforts.[54] One objective of the planning process was to unify the community's approach to development. However, to avoid pulling the chamber of commerce in two directions— downtown business development versus countywide development— the OAEDC was formed separately. Through peer town visits, members of the OAEDC learned of the necessity for consolidated city organization—to meet new industries as well as operate the city more efficiently.[55] For example, Dianne Kiefer, Wapello County Treasurer and a member of the OAEDC, learned the value of coordinating city and county services, such as police and fire, from a peer town visit to Mason City, Iowa. Her committee efforts to consolidate services were not successful in overcoming the unwillingness of officials at all levels to negotiate in open sessions as required by Iowa statute.[56] In spite of examples of unified chambers and development corporations, the Ottumwa chamber of commerce and the economic development corporation remained separate. However, real community development gains were made. The informal network of alliances formed during the strategic planning development process enabled the community as a whole to introduce and pass a $3.5 million bond—the only issue passed in the past 20 years. The funds will be used for downtown development (to create a riverfront recreation and tourist attraction complete with bike trails) and an industrial airport as first steps toward economic development and improved quality of life.[57]

Summary

Community development is comprised of many factors. In addition to having the physical infrastructure to accommodate growth, citizens and leaders alike need training, information, and continued guidance.

Telecommunications infrastructure, such as satellite receiving dishes and electronic networks that extend outside the community, can act as a conduit for development information and planning guidance. Citizens in Ottumwa received leadership training from the ISU Cooperative Extension Service and business start-up advice through the Iowa Economic Development Network. Outside assistance from two state agencies—the Extension Service and the Iowa Department of Economic Development—illustrates the role of government in supplying leadership training and business data bases, which may facilitate rural competition with national and global markets. To a lesser degree, private-sector suppliers of infrastructure assisted in community development. The Iowa-Illinois Gas and Electric Company and US West assisted economic development by taking leadership positions in the OAEDC as well as providing in-kind support and some funds for promotional activities. However, US West has an opportunity to educate local business people in uses of advanced services. TELENET teleconferencing facilitated efficient organizational business for board members of OAEDC, the IDED Area Economic Development Office, and Indian Hills Community College.

While the community of Ottumwa was not successful in implementing the unified development approach desired by the ISU Cooperative Extension Service for effective implementation of the OAEDC strategic development plan, it did effect one major outcome: Citizens formed informal interpersonal networks across institutions in a town fragmented by many development efforts.[58] Cooperative relationships created by the planning process enabled the OAEDC to pass a major community development bond issue. The economy is turning around, and people's attitudes are changing.[59]

AREA COMMUNITY COMMONWEALTH

A group of seven towns in Iowa, one of the states hardest hit by the rural crisis of the 1980s, are implementing an innovative grassroots rural development program called clustering, which is now being emulated across Iowa and four other states. Clustering is a form of community development that addresses both the economic and social dimensions of the rural crisis. The goal of clustering is to empower residents of once separate and competing rural communities to work together as a single community to maintain quality schooling, retain medical services, preserve local retailers, and achieve other economies of scale. As a community development program, the aim of clustering is to preserve or increase the standard of living and the quality of life in rural communities by transforming rural residents' conception of community. As one of the cluster leaders said, "We are seven isolated towns that want to become one community with seven neighborhoods."[60]

Telecommunications plays a role in clustering because it can foster a new sense of community by increasing the level of interactive communication between people who live in separate towns. This section will illustrate a case in which lack of access to affordable telecommunications resources—specifically, telephones—hinders the efforts of a grassroots development project to revitalize a rural community.

To the 445 residents of Thornton, Iowa, the effects of the rural crisis of the 1980s were devastating. They did not need news accounts to know that something was wrong; all they had to do was to look around their community. Farmers were defaulting on their loans, banks were failing, local industries were laying off workers, public infrastructures and services such as schools and medical services were declining, and Main Street retailers were closing their stores. The crisis affected Thornton as well as the nearby towns of Swelsdale, Dougherty, Messervey, Rockwell, Sheffield, and Chapin. The residents of these towns realized that their communities could easily become ghost towns because they, and their neighbors, were losing more than their jobs: they were losing their hopes as well as their sense of community.

The prospects of these seven towns are shared by many Iowa towns. As a state, Iowa's economy, politics, and society historically have been closely linked to the fate of agriculture and rural America. In 1980, more than 40 percent of Iowa's population lived in rural areas.[61] The vast majority of Iowa's rural residents live in small towns that are relatively close to each other. Of Iowa's approximately 985 municipalities, more than 888 have fewer than 5,000 people.[62]

Towns such as Thornton face a daunting task in attempting to survive in the global marketplace. Their small size is a major barrier to economic development. On one hand, their size precludes their achieving the economies of scale in public services and infrastructures that would enable them to develop a diversified economic base. On the other hand, small towns such as Thornton lack the human resources or the expertise to apply for federal or state assistance. Furthermore, small towns such as Thornton that attempt to attract outside businesses to the area are at a distinct disadvantage because they compete not only with neighboring towns but with larger nearby towns that have more resources, such as Mason City with a population of 28,000.

In addition to being unable to attract outside business to the area, Thornton was suffering from "capital flight," because local residents shopped at large chain-owned retail stores in Mason City instead of patronizing the local retail stores. As a result, retail stores closed in Thornton, which created additional strains on the local economy.[63] In Iowa alone, 605 rural groceries, a third of those that existed ten years ago, have disappeared from the rural retail landscape.[64]

Development experts predict that the days of bustling, independent, and self-sustaining small rural towns are waning.[65] On their own, small towns cannot compete in the international economy of the global village. However, an innovative grassroots development strategy that is being implemented in Thornton offers lessons that could work elsewhere.

Community Development Strategy

Under the auspices of a program sponsored by the ISU Cooperative Extension Service, called Tomorrow's Leaders Today (TLT), representatives and leaders of the seven towns in 1987 began a process that led to clustering. Clustering is a form of grassroots regionalism. While regionalism attempts to overcome barriers by pooling resources from a fairly large geographic area and population to work toward a common goal, clustering applies the concept of regionalism on a much smaller scale. Clusters are made up of two to seven small communities or towns that often encompass an area smaller than a county and that can cut across county and school district boundaries.[66]

Thornton is part of a cluster called the Area Community Commonwealth (ACC), which encompasses seven towns within a 36-square-mile area intersected by Interstate 35. The largest town in the ACC cluster has a population of about 1,200, and the total population for the cluster is 6,045. Most clusters in Iowa have populations under 2,500.[67] The ACC is the first and most advanced of the clusters. Unlike many rural towns, the seven towns that form the ACC cluster have learned how to set aside economic rivalry and to work for the community together.

The broad goal behind clustering is to promote economic and community development within the clusters by empowering residents to share human and material resources, which creates an atmosphere more conducive to business creation and retention. Some of the benefits that have accrued to the ACC towns from clustering include making loans to four start-up businesses: a bottling plant, a manufacturer of curbside recycling equipment, a cylinder factory, and a doll company. Two of the ACC towns have pooled their finances and are sharing a police officer and emergency rescue equipment. School districts are swapping junior high school students to assure that each will have full classes in the grade levels they offer.[68] ACC towns were able to carry out a needs assessment program that enabled them to apply for, and receive, a $50,000 state development grant. In Dougherty (population 133) the opening of Larry's Garage was helped by an ACC loan. When a thief stole $1,300 worth of tires from the garage, the community raised $700 to help cover the loss. In politics, the seven communities speaking as one have more clout when they deal with Mason City, state institutions, and legislators.

Clusters are not formed overnight or spontaneously; they are the result of an extended leadership development and training program. Tomorrow's Leaders Today is organized by the ISU CES and funded by the W. K. Kellogg Foundation. Communities that wish to form clusters, in collaboration with extension agents, select representatives and leaders who take part in a nine-month educational program.

The TLT curriculum involves more than 40 hours of instruction and workshops conducted in ten sessions. The TLT program has three main objectives:

1. To educate and empower emerging community leaders and help them identify and mobilize resources to address communities' issues.
2. To work in clusters.
3. To provide continuing education to program graduates who share their expertise in their own and neighboring communities.[69]

Most of the classes are conducted in the local community or at the ISU campus in Ames. As part of the TLT program, participants learn to work in groups, to identify with their community, and to conduct a needs and resource assessment of their communities. At the end of the program, the clusters decide whether to work together. Between 1988 and 1990, 16 clusters completed the TLT program. Not all clusters have been successful.[70]

When the ACC cluster graduated from the TLT program, its ability to mobilize the seven communities for economic development and to raise funds was quickly put to the test. The Disney Corporation went to Iowa searching for a place to plant a huge cornfield in the shape of Mickey Mouse in order to celebrate Disney's sixtieth anniversary. The ACC was able to convince Disney that it was capable of hosting the event. With a three-week deadline, the ACC divided up organizing tasks among the seven towns. More than 100,000 people attended the event, which was held in Sheffield. The celebration was a success, Disney was pleased with the competent organizing by the ACC, and the ACC was able to raise more than $48,000, which provided the seed money for subsequent ACC projects.

The ACC cluster has established the following goals:

1. To consolidate educational resources.
2. To create a revolving loan fund that would be used to foster local business creation and retention.
3. To publish an ACC-wide business telephone directory. Currently there are three different directories for the seven communities, which are serviced by Centel, Teleconnect, and Rockwell Telephone Company.
4. To establish a day-care center.
5. To acquire extended area service for the seven communities.[71]

Telecommunications and Clustering

Clustering, like most community development programs, is a communication-intensive process aimed at increasing interaction and information sharing within a community as well as between the community and the outside world. The telecommunications needs of clustering can be examined in terms of telecommunications infrastructure and the provision of information to community leaders and activists.

The importance of telephone access within clusters is evident in the initial needs assessment survey that the ACC conducted. Two of five priority goals for the ACC cluster were extended area service for the cluster and a clusterwide telephone directory.[72] Within the ACC cluster, Thornton can call only two out of the other six towns as a local call. In order to call the remaining four, townspeople in Thornton must place a long-distance call. Similarly, most of the calls between the seven towns in the ACC cluster are long-distance toll calls.[73] Long-distance charges are a problem because they hinder the sharing of public services and accessing businesses between the clustering towns. The charges also hinder the development of a sense of community between the towns because people are less likely to share information and to communicate with each other. According to cluster leaders, telephone usage has increased as a result of clustering due to pooling of educational and medical services. In 1988, students from Messervey-Thornton School District began attending school in Sheffield, and seventh- and eighth-graders from Sheffield and Chapin attended school in Thornton. Phone usage increased due to school business and social interaction among students. The cluster's only medical center with a doctor is located in Sheffield, which requires a long-distance call for most of the cluster towns.

The goal of obtaining EAS for the cluster was used as an organizing tool for the ACC. The ACC conducted a survey of people in the cluster to determine demand for EAS and then proceeded to collect a petition requesting the local telephone companies and the Iowa PUC to establish EAS. The ACC expects that it will take at least three years for the PUC to resolve this issue. Meanwhile, clustering will continue, but it is greatly inhibited by the lack of EAS within the cluster.

Summary

Clustering is an effective form of community development for small towns that seek to achieve economies of scale. One of the most important driving forces behind clustering is the training and development of individuals who will assume leadership positions within their communities. State institutions, especially state extension services, play a key role in developing these community leaders.

Clustering is an information-intensive activity. For clustering to succeed, the level of interaction and communication within a community needs to increase. Telephones can assist in increasing interaction between clustering towns. Clustering, which is driven by meeting human needs and developing human resources, can be limited by lack of adequate telecommunications infrastructure, that is, extended area service. In other words, even grassroots development programs have a significant telecommunications component to them.

Institutions such as state extension services have access to more telecommunications resources than cluster leaders. These institutions can serve as gateways or nodes for cluster leaders to access sophisticated telecommunications resources. The telecommunications resources of the extension services are not being used by clustering communities.

Part of the process of clustering requires an assessment of community resources and needs. In order to carry out this assessment, clustering communities need economic and demographic information about their communities and the outside world. Clustering communities are capable of collecting some of the local information, but they cannot readily access information on state, national, and international economic trends that would enable them to find an economic niche in the global economy. National and state institutions have fairly extensive electronic database networks that could assist local communities. These electronic data bases are fairly well developed in the field of agriculture but underdeveloped in the kind of information useful in community organizing.

The Iowa extension service is slowly shifting its emphasis from agriculture to community rural development. But extension agents who specialize in agriculture far outnumber those whose area of expertise is community development.

KEARNEY, NEBRASKA

Kearney was the seventh largest city in Nebraska, according to the census of 1980, but became the fifth largest according to the 1990 census.[74] Its population in 1987 was 23,815. Buffalo County, where Kearney is located, has a population of 36,000.[75]

A substantial portion of the Kearney labor force is employed by large organizations. These include Kearney State College, with 1,346 employees; Good Samaritan Hospital, 750; Eaton Corporation, 649; Baldwin Filters, 673; Cabela's, 535; and Kearney Public Schools, 531.[76] From these numbers, one can identify the education sector as an important employer within the community. In fact, the educational system is not only a large source of jobs but also a major supplier of the labor force. The approximately 10,000 students from Kearney State College represent one of the major sources of workers for companies located in the city. Generally, these students work in part-time jobs in restaurants, hotels, fast-food chains, telemarketing companies, or the like. Average wages in Kearney for different job categories range from five to ten dollars per hour.[77]

Restaurants and lodging represent important economic activities to the city and bring people and money to Kearney. Many factors make the restaurant lodging business viable in Kearney. First, the short travel distance to Denver, Kansas City, and Lincoln encourages people traveling to and from these cities to stop in Kearney. Second, Kearney is located along Interstate 80, which crosses the country and connects the East Coast to the West Coast. Third, the central Nebraska location of Kearney favors it as a site for statewide conferences. The number of overnight conferences reaches as many as 250 a year. Finally, Kearney has its attractions, such as an art museum, an auto museum, a state park, a state college, two hospitals, churches, and a historical fort, Fort Kearney. All of these factors bring many people to Kearney.[78]

Despite a sophisticated infrastructure, Kearney still has many problems to solve. The most crucial are related to the labor force and housing.[79] Kearney, like many other small towns, has some difficulty in maintaining a reliable supply of qualified workers. Generally, workers and students move from small cities to large ones where better job opportunities are available. They may also be attracted by the cultural entertainment offered in larger cities. Besides a shortage of qualified workers, Kearney has problems with housing. In particular, the demand for houses is greater than the supply, in spite of the fact that Kearney State College provides dormitories to its students and faculty members. Although new home construction is at record levels, rental and low-cost housing construction has lagged.

In order to address the housing problem and to maintain a qualified labor force, Kearney entities and community leaders have been working to strengthen the city's economic base by increasing the relative participation of sectors of the economy other than agriculture. Yet Kearney has been very selective about attracting business to its borders. The unemployment rate has been around 2.7 percent, and the city has a saturated labor market. Therefore, companies that are looking only for a site where labor is cheap receive no attention from the Kearney community. City leaders are interested only in attracting enterprises that will bring benefits to the city in terms of labor force and an improved standard of living.[80] Institutions involved in recruiting business have decided not to pursue companies that would bring only economic growth, and not economic development, to the community. In other words, Kearney's institutions are very concerned that the yields of any new economic activity will be distributed among Kearney inhabitants. Such distribution more likely will occur with firms that pay high wages; high wages will enable residents to increase their savings and will make it possible for them to afford to purchase homes. Kearney's aim is to increase home ownership from the current rate of 55 percent.

The Kearney Area Chamber of Commerce was the leader in the city's initial recruitment effort. In 1986, it happened that a 200,000-square-foot building, owned by a member of the chamber and leased to Rockwell, became vacant. To sell the building, the chamber placed advertisements in a national business magazine. Cabela's, a tele-marketing catalog retail company owned by a Nebraskan who was searching in Nebraska for a warehouse and a telemarketing site, inquired about the building.[81] Cabela's needed a site that offered more opportunity for expansion than Sidney, a small Nebraska town of 6,000 inhabitants where it had its headquarters. The chamber prepared an economic package that included a zoning ordinance waiver for Cabela's. For a good price, Cabela's decided to buy the building and make it a retail and warehouse center.

Factors other than the building were also influential in Cabela's decision. Kearney offered an advantage over other cities in the labor force supply that Kearney State College could provide. The town's 10,000 college students could be easily employed and trained to fill part-time jobs. The chamber recruited Cabela's, however, without being aware of its own telemarketing potential.

With the success of recruiting Cabela's in mind, the president of the Kearney Area Chamber of Commerce, Bruce Blankenship, and the president of the Buffalo County Economic Development Council (BCEDC—an institution formed in January 1986),[82] Steve Buttress, adopted a two-part strategy. The first part of the strategy consists of the aggressive recruitment of high-technology companies or enterprises that will bring with them an infrastructure to be shared with other companies in Kearney. The second part of the strategy is to absorb and spread throughout the existing ecomony the telecommunications technology coming with the new companies. In the long term, this strategy will be reflected in a more qualified labor force, better wages, and, consequently, a better standard of living.

Cabela's reinforced Buttress's idea that telecommunications technology is important for economic development. In conjunction with the chamber, GTE, the local exchange companies, and others, Buttress started to recruit telemarketing companies to Kearney at a telemarketing trade show in Atlanta. With the help of David Waldron, president of EMRG (a holding company founded in Kearney in 1985 that sells products through telecommunications),[83] Buttress recruited a telemarketing company, WATS, to Kearney in 1988. Moreover, he worked with telephone companies to upgrade their infrastructure. As a result of this personal effort and the telemarketing business, all major long-distance providers were brought to Kearney: MCI, US Sprint, US West, GTE, and AT&T. AT&T even installed a point of presence at Cabela's.[84] Cabela's can now use AT&T long-distance service at greatly reduced rates. There is capacity for other businesses such as EMRG. These companies generate substantial telephone traffic, although much of it bypasses the local exchange company.

By 1990, the first part of the economic strategy was completed and the second was started. For the second phase, attention is focused on ensuring that existing firms use the full capabilities of existing technology infrastructure. This represents a shift from the earlier focus on attracting more telemarketing companies, which no longer helps in expanding and diversifying the economic base.[85]

In order to spread the technology attracted with telemarketing firms, the BCEDC and the Kearney chamber have been working together with Kearney State College. As a result, in 1988 a telecommunications management degree program was created at the college. Students in this program have the ability to gain practical experience by working in local telemarketing companies. In addition, the initiative has the purpose of teaching businesses how to use the telecommunications infrastructure. The ideal situation will be reached when business in Kearney interacts with the world economy.[86]

Summary

The attraction of telecommunications-intensive users to Kearney, part of the community's efforts to broaden its economic base, has opened new horizons. In particular, it has made the community realize the growing importance of telecommunications to business and to the community's quality of life. Through the utilization of a telecommunications network, which includes all major telephone carriers and sophisticated equipment, Kearney has the potential to become accessible to other markets and to attract companies and people willing to move to rural areas. With this potential in mind, Kearney authorities have worked together to create a college program in telecommunications which teaches businesspeople how to use telecommunications infrastructure to expand their businesses. These accomplishments have put Kearney a step ahead of other cities with planning programs, especially considering that telecommunications has been restricted to telephone users in other areas. Kearney's unique planning brings to the community high expectations of growth.

EAGLE PASS, TEXAS

Eagle Pass, the seat of Maverick County, is located on the Mexican border midway between El Paso and Laredo. It was selected as a community research site because of the unique location next to its industry-rich Mexican neighbor, Piedras Negras. Eagle Pass represents a rural city (population, 28,000; Maverick County population, 40,000) in transition from a traditional reliance on agriculture and Mexican trade to a service and manufacturing economy that is heavily influenced by the commercial border traffic generated by the industries across the border. Population estimates for Piedras Negras range from 212,000[87] to 300,000[88]—roughly ten times the size of Eagle Pass—and the unemployment rate is below 2 percent. In Eagle Pass the unemployment rate is approaching 30 percent and the average age of residents is 24, which together suggest the need and potential for economic development. During the 1980s, Eagle Pass suffered from two major events that affected all of Texas: the devaluation of the Mexican peso and the collapse of the oil-based economy. According to the current city manager, Oscar Rodriguez, in 1982 the city laid off 40 percent of its employees due to the peso devaluation.[89]

Location Factors

Unlike other Texas border cities, which dominate the transborder economy of their Mexican counterparts, Eagle Pass is intimately bound to the destiny of Piedras Negras.[90] To begin with, the Hispanic language and culture dominate life on both sides of the border. In contrast to other pairs of cities along the U.S.-Mexican border, Eagle Pass is situated to serve cities and transportation from Mexico. The Southern Pacific Railroad connects at Eagle Pass with the Mexican National Railroad. Motor freight traffic is steady both ways. In addition to being directly on the border with Mexico, Eagle Pass is the point of access for a large region of other small communities on the U.S. side—Crystal City, Carrizo Springs, and Uvalde—all 40 to 70 miles away and connected by major highways to Eagle Pass.

The dependency of Eagle Pass upon Piedras Negras is further exemplified by the effect of the peso devaluation on jobs at city hall. Sales tax from retail trade gives the city 40 percent of its budget.[91] Advertising sales in media are placed with agencies on both sides of the border.[92] Mexican industries provide middle management jobs for U.S. as well as Mexican citizens, many of whom live in Eagle Pass.[93] A steady flow of steel products, cattle, and gas comes from the Mexican interior.[94] The border presents special opportunities as well as liabilities for the future economic and community development of Eagle Pass. On the one hand, there is increased retail and import/export trade, demand for housing for industry managers, and new multiline installations in businesses and homes as the prosperity in Piedras Negras is shared with Eagle Pass. On the other hand, proximity to the border brings the problems endemic to developing countries such as perennial diseases, government neglect of infrastructure, and the added burden on public services.[95] Nevertheless, according to Arthur Pine, president of the Eagle Pass Chamber of Commerce and executive director of the Maverick County Economic Development Corporation, industry in Piedras Negras holds out the best hope for development in Eagle Pass. Pine expects to see one new job in Eagle Pass for every ten in Piedras Negras.[96]

Transborder Economy

Today the economy of Eagle Pass is growing toward increased international trade as the burgeoning maquiladora industries across the border in Mexico spread their income into Maverick County. Maquiladoras are industries based upon an arrangement in which non-Mexican firms supply materials and markets and Mexican firms supply labor. Parts for assembly are shipped in duty free, and the finished products are subject to duty only on the value added by labor. To date, Piedras Negras has 36 maquiladoras, with another 4 under construction. Textiles are the main industry; other maquiladoras engage in coupon counting, sausage casings, electronics assembly, PVC (polyvinyl chloride) pipe connectors, leather processing, and decorative ceramics. Estimated total employment in the maquiladoras as of December 1989 was 11,356; 16 affiliated U.S. offices or related industries employ 936 in Eagle Pass and the nearby city of Del Rio.[97] The nature of the maquiladora industry makes it a source of transborder telecommunications users—large and small—especially those with technologically sophisticated activities that are information intensive. Local, state, and federal policies of the two countries converge to create some of the issues faced by the telecommunications providers: Southwestern Bell Telephone for local service and typically AT&T for transborder communications. Telefonos de Mexico (TELMEX) handles local and long-distance calls in Piedras Negras.

Telecommunications

The effects of divestiture on service to small businesses in rural areas can be readily seen in Eagle Pass. In 1981 Southwestern Bell installed a 2BESS electronic switch, and it is still the most up to date in the area. Line capacity was increased to 30,720 lines, of which roughly 10,000 are now in use. The breakup of the Bell system in 1984 separated the local exchange companies from the long-distance income, which previously had been funding a large customer service staff and advertising.[98] Under the Modified Final Judgment, Southwestern Bell was restricted to servicing phone lines to maintain dial tone. To cut costs in the face of reduced revenues, Southwestern Bell decreased local staff to one manager and about a half dozen installation and maintenance technicians. "As a result," says Connie Salazar, a Southwestern Bell major accounts executive in Laredo, "except for servicing major accounts—that is, 30 lines or more—there was little incentive for Southwestern Bell's reduced sales force to reach medium and small businesses."[99]

Since April 1989 Southwestern Bell Telephone (the regulated company) can have their same salesperson recommend equipment manufactured by Southwestern Bell Telecommunications (the unregulated equipment company). However, the latter does not have much of a competitive presence in the area. Other equipment vendors have sold key systems without providing maintenance. Thus, since divestiture, small businesses are left to face a variety of equipment providers without advice on how to use the technology more effectively. Even if there were enough Southwestern Bell sales representatives who could attend to small businesses, the lack of advanced infrastructure, such as digital switching, can be a detriment to attracting large telecommunications-intensive businesses. The present capacity of the telephone company is adequate for most small businesses; however, it may lack the switching power to have advanced services beyond fast dialing, call forwarding, call waiting, and a form of Centrex.

Eagle Pass has access to seven long-distance carriers and VSAT dishes attached to several chain grocery and department stores, indicating that some businesses effectively bypass the long-distance companies. Lacking advice on how to procure or use sophisticated technology, local businesses are left at a competitive disadvantage compared to the retail chains that use VSAT and dedicated lines. To survive, businesses must find a niche, usually in special items and personal service.

Benjamin and Angie Rodriguez took over the Eagle Grocery from her father in 1979. Angie works days as a school nurse and then joins Ben at the grocery until closing. Competition in the grocery business comes from an H.E.B. chain grocery store right across the street and another store close to the newer part of town where the maquiladora managers shop. Eagle Grocery caters to the walk-in and pickup truck traffic that comes across the border bridge for a few special products. Ben says, "H.E.B.? They have a different clientele. They pick up the middle-upper kind of customer. H.E.B. has the advantage for wholesale. But we sell six thousand gallons of milk [a week] . . . four thousand cases of chicken [a week] . . . all walk-in trade. The quality in Piedras Negras is not as good and prices are not as good."[100]

Since September 1989 the Rodriguezes have been using a computer spreadsheet and ledger to improve their operating efficiency. Typically, small-business customers either do not know where to get what they want or do not know what they can purchase to become more competitive. Salazar claims that business customers such as the Rodriguezes could be further helped through a computer that joins the cash register to accounting services. "Other gateway services could save in one area, and savings could be used to bolster another," she recommends.[101]

Transborder Telecommunications

Curiously, the maquiladora arrangement, created to encourage business along the U.S.-Mexican frontier, failed to include provisions for the communications infrastructure to facilitate the enhanced business across the border. The picture that emerges for a businessperson needing telecommunications to interact with the maquiladoras is one of high costs due to uncoordinated installations, often delayed maintenance, and vastly unequal rates.

Businesses, such as customs brokerages, that depend directly on cross-border traffic realize the need for telecommunications linked to computers but find barriers in getting served. Raymundo Gonzalez, a customs broker in Eagle Pass, points out—as did many other residents of Eagle Pass—that a phone call to Piedras Negras costs about $2.60 for three minutes because of a special tariff, while the same call from the opposite direction costs only 40 cents. Eduardo Barrera, a communications scholar specializing in maquiladoras, reports that TEL-MEX and AT&T are able to provide dedicated lines for voice and data across the border; however, lack of planning on the part of maquiladora site planners has resulted in "a cobweb of lines that offers a poorer quality of service and is more expensive to maintain and upgrade for both provider and user."[102] Referring to the 80 regular long-distance duplex lines, Barrera adds, "TELMEX complains that the maintainance [sic] and repair of these lines is very problematic because of an unclear delimitation of responsibilities between AT&T and Southwestern Bell."[103]

The pressing need for cross-border communication is illustrated by a variety of alternatives to the switched network. Barrera's study also notes that "maquiladoras in other border regions have met their need for more advanced services by using microwave links and cellular, the latter being especially popular all along the border—except in the middle Rio Grande region." He states, "Half of the units being served by the providers in cities like El Paso are actually on the Mexican side. Bypass of the public network in Eagle Pass–Piedras Negras has taken other forms that may not be as sophisticated [as cellular] but are equally ingenious."[104] Some of the other bypass devices include mobile radio telephones, high-powered wireless telephones, walkie-talkies, and unique frequency FM radios.[105] A local electronics dealer in Eagle Pass reports that he has sold many radios to people from Mexico and walkie-talkies with programmable frequencies to ranchers, doctors, and an attorney.[106]

Education

Local economic developers understand that expansion of commerce and diversity of occupations are based upon training youth and other workers, both employed and unemployed. School superintendent Frank Chisum would like to see a technical training center in Eagle Pass, perhaps organized by the council of governments and used by Crystal City, Uvalde, Carrizo Springs, and Portula. Chisum also would like to see the training center linked up with maquiladoras in Piedras Negras. "The entire region needs the capacity to produce a set of industrial skills which they do not now have," says Paul Edwards, director of economic development of the Middle Rio Grande Development Council (MRGDC) in Uvalde.[107] Southwest Texas Junior College in Uvalde offers the first two years of college and some vocational courses. Sul Ross University offers night classes leading to bachelor's and master's degrees in education, general studies, and business. However, vocational courses to prepare students for careers in the maquiladoras are not available in Eagle Pass or anywhere else in the region. Barriers to educational development include lack of funds to purchase interactive learning equipment and transmission facilities as well as lack of cooperative agreements between the cities and schools in the region. A positive feature is that Southwestern Bell serves most of the region, thus averting the interexchange tolls commonly faced by rural communities. Clearly, Eagle Pass and the entire middle Rio Grande area need a comprehensive strategic plan. Development of Eagle Pass's industrial sector and the educational infrastructure needed to fuel a diversified economy most likely will lean heavily on an integrated and carefully planned telecommunications infrastructure.

Summary

Two assets for regional development are Eagle Pass's role as a portal for the area and the size of the Southwestern Bell LATA, which includes most of the cities in the region. The presence of maquiladoras has created a new form of marketplace where communications and transportation are essential. A major development strategy is to "capture" goods moving to or from the maquiladoras in order to add value to the goods or to supply the maquiladoras with intermediate goods and services. Because their existence is predicated on the international transshipment of parts and products, maquiladoras and their support community need much more telecommunications infrastructure than a factory in rural America.

As international maquiladora trade brings Eagle Pass into the global marketplace, the ability of the telecommunications infrastructure to provide market information, centralized accounting services, distance education, and branch industry communication will be a key factor in sustaining Eagle Pass's growth and triumph over unemployment. Partnering of the major telecommunications users, such as the manufacturing plants, schools, government, and hospital, may provide the aggregate demand for investment in infrastructure upgrades. Specifically, for community development, technical training delivered through a regional distance learning network may provide the basis for investment in appropriate telecommunications technology as well as to train individuals for work in the maquiladoras. However, where the telecommunications infrastructure is inadequate or meets price or regulatory barriers, the pressure for cross-border communications will continue to result in a variety of unintegrated broadband alternatives.

An upgraded telecommunications system—like roads—is needed to fuel not only economic development in the region but a recovery from the chronic unemployment, poverty, and lack of up-to-date education that have plagued the Eagle Pass community. Without an advanced public network for education—and businesses large and small—people lack the competitive benefits of technology, and therefore they stay behind.

As a result of the needs for cross-border computer and telephone communications for trade and the need for a distance learning network for technological education in the region, tremendous pressure is building for a local strategic plan as well as a telecommunications infrastructure upgrade.

Paul Edwards of MRGDC has talked with developers about twin industrial parks on the border, similar to those already in San Diego–Tijuana. Edwards's plan is to uplink to available capacity on the Mexican satellite to create a direct connection with the Far East (Tokyo and Taiwan). In addition, a package of services could be offered, such as links between management, designers, and manufacturers in the United States and the assembly plant on the Mexican side. Such a telecommunications system would accommodate just-in-time manufacturing for the Japanese.[108] Market forces may continue to create cross-border communication options, but the benefits of the options will likely accrue to the specific interests that create them and not satisfy the overwhelming needs for community health and education. The variety of telecommunications alternatives being used in the Eagle Pass–Piedras Negras area point not only to the needs of business but to the necessity for low-cost communications to service the two communities joined by common language, culture, and public-service needs such as education, health, and fire protection. Further study should be given to meeting immediate cross-border communication needs. Certainly a toll-free phone zone along the U.S.-Mexican frontier would greatly facilitate community development, but it would not obviate the need for sophisticated telecommunications to interact with the maquiladoras.

Cooperation and greater unity are needed among community leaders in order to do the strategic planning necessary to integrate development efforts efficiently. The application of telecommunications technology takes on a regional public-service perspective that will require state and federal facilitating policy to meet the unique problems presented by the border. Education, business, and government in the middle Rio Grande region could benefit from the kind of leadership training programs promulgated by the Cooperative Extension Service at Iowa State University, as reported elsewhere in this chapter. It is recommended that the Texas CES allocate some of its agriculture extension resources to community leadership training.

A solution is needed to address the cost associated with installing sophisticated telecommunications to aid industry and education. Eagle Pass and the surrounding region may not be large enough to support an upgraded telecommunications infrastructure for public services. But a combination of public-sector industry and trade, comprising two-thirds of the employment in the county, may be able to achieve the economy of scale necessary. More analysis of the region's resources, such as hospitals, banks, manufacturing, and warehousing, might provide a better picture of the feasibility of a regionally diversified economy linked through telecommunications. A policy recommendation would be to use public monies to upgrade the telecommunications system, an infrastructure as important as roads, to improve commerce.

While the public sector may benefit by sponsoring a telecommunications upgrade, small businesses, governments, and educators still need a full-service telecommunications provider capable of supplying advice, service, and equipment to ensure that the public investment is well utilized.

Recognition is needed from the U.S. Congress that the U.S.-Mexican border—and Eagle Pass–Piedras Negras in particular—acts as a gateway for a region of burgeoning commerce and that the social problems of poverty, education, and chronic unemployment are intimately linked to global competition. Telecommunications may offer to meet many of these problems by providing rapid, efficient, cost-effective, and reliable links between needs and the resources for meeting them. As the Eagle Pass school superintendent, Frank Chisum, said, "Whatever we do we need to connect ourselves to Mexico."[109]

CONCLUSIONS

A number of major themes emerged from our study of these six communities. While all the communities are classified as rural, they are extremely diverse. Each of the six communities faced very different barriers when it came to promoting community development, and therefore each one of them pursued different development strategies. Diversity characterized not only the problems and the development strategies pursued by each community but also the role communications played in this process.

In all six sites, the key to successful community development was the presence of visionary community leaders who were willing to spend much time and energy in planning, promoting, and implementing community development. Individuals such as Chris Nannenga and Steve Buttress were the driving force behind the development efforts in Thornton and Kearney. Dale Uehling provided important activities in many development programs, especially in rallying leaders to the strategic planning training offered to Ottumwa. These leaders were the indispensable cornerstones upon which the process of community development was built. The roles these leaders played varied according to the community needs. These leaders acted as catalysts for action in their communities by providing a vision of what was possible and inspiring the community to act; they mobilized and harnessed physical and human resources from within the community; they sought assistance from outside the community, and they performed countless other tasks. For example, in Thornton, Nannenga not only helped develop the idea of clustering, but for more than three years helped organize and empower the residents of the ACC cluster.

Within a given community there is a hierarchy of telecommunications needs. Those at the top of the hierarchy need access to more advanced telecommunications resources than those at lower levels. Within the six communities we examined, businesses and community leaders occupy the top of the hierarchy, while the community at large occupies the lower rungs in the hierarchy. This finding could have an impact on telecommunications policy because it suggests that, short of having a communitywide advanced telecommunications infrastructure, the target audience in rural areas for advanced telecommunications equipment are those who occupy the higher levels in the hierarchy of needs. This was illustrated in the cases of both Thornton and Ottumwa, in which the community leaders and activists needed to access advanced telecommunications resources, such as electronic data bases and teleconferencing, in order to implement their development strategies.

Telecommunications played a significant role in the development efforts of five communities and has a potentially important role in Eagle Pass. In Dahlonega and Ottumwa, telecommunications helped create a setting within which planning, training, and implementation of community development could take place. In Kearney, telecommunications acted as the engine for economic development, while in Thornton, Eagle Pass, and Dahlonega, telecommunications regulation remains a barrier to development efforts. In Hailey, telecommunications is being used as a springboard for future economic development by attracting tourists and small telecommunications-intensive companies.

Community development is a communications-intensive process aimed at increasing interaction within a community. The most important component of this increased interaction is that people and institutions within a community begin to cooperate, form alliances, and share resources for the betterment of the community as a whole. The most salient aspect of this interaction takes place on a person-to-person level. Telecommunications plays a role in increasing interaction by mobilizing people who live in widely dispersed rural communities. Telecommunications can either enhance or hinder the process of interaction. Thornton and Dahlonega are two cases in which lack of extended area service is acting as a barrier to community development. In Eagle Pass, the absence of inexpensive service agreements across the international boundary and the lack of a one-stop service and equipment provider following divestiture pose serious restraints to the development of business.

In addition to increased interaction within the six communities, the community development process eventually reached a stage in which it was necessary to increase the interaction between a given community and the outside world. Within the context of the emerging information age and the increasingly integrated world economy, telecommunications plays a key role. The ties of Eagle Pass to Mexico, the region, and the global economy are abundantly clear. The need for increased interaction between the rural communities and the outside world can be driven by a number of factors, such as attracting outside investment and companies to a community, as in the cases of Kearney, Eagle Pass, and Dahlonega, serving clients that are spread across the globe, as in the cases of Power Engineers in Hailey and maquiladora branch offices in Eagle Pass, or accessing training programs and expertise from outside the community, as in the cases of Dahlonega and Ottumwa.

Public and private institutions serve as gateways or access points through which community leaders access advanced telecommunications resources. This was clearly the case in the two Iowa communities in which the Iowa State University CES encouraged and allowed community leaders to use its satellite and telephone network, which would not have been accessible otherwise. If states or communities do not have the financial resources to make advanced telecommunications available to the entire community, then public and private institutions could be the focal point of telecommunications upgrades that could benefit the entire community.

Our findings indicate that telecommunications is a necessary but not sufficient condition for rural economic development. Even in the case of Kearney, in which telecommunications played a prominent role in economic development, community development would not have succeeded without the presence of visionary leadership and an educated work force willing to work.

Although human resources were the key to development in all six communities, access to an adequate physical infrastructure was also important. The indispensable physical infrastructure encompasses roads, air service, sewage and water systems, health care, educational facilities, and telecommunications. A serious deficiency in any of these categories will be a barrier to development.

Leaders in the sites we examined were successful in their efforts to mobilize a community for economic development only because they could call upon qualified individuals. For example, Buttress's efforts to attract companies to Kearney were successful in large measure because the community had a sufficiently large, educated labor force that was willing to work part time. In Dahlonega, the creative and motivated chamber of commerce vice-president, Cullen Larson, was able to implement and supervise the plans of county commissioner J. B. Jones. In the Hailey area, community members led successful drives based on organizational skills and "know-how," Clarence Stillwill formed a strategic development "lobby" to influence long-term planning, and Dick Fenton has endlessly supported an airport upgrade. Cooperative extension district director Dale Uehling successfully gathered community leaders and citizens to form an effective power base to initiate planned community development. Eagle Pass stands out by its need to rally community leadership and upgrade the skill proficiency of its residents.

Although all six communities experienced economic duress during the 1980s, the residents of the communities and their leaders did not seek economic development at any cost. These communities implemented community development strategies aimed at increasing the standard of living (i.e., by creating jobs and increasing income) as well as preserving or improving the quality of life within their communities. For example, Kearney was very selective when it came to inviting outside companies to set up shop in the area. A driving force behind Kearney's selectivity was the need to ensure that the benefits of having a given company relocate to Kearney would accrue to a wide segment of the population. Hailey is also very selective in attracting new business. While light manufacturing would be considered by the development authorities, all industries must meet strict environmental qualifications.

Appendix 5.1   Extended Area Service in Hutto, Texas

Hutto, Texas, is a rural community seeking extended area service to promote economic development. Incorporated in 1940, Hutto is a very small rural town (population 1,102) located approximately 15 miles northeast of Austin, near Georgetown. It is primarily a bedroom and retiree community, though at one time farmers from miles around would bring their cotton to the town's gin for processing and baling. Most of its citizens have chosen to live there for the "slow, calm, and easy" life that it offers; it is an attractive haven for the frustrated city dweller. Hutto has a small downtown with a number of businesses, including a grocery store, an auto parts store, a restaurant, and a bank.

Times are hard for Hutto. Businesses are not doing well and the town has seen little growth over the past decade. Young people are moving from Hutto to the neighboring communities of Pflugerville, Round Rock, and Austin, where there are more employment opportunities. Town leaders are worried. In their view, economic development is needed to save the future well-being of their town. They note that despite its positive small-town attributes, the town is operating under capacity and desperately needs some development.[110]

Ironically, at the same time that Hutto saw its economy dwindle, it watched the neighboring communities of Pflugerville and Round Rock experience rapid growth. Hutto business leaders wondered why they were being overlooked for development. What was it that made them less competitive? They concluded that they were not as competitive as their neighbors because they were not a part of the Austin Local Calling Area (LCA) (as were Pflugerville and Round Rock). Not being in the Austin LCA meant that any call with a destination outside of Hutto, including Austin, was a toll call. Thus, businesses might not want to move to Hutto because of higher telephone bills. Moreover, existing local businesses were also at a disadvantage. Their growth and prosperity were being hindered by the lack of extended area service. EAS is a special telephone service that converts long-distance calls into local, nontoll calls for people in one city who regularly make calls to a nearby city. Frustrated with this situation, the Hutto business community established an EAS committee in 1985 and filed for EAS with the Public Utility Commission (PUC) of Texas.

In 1988–89, Hutto signed an agreement with Southwestern Bell, the BOC that serves the Austin LCA. In it, Southwestern Bell agreed to include Hutto in the Austin LCA and to offer EAS on an optional basis, conditional on the BOC's settlement on an overearnings case with the Texas PUC. The settlement (known as Texas First) was signed on February 2, 1990. While EAS eliminates long-distance charges for certain calls, receipt of such service means a monthly flat-rate charge in addition to the basic charge for local calls.[111] In fact, rates will be considerably higher than what is currently available in the Austin LCA ($36 versus $8). Hutto had joined 32 other communities around the state seeking extended metropolitan service calling, which would allow them to be a part of the calling area of their respective large metropolitan towns.[112] EAS was approved on an optional basis by the Texas PUC between Rockwall and Dallas (Docket #5954) on September 25, 1986. This action allowed Rockwall residents and businesses to make and receive calls from Dallas on a flat-rate basis instead of paying long-distance tolls. This was the first EAS request approved by the PUC since its creation in 1975.[113]

Whether Hutto would benefit from EAS is a function of general customer welfare and economic development. In terms of general customer welfare, the effect of EAS depends on (1) the increased consumer surplus arising from reducing the price of what were previously toll calls, (2) the lost producer surplus generated by reducing the price of previously interexchange calls to zero, (3) the change in the cost associated with the transition to EAS, and (4) any change in the fixed costs due to the implementation of EAS.[114] The merits of any specific EAS proposal, however, will depend upon the particular circumstances surrounding the EAS proposal and the economic condition of the area in question.

In terms of economic development, the benefits of EAS are disputed. Almost no empirical evidence exists to corroborate or refute the claim that EAS benefits development. Thus, the question of whether EAS would bring economic development to Hutto is a difficult one because it is not at all clear that new firms would be attracted to an EAS area or that firms would expand more rapidly under an EAS pricing structure than under either a usage-sensitive pricing structure or the flat-rate/toll hybrid system currently in place.

A major argument used in favor of EAS is that, while it might make telephone service more expensive due to the surcharge of the EAS privilege, it is worthwhile because telephone quality will be upgraded and residents will have access to advanced features and services. However, it is uncertain whether these "advances" are needed. In the case of Hutto, it is clear that most residents and businesses use only basic telephone services. Calls outside of the Hutto LCA are primarily made for social purposes—to friends and relatives—and occasionally for business purposes. Even business establishments, primarily because they are small and serve the local residents, do not use their telephones for anything other than basic telephone service. A few businesses and residents, however, do claim that their calling patterns would definitely change if included in the Austin LCA.

A final question is whether residents are willing to pay extra for EAS. The consensus in Hutto is that residents would be willing to pay only a little more (businesspersons would be more willing). EAS committee members made it clear that if EAS were implemented in Hutto, it would have to be on an optional basis only. Elderly retired residents do not want to see hikes in their telephone bills.

In sum, the effect of EAS on economic development is uncertain. An extensive study might help clarify the uncertainty. Nonetheless, the business community feels that EAS is vital, even though few residents are willing to pay significantly more for the added services.

Appendix 5.2 U.S. Department of Agriculture

The role of federal agencies, in particular the Extension Service (ES), is to develop program and policy priorities and then work with state land grant universities to research and implement the actual extension work of community development. Policy guidance is in the form of initiatives that have been determined through state-level advisory boards and research. The USDA also funds research on agricultural management and practices through the land grant universities.

Partnering

The ES of the USDA uses on-line computer and satellite telecommunications to stay in contact with extension services at state land grant universities. As the economy of rural America experiences profound structural shifts, the USDA tries to keep all the states focused on national initiatives, including rural development and revitalization. These initiatives are used by the state land grant extension services to develop programs to meet specific community problems.

The USDA, Soil Conservation Service, and Small Business Administration are the federal agencies most in evidence in rural American counties. Where agriculture is a major economic activity, the county extension agent and district conservationist provide crop prices, inspection of crops for shipping, and soil and water conservation advice, in addition to running adult education and 4-H activities, among many other programs.

In 1987, major decisions were made between states and the federal government that recognized the structural changes in rural America, and out of those decisions a partnership notion developed between the federal and state cooperative extension services. This has led to a much more focused agenda. Historically, the Cooperative Extension Service (CES), which encompasses both USDA activities and state extension activities, has tended to be all things to all people. Being able to be responsive has been a strength, but Congress wants the CES to deliver on high-priority national problems and issue areas.[115] As a result of a series of hearings in 1984, the CES can cooperate programmatically on anything that federal and state partner boards can come to agreement on. The number of federal initiatives have been reduced to five: (1) water quality, (2) rural development and revitalization, (3) youth at risk, (4) competitiveness of American agriculture (concentration on sustainable agriculture and globalization), and (5) improving nutrition, diet, and health (with a heavy focus on food safety).[116] These initiatives affect either economic development or quality of life. Lacking a federal office charged with developing a national economic development program and an agency charged with carrying out rural development initiatives, the USDA is trying to focus federal dollars in these areas. The CES has done some partnering in the past, but efforts since 1986 have been extensive. For example, water quality efforts have been jointly sponsored by the CES, the Soil Conservation Service, the Agricultural Research Service, and local health and human services. A large percentage of states have adopted this focused agenda and have set their own grassroots policy priorities. The similarity between state agendas and the federal agenda is the first of its kind.[117]

One ES division important to community development and telecommunications is the USDA's Communication, Information, and Technology (CIT) Division. This small decentralized division, part of the Science and Education Agency of the USDA, is directed by Dr. Janet Poley. Its role is to stay at the cutting edge in the communications-technology area; provide coordination, leadership, and—in some cases—communication support to the CES; and to advise state partners. A small agency with a staff of 30 people, CIT maintains congressional linkages and keeps abreast of state programs helping to direct funds. Acting as a clearinghouse for research and development, ES/CIT staff administers cooperative agreements with state land grant universities to conduct testing and to develop materials, data bases, and public awareness information. Task force teams, formed out of the USDA at the federal level, become the real extensions of the ES. Poley's objective is to keep older technological systems compatible with new purchases and upgrades. Her office is trying to improve information delivery at the county extension level through a combination of networks, PC, CD-ROM, and laser disc technology and to encourage the CES to take advantage of some of the technologies that are on the horizon.[118]

Rural Revitalization

The focus of rural revitalization is on small business development. A large part of CIT's efforts is directed toward changing the awareness of people at the USDA, in the media, and in education—through workshops at the state level—to recognize that rural America is not solely agriculture and that many of its problems are not directly linked to agriculture. The ES faces the real challenge of securing coordination of agencies ranging from the federal to the local level. The CES is itself a decentralized agency that provides development direction only through grants, educational programs, and publications. State CES agencies then apply ideas and information as they wish.[119]

Goals of CIT in support of rural revitalization are as follows:

1. Availability of multimedia—including audio/video, up/downlink, interactive—in every county office.
2. Information sharing across regions, states, and nations.
3. "Decision support" for agricultural producers to integrate agricultural production data with ecological considerations.
4. One hundred-percent computer adoption among rural residents.
5. Cooperation with states to do national mapping of communications technologies.

NOTES

1. U.S. Department of Agriculture, Economic Research Service, Agriculture and Rural Economy Division, *Rural Economic Development in the 1980s: Preparing for the Future*, ERS Staff Report AGE870724 (Washington, D.C., 1987), p. viii.

2. Ibid., p. ix.

3. Ibid., p. x.

4. Ibid.

5. Margaret G. Thomas, "Countywide Economic Development Programs—Lumpkin County, Georgia," in *Profiles in Rural Economic Development* (Kansas City, Mo.: Midwest Research Institute, April 1988), pp. 117–18.

6. Ann E. O'Neill et al., *Tourism in Northeast Georgia: Markets, Opportunities, and Recommendations*, vol. 1 (Atlanta: Georgia Tech Research Corporation, October 1989), p. 21.

7. Georgia Department of Industry, Trade, and Tourism, "Lumpkin County Area Industry Mix by Employment," in *Georgia Economic Profile* (Atlanta, 1988).

8. Cullen Larson, "A Practical View of Consolidation," *Georgia County Government Magazine*, October 1986, p. 51.

9. Ibid.

10. Thomas, "Countywide Economic Development Programs," p. 117.

11. Interview with Cullen Larson, Executive Vice-President, Dahlonega–Lumpkin County Chamber of Commerce, Dahlonega, Georgia, July 27, 1990.

12. Interview with Bill Halderson, Owner, Halderson Executive Search Firm, Dahlonega, Georgia, January 5, 1990.

13. United States Telephone Association, *Phone Facts '89 for the Year 1988* (Washington, D.C., July 5, 1990) (brochure); interview questionnaire completed by Standard Telephone Company, Cornelia, Georgia, January 1990.

14. Standard Telephone Company, "1988 Progress Report" (Cornelia, Ga., February 1, 1989) (press release).

15. Speech by Jim Johnson, Executive Vice-President, Standard Telephone Company, Cornelia, Georgia, to Dahlonega Rotary Club, Dahlonega, Georgia, June 7, 1988.

16. "Do Communications Problems Hurt Our Economic Development Potential?" *Georgia County Government Magazine*, December 1989, p. 3.

17. Counties include Lumpkin, Dawson, Hall, Union, and White.

18. "Do Communications Problems Hurt Our Economic Development Potential?" p. 3.

19. In fact, Jones had no telephone until after a man walked on the moon; interview with Larson.

20. Ibid.

21. Larson, "A Practical View of Consolidation," p. 53.

22. Telephone interview with Perry Swisher, Commissioner, Idaho Public Utility Commission, Boise, Idaho, November 21, 1989.

23. Sun Valley/Ketchum Chamber of Commerce, *Guide to Wood River Valley Businesses*, n.d.

24. Interview with Swisher.

25. *Guide to Wood River Valley Businesses.*

26. Interview with Terry Elderidge, Local US West Representative, Hailey, Idaho, January 13, 1990.

27. Interview with Clarence Stilwill, Co-Publisher, Peak Media, Inc., Hailey, Idaho, January 10, 1990.

28. *Guide to Wood River Valley Businesses.*

29. Interview with Don Murray, Network Coordinator, Division for Community Progress, Iowa Department of Economic Development, Des Moines, Iowa, January 10, 1990.

30. Ibid.

31. Interview with Laura Mosena, Director, Area Economic Development Office, Regional Satellite Center, Indian Hills Community College, Ottumwa, Iowa, January 12, 1990.

32. Region XV Satellite Center for Economic Development, Wapello County fact sheet, Ottumwa, Iowa, 1987 (promotional flyer).

33. Interview with Steve Welker, Editor, *Ottumwa Courier*, Ottumwa, Iowa, January 12, 1990.

34. Telephone interview with Mosena, March 28, 1990.

35. Interview with Carl Radosevich, Mayor, Ottumwa, Iowa, January 12, 1990.

36. Region XV Satellite Center for Economic Development, Wapello County fact sheet.

37. Interview with Tom Quinn, Community Extension Development Specialist, Iowa Cooperative Extension Service, Wapello County Extension Office, Ottumwa, Iowa, January 12, 1990.

38. Region XV Satellite Center for Economic Development, Wapello County fact sheet.

39. Interview with Chris Swanson, President, Ottumwa Area Economic Development Corporation, Ottumwa, Iowa, January 12, 1990.

40. Region XV Satellite Center for Economic Development, Wapello County fact sheet.

41. Interview with Welker.

42. Interview with Mosena, January 12, 1990.

43. Interview with Swanson.

44. Throughout rural America, agricultural extension agents are reportedly held in high esteem. Not only do they become well acquainted with families through their sponsorship of 4-H clubs, but they know each agricultural producer and offer important advice on how to best manage farm or livestock production. Their persuasive role in the community is enhanced by their working code, which dictates that they offer information, training, and advice but leave the choice of action to their clients.

45. Interview with Dale Uehling, District Director, Iowa Cooperative Extension Service, Wapello County Extension Office, Ottumwa, Iowa, January 12, 1990.

46. Ibid.

47. Interview with Radosevich.

48. Interview with Murray.

49. Interview with Mosena, January 12, 1990.

50. Interview with Deborah Coates, Manager, EXNET and Software Services, Cooperative Extension Service, Iowa State University, Ames, Iowa, January 9, 1990. The potential for interactive services on EXNET exists but is underutilized; several interviewees professed only their secretaries use it for electronic mail. The statement was frequently heard that, when the dean of extension got on EXNET, so would the rest of Iowa's CES.

51. Interview with Mosena, January 12, 1990.

52. Interview with Radosevich.

53. Interview with Dave Hammond, Director, Community Resource Development, Iowa Cooperative Extension Service, Iowa State University, Ames, Iowa, January 8, 1990.

54. Interview with Radosevich.

55. Interview with Welker.

56. Interview with Dianne Kiefer, Wapello County Treasurer, Ottumwa, Iowa, January 12, 1990.

57. Interview with Radosevich.

58. Ibid.

59. Interview with Quinn.

60. Interview with Chris Nannenga, Secretary, Area Community Commonwealth, Thornton, Iowa, January 11, 1990.

61. 1990 New York Times Almanac (New York: New York Times, 1989), p. 607.

62. Interview with Nannenga.

63. Ibid.

64. Rogers Worthington, "Little Towns Look at Bigger Picture," *Chicago Tribune*, September 11, 1989, p. 3.

65. Comments made at the Texas Rural Development Policy Workshop, Austin, Texas, November 13, 1989.

66. Interview with Bob Cole, Director, Iowa Cooperative Extension Service, Iowa State University, Mason City, Iowa, January 18, 1990.

67. "Iowa Group Demonstrates Power in Numbers," *NATaT Reporter*, p. 6.

68. Rogers Worthington, "Rural Towns Unite to Save Way of Life," *Billings Gazette*, June 11, 1989, p. 1.

69. Iowa State University, *TLT Overview* (Ames, Iowa, June 11, 1989) (pamphlet).

70. Interview with Dave Hammond, Director, Community Resource Development Program, Iowa State University, Ames, Iowa, January 9, 1990.

71. Interview with Nannenga.

72. Ibid.

73. Centel, which is based in Fort Dodge, serves Messervy, Thornton, Swalesdale, Sheffield, and Chapin. Rockwell and Dougherty and two other towns in the ACC cluster are served by the Rockwell Cooperative Telephone Association.

74. Interview with Bruce Blankenship, President, Kearney Area Chamber of Commerce, April 19, 1991.

75. The Kearney Area Chamber of Commerce and the Economic Development Council of Buffalo County, Inc., *Nebraska Community Profile* (Kearney, Nebr., December 1989) (pamphlet).

76. Ibid.

77. Interview with Steve Buttress, President, Buffalo County Economic Development Council, Kearney, Nebraska, January 10, 1990.

78. Interview with Blankenship.

79. Ibid.; interview with Buttress.

80. Ibid.

81. Cabela's is the subject of a case study in Chapter 2.

82. The Buffalo County Economic Development Council is a nonprofit organization. Its members are contracted by the city because of legal requirements. It is funded one-third by the local government (city), one-third by the county, and one-third by the Kearney Area Chamber of Commerce. Its board consists of two representatives from the city, two from the county, and two from the chamber of commerce.

83. EMRG is more fully discussed in Chapter 2.

84. Interview with Buttress.

85. Ibid.

86. Ibid.

87. Maverick County Development Corporation, *Eagle Pass and Maverick County* (Eagle Pass, Tex.) (pamphlet.)

88. Interview with Juan Manuel Wheeler, Jr., Programming Director, WWTV-Cable Channel 7, Eagle Pass, Texas, February 23, 1990.

89. Interview with Oscar Rodriguez, City Manager, Eagle Pass, Texas, February 23, 1990.

90. Ibid.

91. Ibid.

92. Interview with Wheeler.

93. Interview with Arthur Pine, President, Eagle Pass Chamber of Commerce, and Executive Director, Maverick County Economic Development Corporation, Eagle Pass, Texas, February 22, 1990.

94. Interview with Rodriguez.

95. Interview with Reymundo Rodriguez, Executive Associate, Hogg Foundation, University of Texas at Austin, Austin, Texas, January 8, 1990.

96. Interview with Pine.

97. Maverick County Economic Development Corporation, *Maquiladoras* (Eagle Pass, Tex.) (pamphlet).

98. Interview with Connie R. Salazar, Account Executive, Southwestern Bell Telephone, San Antonio, Texas, May 25, 1990.

99. Ibid.

100. Interview with Benjamin and Angie Rodriguez, Owners, Eagle Grocery, Eagle Pass, Texas, February 22, 1990.

101. Interview with Salazar.

102. Eduardo Barrera, "Piedras Negras: An Exceptional Interdependence," 1990 (manuscript).

103. Ibid., p. 4.

104. Ibid.

105. Ibid.

106. Telephone interview with Frank De La Cerda, Owner, Frank's Custom Auto and Electronics, Eagle Pass, Texas, June 25, 1990.

107. Telephone interview with Paul Edwards, Director of Economic Development, Middle Rio Grande Development Council, Uvalde, Texas, June 1990.

108. Ibid.

109. Interview with Frank Chisum, Eagle Pass School Superintendent, Eagle Pass, Texas, February 22, 1990.

110. Observations in this section are based on an informal survey of the following Hutto business leaders and residents: Mr. and Mrs. Rosplock, residents; Ron Whitfield, resident and local businessperson; Jim Gage, resident; Doyle Hobbs, member EAS Committee and local businessperson; Randy Pimpler, local businessperson and nonresident; Mr. Schmidt, local businessperson; Mike Fowler, member EAS committee and resident; Mr. and Mrs. Pritchard, residents; Billy Sanders, resident; Mr. and Mrs. Hanstrom, residents and retirees; and Earl Klanttenhoff, member EAS committee and businessperson.

111. Press Release, Public Utility Commission of Texas, Austin, Texas, March 7, 1990, p. 1.

112. Telephone interview with Betty Suthard, Public Information Officer, Public Utility Commission of Texas, Austin, Texas, March 13, 1990.

113. Public Utility Commission of Texas, *Annual Report, 1987* (Austin, Tex., 1988), p. 3.

114. John W. Mayo and Joseph Z. Flynn, "The Economic Effects of Local Telephone Pricing Options," Center for Business and Economic Research, College of Business Administration, University of Tennessee, Knoxville, Tennessee, 1988.

115. Interview with Dr. Janet Poley, Director, Communication, Information, and Technology Division, USDA Science and Education Agencies, Cooperative Extension Service, U.S. Department of Agriculture, Washington, D.C., December 7, 1989.

116. Ibid.

117. Ibid.

118. Ibid.

119. Ibid.

6

Conclusions

Richard Cutler and Harmeet S. Sawhney

This study of the uses of telecommunications systems in rural areas was prompted by two factors: first, the recognition that rural regions of the country are suffering economic duress, and, second, the widely held expectation that the newest generation of telecommunications technology and its role in an information economy may provide new opportunities for ameliorating some of the difficulties facing sparsely populated and remote parts of the country. The potential of telecommunications has been realized in many communities, and this study has attempted to describe and analyze a number of them. Many discussions of telecommunications speculate on larger issues such as the information age, structural change, or social equity; our approach directed attention to the micro level—where the impact of rural telecommunications is first felt. Studying the innovations made by the site communities has provided insights into important areas of policy considerations, namely the benefits of telecommunications investments, the mechanics of implementing an infrastructure strategy, and the relationship between economic and community development and telecommunications strategies.

Our study was framed by the following research questions:

1. What innovative applications of telecommunications for rural development can be identified in the United States at this time?

2. Why and how do these innovative applications occur?
3. What are the generalizations and policy implications of these innovative applications for national, state, or regional planning as well as for regulating telecommunications?

Our 37 research sites included examples of public services (education, health, agricultural extension), businesses (retailing, natural resource processing, decentralized manufacturing), communities, and telecommunications service providers. The following sections discuss our findings and recommendations.

INNOVATIVE APPLICATIONS OF TELECOMMUNICATIONS FOR RURAL DEVELOPMENT

Rural Business

Telecommunications provides a competitive advantage for retail businesses and manufacturing. Large companies with rural branches can provide their own communications to augment or substitute for the public network. Maintaining some internal control over aspects of one's communication network is common (Weyerhaeuser and Deere), and some businesses are moving toward total bypass of public facilities (Wal-Mart). The managements of large firms make communications decisions based on an assessment of what competitive advantages they can reap through the alternatives available to them; the advantages of the communications systems we examined indicate that cost savings may be an initial impetus for deploying specialized networks, but it is not the only advantage and in the long run may not even be the primary advantage. For some, telecommunications enables them to locate to rural areas; for others, telecommunications enables them to maintain their rural presence.

Businesses appreciate the ability to customize their own networks. By owning their own facilities or by designing their own communication protocols that can operate on leased trunks, businesses can quickly make the service changes they require. We found such businesses give little thought to the long-term implications of moving their traffic from the local provider.

We point out that this study did not systematically examine how small businesses depend on or may utilize telecommunications. Our small business case (EMRG) and medium-sized business case (Cabela's) cannot represent the typical situation of Main Street businesses. Generally, lacking information on what telecommunications facilities or information networks are available, and lacking adequate infrastructure to provide access to modern services, small (especially retail) businesses in rural areas are captive to the LEC. This suggests that the local telco may have a major role in educating local businesses about the potential of telecommunications to enhance their operations.

The impact of business telecommunications applications in rural areas is decidedly mixed. Large retail firms such as Wal-Mart, able to operate efficiently in rural areas in part because of their sophisticated VSAT network, draw more revenue and provide cheaper goods to an area, but at the expense of local businesses. Large manufacturing companies provide jobs and may influence telephone-rate bargaining power for the entire community. Smaller businesses may take advantage of some of the advanced telecommunications infrastructure that larger businesses attract to rural areas, thereby improving the prospects for sustained rural business growth and providing smaller employment gains. Sharing infrastructure investment in the public network or sharing private network capacity may provide solutions that benefit large businesses and the communities in which they locate.

Rural Public Services

Our findings concerning ways in which communities have tackled their educational needs focused on two alternative models: sharing local resources (as in the Minnesota school systems) and using satellite-based distance instructional systems. Our study indicates that there are advantages to both; different communities will profit from different approaches. Our general observation is that distance learning via telecommunications offers an expanded range of educational resources to dispersed communities, no matter which model is adopted.

It is clear that the Minnesota model must rely on a concerted regional effort, while TI-IN enables single schools or school districts to take action. Although there is debate as to whether education should be provided and controlled locally or through national networks, our research suggests both systems can be used with positive results. The drawbacks to the centralized concept include difficulties in scheduling classes to meet satellite feeds in different time zones, resistance to education provided by "outsiders," and sometimes cost. Nevertheless, the course offerings are substantial and the cost is affordable for most school districts. In the alternative model, linked local sites provide a seemingly effective interactive teaching environment and enhance the sense of community power over educational offerings. However, local control of educational resources, including the physical infrastructure, is a factor that may inhibit the emergence of regional networks.

The case of the Geisinger Clinic illustrated that rural health services can benefit from the efficiencies realized by centralized functions such as accounting, billing, and technically intensive services. Telecommunications can also support decentralized diagnostic services. In a sense, our medical case illustrated again the benefits of centralizing and sharing certain facilities in response to demand that was "naturally" fragmented within the region. The economies of scale afforded by the centralized service benefited all concerned.

Our cases examining the agricultural extension service illustrated that some of the most highly developed information networks in rural America serve specific agricultural needs. In contrast, the more diffuse *community* development needs are often hard to identify and serve with information networks. Consequently, if information networks are to serve rural areas, potential users need (1) education on how to work with them, (2) easy access to them, and (3) reassurance that they carry relevant information. This assumes that such networks do indeed have useful information.

Education, health, and diverse community services to rural areas generally lag behind those common in urban areas. Telecommunications may compensate for the absence of some of the factors that make services more economical in urbanized areas by providing the economies of scale necessary to sustain services financially. By linking communities through networks so that training, data bases and information, and other amenities can be delivered to regions that otherwise would lack access to them, telecommunications has clear abilities for helping rural regions obtain better services.

Small Rural Telecommunications Companies

In order to provide service to rural areas, local telecommunications providers must surmount obstacles as diverse as high costs (relative to density) and difficult physical terrain, which adds to the cost and difficulty of providing service. Two general coping strategies are illustrated in our cases: exploiting in-house expertise to create new, useful applications and fighting for the elements in the regulatory domain that protect rural companies. The strategies small rural telephone companies adopt result from a combination of many different factors: a particular individual's vision, local economic necessities and opportunities, regulatory changes, proximity to other telcos, and the ability to undertake cooperative activity.

Innovative cooperative efforts by providers have demonstrated the feasibility of bringing outside services to rural areas. Not only are some rural telcos offering consolidated (and therefore more economical) services, such as accounting and billing, to other telcos, but their field trials point to the possible consolidation of all wired services: cable, phone, and power. Locally owned independent companies seem to be responsive to local conditions, perhaps because sometimes they are owned by members of the local community.

Nevertheless, small independent companies appeared to be generally information deficient when it came to accessing technical information. Professional associations are a good source of information for them; however, the associations themselves may be limited. At a minimum, the provider must be motivated to seek the sort of information that could be useful for improving service.

Small phone companies were concerned about the perceived imminent erosion of support mechanisms, such as REA funding and cost pooling, at the same time that they are under pressure to upgrade rural plants. Demand for improved services, which might require upgraded plants, may come from former urban dwellers or urbanites with second homes in rural areas (for example, Taconic customers desired direct-dial service for international calls, and North Pittsburgh customers desired EAS). These companies worried that an expanded concept of universal service will be mandated at the same time that funding mechanisms are withdrawn. Nevertheless, the phone companies realize that they could play a larger role in rural communities because they are in the best position today to bring rural America into the information age.

Given the uncertain future of traditional funding mechanisms, some telcos are looking to other lines of revenue and creative capitalization in the telecommunications market. Selling consolidated services (Iowa Network Services) and turning to the local community for bond funding (Clear Lake Telephone Company) are examples of such creative funding sources.

Telecommunications and Community Development

Telecommunications can affect community development in several ways. First, many communities look to business growth to fuel community development, and telephone toll rates can have a direct effect on the cost of doing business. The case of Hailey, Idaho, shows that local telcos may participate in community development by upgrading services in order to attract businesses. Alternatively, the absence of extended area dialing (e.g., Hutto, Texas, and Dahlonega, Georgia) or low-cost cross-border service (Eagle Pass, Texas) could inhibit local business opportunities.

A business may be attracted initially to a rural location because of favorable labor or other resources, but with good planning and tele-communications infrastructure upgrading, abetted by business pres-ence, other aspects of the local economy can be developed. For example, in Kearney, the initial advantages of telemarketers' locating to the community—the subsequent increase in jobs and upgraded telecommunications facilities—are being funneled into new ideas for improving public services and creating or facilitating still other busi-nesses (which may exploit the high-capacity telecommunications links that now exist).

Second, telecommunications can affect the process of community planning. In the Thornton, Iowa, region, for example, the process of community "clustering" was inhibited by the toll charges exacted by the local phone companies; the distance between the small rural towns in the area meant that communication costs would be higher. Obtain-ing extended area service for rural areas may have to be considered as community development efforts progress. Ottumwa, Iowa, illustrates a different role for telecommunications in community planning in that access to various "external" electronic information services furthered the process of community organizing.

Cooperation among those promoting local development can make geographic location—too often seen as a cause of local problems—an advantage; cooperative action may overcome local distance and other resource barriers. These cases illustrated how telecommunications may be one of the tools used to break those barriers by addressing certain economic opportunities as well as by enhancing local planning through leadership training and satellite-based town meetings. While it is too soon to say exactly what the upgraded network facilities (facilitated by PUC actions) will do for Idaho, the case of Hailey suggests that new populations and new economic activities may be-come feasible with such deployment.

However, infrastructure alone is not enough for community development. Lack of local leadership can stall development in spite of training and advanced communications capabilities. A well-developed community strategy, such as clustering, or efforts to attract certain types of businesses can be impeded if there is insufficient local community support for or involvement in them. In the best of situa-tions, when growth occurs, local strategic planning pays off by pre-paring the community to take advantage of newly available economies of scale or scope. Telecommunications capabilities and participation of telco personnel in community leadership may be a catalyst for such opportunities.

ORIGINS OF INNOVATIVE APPLICATIONS

The cases examined in this study suggest at least three sources of rural innovations. First, many of the innovations depended on discovering ways to aggregate demand, thereby creating the economies of scale typically absent in rural areas. Second, creating partnerships provided an institutional mechanism to exploit potential scale economies and to gain a critical mass of resources to do so. Third, leadership, sometimes local and sometimes regional, was critical in several cases; certain individuals must be credited with having the vision and the talent to formulate and execute novel plans.

Aggregation and Partnerships

One challenge in rural areas is to organize the limited resources in a manner that can justify and support modern technological infrastructure and concomitant services. Several salient examples of aggregating demand and capacity are evident in the cases studied here. For example, both PalmettoNet in South Carolina and Iowa Network Services represent group enterprise. The first capitalized on the complementary nature of contiguous LEC territories to bring an advanced network into service areas, and the other provided enhanced services, including equal access, by linking 128 rural telephone companies so that they could afford a centralized technology providing that capability. Geisinger Medical Center likewise represents an effort to centralize technology and expertise; the benefits of the economies thus obtained could be extended (or in a fashion decentralized) to a larger region.

Organizing to share existing resources is a related strategy. When the schools in Minnesota shared courses, they created scale economies and a set of conditions that benefited all concerned. And as EMRG and other Kearney companies move closer to "piggybacking" on the AT&T POP at Cabela's, so too will their sharing introduce both new opportunities and reduced unit costs. These examples epitomize the way capacious telecommunications infrastructure can be used by enterprising and creative organizations. It is perhaps such organizational innovations that hold the greatest potential for rural America because they rely more on new thinking than on additional resources. These innovations basically are new ways of organizing the cooperative spirit often present in rural areas. The technologies simply provide opportunities for new ways to cooperate.

The challenge is to foster new organizational forms that harness the potential of such telecommunications technologies. A bright spot in such efforts is the distance-reducing power of telecommunications technologies, which facilitates larger cooperative efforts across greater regions.

Communication technologies in themselves provide new opportunities for aggregation. The special capabilities of satellites, particularly their distance insensitivity, are crucial for the sorts of capabilities utilized by Wal-Mart and TI-IN. For businesses with far-flung branches, satellites offer excellent ways to gather and distribute voice, data, and video communication. The net cost allocated to any single "branch"—whether a school or a retail facility—is relatively low.[1]

Telecommunications facilitates aggregation in another way in the community cases examined here. If communities advocate clustering in order to create scale economies and nurture each other's strengths, telecommunications can help by enabling cheap, extensive "horizontal" communication. In other words, while telecommunications capabilities can bring new opportunities and information into communities—a type of "vertical" communication—it can also encourage deeper, more extensive use of information and resources within the region. Proliferating opportunities for towns to work with each other are directly dependent on good, inexpensive communication systems. The importance of extended area service is clear for such efforts.

Leadership

Our results suggest that a main source of innovation in rural areas rests with visionary individuals who see ways to improve their businesses, communities, or services. For example, the innovative telcos examined here generally were characterized by having at least one creative individual in charge. ENMR, which serves a rather isolated region of the continental United States, has been deploying state-of-the-art infrastructure to a large extent because of its general manager, Robert Harris. Since he joined ENMR in 1974, the company has grown from 600 members to over 10,000, and it has increased its net worth from approximately $1 million to over $80 million. It is one of the first cooperatives to fully deploy SS7. Similarly, Mid-Rivers Telephone Cooperative in Montana serves a huge landmass (about the size of West Virginia) with one of the lowest customer densities in the nation. Yet the company is equipped with the most advanced switching and transmission technologies—almost fully digital switches and hundreds of miles of fiber-optic cable. The impetus behind Mid-Rivers' activities is once again one individual, its general manager, Gerry Anderson. PalmettoNet's innovative organizational configuration, which resulted in a fiber backbone for rural South Carolina, is an idea sponsored by Frank Barnes, president of Rock Hill Telephone Company, and Jim Carlson, general manager of PalmettoNet, who implemented it. So too can the growth and success of Kearney's small business, EMRG, be attributed largely to its founders.

In rural communities leadership seems to face fewer bureaucratic obstacles—some compensation for having fewer resources to work with at the outset. Visionary leaders consequently are sometimes able to enlist other members of the community to back their ideas. For this reason leadership training and community organizing can be especially important to rural areas. Some of Kearney's economic health can be attributed to the combined efforts of Bruce Blankenship, president of the Kearney Area Chamber of Commerce; Steve Buttress, president of the Buffalo County Economic Development Council; David Waldron, president of EMRG; and other members of the Buffalo County Economic Development Council. Their combined plan resulted in a two-stage economic development strategy of first attracting a high-tech enterprise and then capitalizing on the subsequent creation of infrastructure to develop other related businesses. Significantly, their economic development ideas are blended with parallel notions of *community* development, characterized by a more holistic concern for the community's quality of life and internal health and growth.

We see the power of individual efforts to mobilize larger communities or organizations in other areas as well. The transformation of Hailey, Idaho, rests not so much on a local Hailey citizen as on Idaho's PUC and particularly Commissioner Swisher's efforts. These efforts were crucial in channeling US West's overearnings into investment in digital switches for rural Idaho. This regulatory initiative created the infrastructure allowing Power Engineers to relocate in Hailey. Likewise, the Minnesota Distance Learning Network was heartily sponsored and supported by the local exchange companies, consulting firms, and others who donated a great deal of time and facilities to the success of the endeavor.

These are only some of the more salient cases of individually driven innovative activities. There were visible traces of individual initiative in almost all of the cases we studied, lending support to the observation that, although individuals generally play an important role in the innovation process, in rural areas their role is particularly strong. While individual creativity in urban areas is often stifled by the inertia and constraints created by the larger social and organizational systems, the existing organizational forms in rural areas may be more pliable.

Finally, more often than not the visionary is an "outsider" who relocates to a rural area. Robert Harris had worked for many years in the telephone business before joining ENMR; Gerry Anderson, Mid-

Rivers' general manager, is an ex-REA employee; Jim Carlson, PalmettoNet's general manager, is an ex-GTE employee; David Waldron,
president of EMRG, moved from a larger city to Kearney. These rural
"cosmopolites," to use a phrase well developed in the scholarly literature on innovation, possess a potent combination of broad perspective
and a commitment to their new habitat.[2] Similarly, programmatic
attempts to induce change in rural areas may rely on external agencies
such as the USDA's Cooperative Extension Service. Some of our cases
illustrate their success. In Thornton, Iowa, the Iowa State University
Cooperative Extension Service introduced the concept of clustering,
while in Ottumwa, Iowa, it empowered citizens by developing their
strategic planning skills through satellite-based teleconferences. In
many of our cases the innovations were due to an individual or agency
that was "external" in nature.

IMPLICATIONS FOR PUBLIC POLICY

This study documented the multidimensional character of rural
America. This diversity reinforces the notion that there are various
strategies by which new telecommunications opportunities can affect
community development, public services, business applications, and
the business of rural telecommunications service providers. The low
ratio of population to landmass, the very essence of any rural area,
tends to mask the variability inherent in the socioeconomic fabric of
rural America. An appreciation of this heterogeneity makes it obvious
that no single policy is likely to serve all rural interests. To be effective,
any policy framework will have to be flexible enough to cater to the
many faces of rural America.

The rural revitalization policy alternatives dominating federal and
state policy discussions in the late 1980s and early 1990s have focused
on alternatives that basically subsidize certain aspects of the rural
community. For example, the U.S. Senate's 1989 Rural Development
Partnership Act (S. 1036) had several provisions, among them increasing the credit available to rural areas and establishing telecommunications assistance programs that would fund special applications in the
health, education, and business domains.[3] At the same time, several
critics have suggested that the REA be expanded in both funding and
authority in order to take a lead role in ensuring that rural telecommunications infrastructure is constructed.[4] However, these subsidization measures, although well intentioned, should be designed to
complement the dynamics that appear to be crucial to using telecommunications most efficaciously in rural areas. Our conclusions therefore stress a different tack.

While various interest groups have been waging a debate in the policy arena about the appropriate strategy for ameliorating rural difficulties, a number of rural visionaries have gone ahead on their own initiative and carried out innovative ideas. We saw this in the various grassroots initiatives that accounted for several of the events recounted in earlier pages: Cabela's move to Kearney, forming Iowa Network Services or PalmettoNet, Dahlonega's growth planning, and the Minnesota distance education efforts. Such rural innovations are particularly interesting from the policy standpoint because they have sprouted up with little help from external agencies and are, in effect, mini-experiments. Perhaps they have much to offer the policy-making process. Rural America is likely to benefit the most from policies that work toward generating and re-creating on an even larger scale the positive aspects of these innovations. Understanding the processes underlying these innovations helps to identify key points for the most effective channeling of resources into rural America. Many of these rural telecommunications initiatives, though perhaps encouraged by a higher level of government, involve a "bottom-up" strategy and a base of support that nurtures and facilitates local initiatives. It is here that these case studies are particularly exciting.

While telecommunications infrastructure is important for providing opportunities for relieving economic distress in rural America, other factors are also important. This study investigated the factors and strategies for utilizing telecommunications to maintain community development as the base for sustained economic growth. For example, workers need education before and during employment. Medical, recreational, educational, water, and power facilities are needed for productive, healthy citizens. Taken together with telecommunications infrastructure, these factors add up to a solid equity base that is a prerequisite to sustained economic development. Policies that seek a balance between developing physical infrastructure and developing human capital best ensure that the boom and bust cycles characteristic of rural economies will be avoided.

Policymakers have certain options at their disposal for devising strategies that may aid rural areas. Those options should rest on certain fundamental realizations about rural America. A key problem in the economic topography of rural areas is the widely dispersed pockets of demand. Often each pocket in its isolation is not sufficient to support the investment required to "serve" it—whether that investment amounts to extending new high-speed data-transfer lines or building a new high school with the latest facilities. Therefore, policies that have the effect of aggregating demand should be sought.

What makes rural market aggregation particularly interesting in the case of telecommunications infrastructure is the relationship between the technology and the process of aggregation. On the one hand, the aggregation of services and demand is needed to sustain the modern telecommunications infrastructure. On the other hand, the telecommunications technology actually helps the aggregation process through its distance "annihilation" factor. It is the interplay between the technological capabilities and the aggregation process that generates the promise of rural telecommunications.

RECOMMENDATIONS

Several general policy recommendations are relevant to implementing strategies for aggregating demand.

1. *Enable adjacent areas to devise complementary community development activities.* If the telecommunications infrastructure in adjacent areas is developed in a coordinated manner, the individual pieces complement each other to create a regional, substate system.

One direct policy implication for facilitating such efforts is that the basic telecommunications network needs to be planned and regulated on a regional level. This is very different from the traditional approach of regulating on a company-by-company basis. Telecommunications providers' territories and markets are rather arbitrary, and the complementary approach requires a more integrated view of the entire telecommunications system. Regulators may facilitate such developments by eliciting cooperation from disinterested but important entities (such as telecommunications-intensive users or businesses) whose participation may be essential for a regional network.

For those rural communities proximate to urban regions, conscious integration of the rural community's economy with the metropolitan area's agglomerative economy may be warranted. The rural telecommunications infrastructure could be positioned as an extension of the urban system's. Policymakers on both local and regional levels should be conscious of the advantages and disadvantages of such integration. One would not wish to sacrifice the strengths of the rural area by siphoning off its local business potential; however, if the large and small communities can develop their single and unified strengths, integrated planning can be a win-win situation for both.

2. *Facilitate centralization in certain circumstances.* Aggregation may be achieved by actually transferring the resources or the demand to a central point. TI-IN is an example of how satellite-based distribution systems can allow for centralization of resources to meet the educational needs of a dispersed population. INS is an example of how telecommunications technologies permit aggregation of demand at a

central point. Technological developments like remote switching increasingly are going to allow for such centralization. Though there are definite economic benefits that will accrue from such centralization, these developments are going to generate sociopolitical tensions that regulators will have to resolve.[5]

3. *Share resources ("piggybacking")*. It is possible for certain rural entities, which alone do not generate sufficient demand or have enough resources, to capitalize on a symbiotic relationship with a larger entity. EMRG's exploitation of the AT&T POP, which was attracted to Kearney by Cabela's, is an example of how such sharing might work. Bretton Woods' collocation of its facilities within Mount Washington Hotel, its largest client, is another example of sharing resources.

Regulatory efforts may develop incentives for encouraging the resale of excess capacity of private networks in rural areas. Many large rurally based corporations have set up their own networks which often extend to very remote areas. The telecommunications needs of these areas are likely to be slight compared to those of the large corporation operating in the area. Certain specialized needs (e.g., access to specialized information services or high-speed data links) perhaps can be met by using the excess capacity available on the private corporate networks. The profitability of such arrangements may not be very attractive to the corporations owning such networks, but policymakers may be able to devise incentives, such as tax credits, to make them more attractive.

4. *Ensure access to advanced network capabilities*. The past few years have seen a tremendous amount of high-capacity fiber-optic network construction, generally supported by interexchange carriers interconnecting the major metropolitan areas. While "eliminating" the continental distances, these lines by necessity crisscross the rural expanse. From a rural standpoint, it makes sense to connect to these networks. The factors impeding interconnection are both cost and the relatively small demand on the part of rural communities. (Their use is likely to be minuscule compared to the billion-dollar metropolitan markets that these networks interconnect.)[6] A regulatory nudge in the direction of facilitating rural access to these networks may be warranted.

5. *Incorporate the magnet principle in local development*. Obviously, telecommunications-intensive users attract infrastructure. Their demand is great enough to justify certain investments on the provider's part. Local development strategy, particularly as it interacts with whatever state-sponsored initiatives exist, might consider targeting a "magnet" user, one whose demand would justify the attention of service providers. The community could then tailor subsequent development toward activities that would exploit newly justifiable

(and affordable) infrastructure. Kearney, Nebraska, offers an example of such a strategy.

These five policy recommendations, for addressing the situation of fragmented demand aggregation, rely on explicit policy initiatives that break with some of the more traditional ways of viewing rural service areas. Another way of addressing this fragmented demand might be to consider not the geographic dispersal of demand but the fragmentation resulting from service or client structures, which are more often than not artificial.

6. *Facilitate service differentiation.* Insofar as it may make sense for rural areas to have a single integrated system or conduit that transports all of their telecommunications needs, the current situation of allowing certain service providers to engage in only a limited range of businesses may be dysfunctional. The digital technology that allows the mixing of voice, data, and video traffic is ideally suited for service integration. For example, the same single wire could provide not only telephone-like communication services but also access to data bases and video entertainment programming. The ever-increasing transmission capacity of fiber-optic networks makes it attractive to aggregate all of the rural communications demand onto the single channel. For example, on the basis of pure technological or economic criteria, having separate networks for cable and telephony does not make sense in rural areas. This is an issue difficult to resolve in the policy arena, although it has come up repeatedly in the 1989–90 federal legislative session in the context of revising cable legislation. Rural utilities, telephone companies, cable companies, and satellite communication providers may be able to provide better services to rural areas if they can use their existing infrastructure as a platform from which to initiate new ventures. In the interest of getting the best possible mix of services to rural areas, some form of competition in heretofore protected service realms seems warranted.

Lest the most uneconomic of services (e.g., rural residential telephone service) be lost in the competitive fray, we suggest that policymakers devise incentives to ensure that some basic level of telecommunications service will be available to all rural dwellers and businesses. A revised national definition of universal service, beyond the traditional level provided by POTS, may be the answer, benefiting not only rural customers but also low- and moderate-income urban customers.

7. *Provide federal and state communications links to rural areas.* One entity that needs to reach out to every nook and cranny of the country is the government, both federal and state. Yet governments are often the biggest bypassers of the public network. This bypass activity may save one arm of the government a few million dollars, but it exacts costs from another. From the perspective of developing the rural

telecommunications infrastructure, it may make sense that the federal and state government traffic come into the single rural conduit, the public network, or, alternately, that government telecommunications capacity be shared with various categories of rural users.

These aggregation strategies imply a variety of policy actions. In the service of other useful approaches, such as developing partnerships and enhancing leadership, several additional recommendations are pertinent. These are targeted at localities, state-level policymakers, and service providers.

8. *Inculcate community leadership*. Communities should be empowered to form united community leadership and to achieve broad-based citizen commitment to development by providing training and necessary information resources. Programs such as Iowa State University Extension's Tomorrow's Leaders Today may provide an example for future leadership training programs. The strategic use of telecommunications should be considered in order to facilitate community empowerment. Extended area service and easy access to information through computer data bases may be helpful. One pertinent suggestion may be to shift the emphasis and funding away from agricultural information networks that are underutilized to the same district extension offices' efforts for community development training. In-place extension agents could be utilized to gain the competitive advantages that result from localizing information.

9. *Plan to develop communities in tandem with developing telecommunications infrastructure*. Infrastructure planning should parallel the strategic planning efforts of community leaders and citizens. Businesses and services need telecommunications to compete locally, regionally, and internationally; achieving economic health may require modern technology, yet having modern technology does not guarantee its effective use within the community. Technology planning and community planning need to proceed in tandem. All planning for rural development should anticipate capacity for telecommunications businesses and the efficient operation of government, education, and public services. Integrated planning offers the best opportunity for providing telecommunications services at a cost that is appropriate for all ratepayers.

10. *Encourage a broad view of telecommunications at the state level*. A state telecommunications regulatory agency, or some other body, that has the authority to recognize community development problems and make recommendations is needed to effect long-range solutions. For example, state utilities commission staff may solicit cooperatively proposed arrangements between telecommunications, community, and industry players. A rural industry may be allowed to sell excess private telecommunications capacity, thus giving to the community

upgraded capacity for those small-business and professional users who need it, in exchange for some state-granted "reward" or incentive. Properly planned, any upgrade in a rural community could have a considerable impact on the quality, cost, and efficiency of government and education services as well as the health of businesses.

11. *Build human skills.* Rural citizens and the labor force need up-to-date education in computer literacy and communications concepts as well as basic communications skills. States should ensure that all their school districts have access to the same educational materials by integrating distance learning initiatives and providing curriculum guidance.

12. *Identify and respond to community needs.* Local telephone companies need to expand their service horizons to meet larger community needs such as improved services to schools, government, and health facilities. On-line data bases, data processing, distance learning, digitized lab results, and teleconferences can bring up-to-date efficiencies needed to build communities and preserve quality of life.

13. *Adopt an educational mission.* Rather than wait for communities to discover how to use capacities they have never had, telecommunications providers need to educate their ratepayers about more than simply enhanced consumer services. Once upgrades are accomplished, the telecommunications provider should have a stake in seeing that innovative community problem solving maximizes use of its capacity. Diversified activities such as servicing military lines, providing cable television, selling advanced capacities such as SS7, and educating their client/consumer base are some uses providers should consider. State utilities commissions might require evidence of active participation in integrated community planning on the part of the telecommunications provider in exchange for granting certain rate changes or other concessions.

14. *"Market" telecommunications-based opportunities.* Where investment in telecommunications infrastructure capacity is expanded to accommodate unknown future needs, marketing may be needed to hasten adoption in order to achieve economies of scale. Supporting such marketing and local "telecommunications education" efforts should be designed into appropriate incentive structures devised by state or federal regulators.

Finally, in addition to the recommendations directed at the local and state levels and at telecommunications providers, there are various measures that could be undertaken at various levels of authority. The goal of the following suggestions is to encourage renewed investment in business by making available some of the advantages that telecommunications can bring to enterprises of all sorts.

15. *Educate entrepreneurs in using telecommunications-based services.* Helping local entrepreneurs avail themselves of the array of services

and aids available to them through telecommunications-based services or information networks could be a target of opportunity for policymakers at the federal, state, or local levels. Local businesses or organizations could use telecommunications for management, accounting, or vending services to a larger clientele; the same network can link them to sources of local or nonlocal expertise such as college faculty or sophisticated data bases. Such measures may enhance the success rate of existing or start-up small businesses. Training and continuing education for rural entrepreneurs is probably no less important than improving public education in rural areas.

16. *Disseminate information.* Governments at all levels need to create an environment for the rapid dissemination of information. State and local agencies should survey current or potential users for recommendations about what kinds of information are needed. Existing networks should be made available to new audiences involved in development. Development-oriented electronic bulletin boards should target community activists and entrepreneurs and encourage them to discuss problems, ideas, and solutions with other communities. Private information gatekeepers should be encouraged by federal and state governments to localize development information, much as they do agricultural information from the USDA and state extension services.

This study has documented and confirmed the potential that telecommunications holds for rural areas. But it is also clear that the realization of this potential is far from being guaranteed. It will take the collective efforts of all actors—community leaders, telecommunications providers, rural businesses, public-service providers, and policymakers—to establish strategies that are appropriate for local circumstance. We hope that this report will make a contribution to this effort.

NOTES

1. Other cases profiled businesses such as Weyerhaeuser and ENMR, which used terrestrial networks and advanced software protocols to enhance business operations or to exploit new service niches. It may not be too surprising that when simple technological use, as opposed to reorganizing resources or people, characterized a case's dominant innovation, that case was a private business. Private businesses are generally more organizationally primed to recognize and utilize inputs such as telecommunications to achieve improved competitive standing.

2. E. Rogers, *Diffusion of Innovations* (New York: Free Press, 1983).

3. At this writing it appears that portions of S. 1036 have been incorporated into the 1990 farm bill (H.R. 3950). Telecommunications-related provisions have been eliminated from this version of the bill.

4. See, for example, E. Parker et al., *Rural America in the Information Age*, and portions of the federal legislation considered by Congress in the 1989–90 sessions, namely Section 301 of H.R. 3581 and Section 120 of S. 1036.

5. There already are a number of such tensions revolving around centralization, and we do not mean to underestimate the sensitivity of such a strategy. One reason that Minnesotans decided to develop their own network rather than rely on TI-IN was that they did not want their children to be exposed to an education system whose locus of control resided beyond the state's boundaries. Similarly, many independent telcos are apprehensive about entering into SS7 arrangements because they fear loss of control over their subscriber data. On another dimension, the regulators will have to be open to new organizational forms and have an understanding of the regulatory complications arising from the rather unprecedented developments. One of the key factors behind INS's existence has been the supportive role played by the Iowa PUC board in the matter of newer tariffs and other operational issues.

6. EMRG's experience with US Sprint provides an excellent example of this. US Sprint's high-capacity transcontinental line runs just two blocks from EMRG's front door. But US Sprint would not connect Kearney for a "small" $800,000-a-year customer.

Telecommunications Glossary

ACCESS CHARGE Special fee to compensate the local exchange company for use of its network to connect the long-distance network; recently a fixed fee for access has been authorized to be charged to U.S. telephone customers.

ANALOG Representations that bear some physical relationship to the original quantity, usually electrical voltage, frequency, resistance, or mechanical translation or rotation.

ANTENNA Device used to collect and/or radiate radio energy.

BANDWIDTH Width of an electrical transmission path or circuit, in terms of the range of frequencies it can pass; a measure of the volume of communications traffic that the channel can carry. A voice channel typically has a bandwidth of 4,000 cycles per second; a TV channel requires about 6.5 MHz.

BASEBAND Information or message signal whose content extends from a frequency near dc to some finite value. For voice, baseband extends from 300 hertz (Hz) to 3400 Hz. Video baseband is from 50 Hz to 4.2 MHz (NTSC standard).

BAUD Bits per second (bps) in a binary (two-state) telecommunications transmission. Named after Emile Baudot, the inventor of the asynchronous telegraph printer.

BELL-COMPATIBLE   Essentially, conformation of a modem to the standards of the Bell Telephone System.

BINARY   Numbering system having only digits, typically 0 and 1.

BIT   Binary digit. Smallest part of information with values or states of 0 or 1, or yes or no. In electrical communications systems, a bit can be represented by the presence or absence of a pulse.

BOC   Telephone jargon for "Bell operating company," used to refer to divested companies.

BROADBAND CARRIERS   Term to describe high-capacity transmission systems used to carry large blocks of, for instance, telephone channels or one or more video channels. Such broadband systems may be provided by coaxial cables and repeated amplifiers or by microwave radio systems.

BROADBAND COMMUNICATION   Communications system with a bandwidth greater than that of a voiceband. Cable is a broadband communications system with a bandwidth usually from 5 MHz to 450 MHz.

BYPASS   Telephone industry term meaning service that avoids use of the local exchange company network, such as a customer connecting directly into the long-distance network or buying a direct line between offices instead of using the public network.

BYTE   Group of bits processed or operating together. Bytes are often an 8-bit group, but 16-bit and 32-bit bytes are not uncommon.

CABLE TELEVISION   Use of a broadband cable (coaxial cable or optical fiber) to deliver video signals directly to television sets in contrast to over-the-air transmissions. Current systems may have the capability of receiving data inputs from the viewer and of transmitting video signals in two directions, permitting pay services and video conferencing from selected locations.

CAD   Computer Aided Design. Techniques that use computers to help design machinery and electronic components.

CAI   Computer Assisted Instruction.

CAM   Computer Aided Manufacturing.

CARRIER   Signal with given frequency, amplitude, and phase characteristics that is modulated in order to transmit messages.

CARRIER SIGNAL   Tone that you hear when you manually dial into a computer network.

CATHODE RAY TUBE   Called CRT, this is the display unit or screen of your computer.

CCITT   Consultative Committee for International Telephone and Telegraphs, an arm of the International Telecommunications Union (ITU), which establishes voluntary standards for telephone and telegraph interconnections.

CELLULAR RADIO (TELEPHONE)   Radio or telephone system that operates within a grid of low-powered radio sender-receivers. As a user travels to different locations on the grid, different receiver-transmitters automatically support the message traffic. This is the basis for modern cellular telephone systems.

CENTRAL OFFICE   Local switch for a telephone system, sometimes referred to as a wire center.

CENTREX   Referring to both a service and a switch, Centrex entails having a switch located in a telephone company's central office that provides switching services to an institutional user; typically that user requires more than 30 internal lines. Centrex facilitates intra-institutional calling and offers various special calling features.

CHANNEL   Segment of bandwidth that may be used to establish a communications link. A television channel has a bandwidth of 6 MHz, a voice channel of about 4000 Hz.

CHIP   Single device made up of transistors, diodes, and other components, interconnected by chemical process and forming the basic component of microprocessors.

CIRCUIT SWITCHING   Process by which a physical interconnection is made between two circuits or channels.

COAXIAL CABLE   Metal cable consisting of a conductor surrounded by another conductor in the form of a tube that can carry broadband signals by guiding high-frequency electromagnetic radiation.

COMMON CARRIER Organization licensed by the Federal Communications Commission (FCC) and/or by various state public utility commissions to supply communications services to all users at established and stated prices.

COMSAT Communications Satellite Corporation. A private corporation authorized by the Communications Satellite Act of 1962 to represent the United States in international satellite communications and to operate domestic and international satellites.

CPE Telephone jargon for "customer premises equipment," which may often be distinguished from telephone company-owned equipment.

CROSS SUBSIDY Telephone term meaning that funds from one part of the business (e.g., long distance) are used to lower prices in another (local service). A controversy is how to prevent cross subsidy between regulated and unregulated parts of the telephone business.

CRT See cathode ray tube.

DATA BASE Information or files stored in a computer for subsequent retrieval and use. Many of the services obtained from information utilities actually involve accessing large databases.

DCE Data communications equipment. Computer components that are designed to communicate directly to data terminal equipment. (See DTE.)

DEAVERAGING Changing telephone rates so as to reflect true cost differences, thus making rates vary in different parts of a state. (Local rates are typically regulated so that telephone service is not much more expensive in some parts of a state than in others although the costs to the providers may vary greatly; rates are kept at an "average" by having a pool so that high-cost areas are subsidized by low-cost ones. Typically rural telephone companies are against deaveraging because it could cause a major increase in their rates.

DEDICATED LINES Telephone lines leased for a specific term between specific points on a network, usually to provide certain special services not otherwise available on the public-watched network.

DEPRECIATION   As usually defined, the tax "write-off" or credit given in some way for the declining value of equipment investments; in the telephone business, depreciation variations are an important variable in setting rates.

DIGITAL   Function that operates in discrete steps as contrasted to a continuous or analog function. Digital computers manipulate numbers encoded into binary (on-off) forms, while analog computers sum continuously varying forms. Digital communication is the transmission of information using discontinuous, discrete electrical or electromagnetic signals that change in frequency, polarity, or amplitude. Analog intelligence may be encoded for transmission on digital communications systems. (See pulse code modulation.)

DIRECT BROADCAST SATELLITE (DBS)   Satellite system designed with sufficient power so that inexpensive earth stations can be used for direct residential or community reception, thus reducing the need for local loop by allowing use of a receiving antennae with a diameter that is less than one meter.

DIVESTITURE   Break-up of AT&T into separate companies.

DOMINANCE   Telephone industry term meaning whether a company serving an area has such a high percentage of the business that it drives out competition; a current challenge is in how to define and measure dominance.

DOWNLINK   Antenna designed to receive signals from a communications satellite. (See uplink.)

EARTH STATION   Communication station on the surface of the earth used to communicate with a satellite. (Also TVRO, television receive only earth station.)

ELECTRONIC MAIL   The delivery of correspondence, including graphics, by electronic means, usually by the interconnection of computers, word processors, or facsimile equipment.

ESS   Electronic switching system. The Bell System designation for their stored program control switching machines.

FAX Facsimile. A system for the transmission of images. It is a black-and-white reproduction of a document or picture transmitted over a telephone or other transmission system.

FCC Federal Communications Commission. A board of five members (commissioners) appointed by the President and confirmed by the Senate under the provision of the Communications Act of 1934. The FCC has the power to regulate interstate communications.

FIBER OPTICS Glass strands that allow transmission of modulated light waves for communication.

FINAL MILE Communications systems required to get from the earth station to the point at which the information or program is to be received and used. Terrestrial broadcasting from local stations and/or cable television systems provide the final mile for today's satellite networks.

FREQUENCY Number of recurrences of a phenomenon during a specified period of time. Electrical frequency is expressed in hertz, equivalent to cycles per second.

FREQUENCY SPECTRUM Term describing a range of frequencies of electromagnetic waves in radio terms; the range of frequencies useful for radio communication, from about 10 Hz to 3000 GHz.

GATEWAY Ability of one information service to transfer a user to another one, as when one goes from Dow Jones/News Retrieval to MCI Mail.

GEOSTATIONARY SATELLITE Satellite, with a circular orbit 22,400 miles in space, that lies in the satellite plane of the earth's equator and that turns about the polar axis of the earth in the same direction and with the same period as that of the earth's rotation. Thus, the satellite is stationary when it is viewed from the earth.

GIGAHERTZ (GHz) Billion cycles per second.

HARDWARE Electrical and mechanical equipment used in telecommunications and computer systems. (See software; firmware.)

HEADEND Electronic control center of the cable television system where weaving signals are amplified, filtered, or converted as necessary. The headend is usually located at or near the antenna site.

HERTZ (Hz) Frequency of an electric or electromagnetic wave in cycles per second, named after Heinrich Hertz, who detected such waves in 1883.

INFORMATION UTILITY Term increasingly used to refer to services that offer a wide variety of information, communications, and computing services to subscribers; examples are The Source, Compuerve, or Dow Jones News/Retrieval.

INSTITUTIONAL LOOP Separate cable for a CATV system designed to serve public institutions or businesses usually with two-way video and data services.

INTEREXCHANGE CARRIER (IXC) Telephone companies (e.g., AT&T, MCI, US Sprint) that connect local exchanges and local access and transport areas (LATAs) to one another (i.e., they provide interLATA service); a highly competitive part of the telephone business.

INTERFACE Devices that operate at a common boundary of adjacent components or systems and that enable these components or systems to interchange information.

ISDN Integrated Services Digital Network; a set of standards for integrating voice, data, and image communication; a service now being promoted by AT&T and some regional telephone companies.

K 1024 bytes of information, or roughly the same number of symbols, or digits.

KILOHERTZ (KHz) Thousand cycles per second.

LAN See local area network.

LASER Light amplification by simulated emission of radiation. An intense beam that can be modulated for communications.

LATA Local Access and Transport Area. A telephone service region incorporating local exchanges, yet usually smaller than a state. Typically it is serviced by a given telephone company for local services, and by interexchange carriers for some intraLATA and all interLATA service.

LOCAL AREA NETWORK (LAN) Special linkage of computers or other communications devices into their own network for use by an individual or organization. Local area networks are part of the modern trend of office communications systems.

LOCAL EXCHANGE CARRIER (LEC) Telephone company that supports local dial tone, typically a regulated monopoly. LECs are responsible for traffic within LATAs (local access and transport areas).

LMS Local Measured Service. Method of telephone rate calculation that is sensitive to the amount of usage rather than a flat rate.

LOOP Wire pair that extends from a telephone central office to a telephone instrument. The coaxial cable in broadband or CATV system that passes by each building or residence on a street and connects with the trunk cable at a neighborhood node is often called the "subscriber loop" or "local loop."

MAQUILADORA Generally, U.S. manufacturing plants built near the U.S.-Mexico border, on the Mexican side. The maquiladora (or maquila for short) industry has replaced tourism as Mexico's second-largest source of income.

MEGAHERTZ (MHz) Million cycles per second.

MEMORY One of the basic components of a central processing unit (CPU). It stores information for future use.

MFJ Modified Final Judgment (1982). This ended the antitrust case against American Telephone & Telegraph Company (AT&T) and broke up the Bell system.

MICROCHIP Electronic circuit with multiple solid-state devices engraved through photolithographic or microbeam processes on one substrate. (See microcomputer; microprocessor.)

MICROCOMPUTER Set of microchips that can perform all of the functions of a digital stored-program computer. (See microprocessor.)

MICROPROCESSOR Microchip that performs the logic functions of a digital computer.

MICROSECOND One millionth of a second.

MICROWAVE Shortwave lengths from 1 GHz to 30 GHz. Used for radio, television, and satellite systems.

MILLISECOND One thousandth of a second.

MINICOMPUTER In general, a stationary computer that has more computer power than a microcomputer but less than a large mainframe computer.

MOU (Minute of Use) Usage measure used in the telephone business to calculate certain rates.

MODEM Short for modulator-demodulator. The equipment that you use to link your computer to a telephone line.

MODULATION Process of modifying the characteristics of a propagating signal, such as a carrier, so that it represents the instantaneous changes of another signal. The carrier wave can change its amplitude (AM), its frequency (FM), its phase, or its duration (pulse code modulation), or combinations of these.

MONITOR (VIDEO) Usually refers to the video screen on a computer but has more technical meanings as well.

MULTIPLEXING Process of combining two or more signals from separate sources into a single signal for sending on a transmission system from which the original signals may be recovered.

NANOSECOND One billionth of a second.

NARROWBAND COMMUNICATION Communication system capable of carrying only voice or relatively slow-speed computer signals.

NETWORK Circuits over which computers or other devices may be connected with one another, such as over the telephone network. One can also speak of computer networking.

NODE Point at which terminals and other computers and telecommunications equipment are connected to the transmissions network.

OFF-LINE Equipment not connected to a telecommunications system or an operating computer system.

ON-LINE Device normally connected to a microcomputer that permits it to run various programs and handle scheduling, control of printers, terminals, memory devices, and so forth. (See CP/M; MS/DOS.)

OPTICAL FIBER   A thin flexible glass fiber the size of a human hair that can transmit light waves capable of carrying large amounts of information.

PABX   See PBX.

PBX   Private branch exchange that may or may not be automated. Also called PABX (private automatic branch exchange).

PACKET SWITCHING   Technique of switching digital signals with computers wherein the signal stream is broken into packets and reassembled in the correct sequence at the destination.

POOLING ("Revenue Pooling")   Telephone industry term meaning setting up special collections of funds for intended cross subsidy, as in averaging rates between high-cost rural services and less-expensive urban ones.

PORT   Place for communication signal entrance or exit to and from a computer.

POTS   Jargon for "plain old telephone service."

PUBLIC SWITCHED TELEPHONE NETWORK   More formal name given to the commercial telephone business in the United States. It includes all the operating companies.

PUC   Public Utility Commission, usually the entity that sets telephone rates in a state.

PULSE CODE MODULATIONS (PCM)   Technique by which a signal is periodically sampled, and each sample is then quantitized and transmitted as a signal binary code.

REGIONAL HOLDING COMPANIES (RHC)   Companies formed to take over the individual Bell System operating companies at divestiture. There are seven (e.g., Pacific Telesis).

REVENUE POOLING   Telephone industry term referring to setting up special collections of funds intended to offset cost disparities, as in averaging rates between high-cost rural services and less-expensive urban ones.

SEPARATIONS   Telephone industry term meaning methods for dividing costs, revenues, and so forth, between different types of carriers, especially between long-distance and local exchanges.

SLOW-SCAN TELEVISION   Technique of placing video signals on a narrowband circuit, such as telephone lines, which results in a picture changing every few seconds.

SOFTWARE   Written instructions that direct a computer program. Any written material or script for use on a communications system or the program produced from the script. (See hardware, firmware.)

T CARRIER   Family of carriers with various circuit capacities. The capacity of T1 is equal to 24 circuits.

TARIFF   Published rate for a service, equipment, or facility established by the communications common carrier.

TELCO   Jargon for "telephone company."

TELECOMMUTING   Use of computers and telecommunications to enable people to work at home. More broadly, the substitution of telecommunications for transportation.

TELECONFERENCE   Simultaneous visual and/or sound interconnection that allows individuals in two or more locations to see and talk to one another in a long-distance conference arrangement.

TELEMARKETING   Method of marketing that emphasizes the creative use of the telephone and other telecommunications systems.

TELETEXT   Generic name for a set of systems that transmit alphanumeric and simple graphical information over the broadcast (or one-way cable) signal, using spare line capacity in the signal for display on a suitably modified TV receiver.

TELEX   Dial-up telegraph service.

TERMINAL   Point at which a communication can either leave or enter a communications network.

TERMINAL EMULATOR Use of a personal computer to act as a dumb terminal; this requires special software or firmware.

TIMESHARING Computer support of two or more users. The large computers used by the information utilities can accommodate many users simultaneously who are said to be timesharing on the system.

TRANSPONDER Electronic circuit of a satellite that receives a signal from the transmitting earth station, amplifies it, and transmits it to earth at a different frequency.

TRUNK Main cable that runs from the head end to a local node, then connects to the drop running to a home in a cable television system; a main circuit connected to local central offices with regional or intercity switches in telephone systems.

TWISTED PAIR Term given to the two wires that connect local telephone circuits to the telephone central office.

UPLINK Communications link from the transmitting earth station to the satellite.

UPLOAD To transfer information out of the memory or disc file of your computer to another computer.

VIDEOTEXT Generic name for a computer system that transmits alphanumeric and simple graphics information over the ordinary telephone line for display on a video monitor.

VLSI Very large scale integration. Single integrated circuits that contain more than 100,000 logic gates on one microchip (see LSI).

WATS Wide area telephone service. A service offered by telephone companies in the United States that permits customers to make dial calls to telephones in a specific area for a flat monthly charge, or to receive calls collect at a flat monthly charge.

Selected Bibliography

Bauer, Jeffrey C., and Eileen M. Weis. "Rural America and the Revolution in Health Care," *Rural Development Perspectives* 5, no. 3 (June 1989), pp. 2–6.

Brock, G. *The Telecommunications Industry: The Dynamics of Market Structure* (Cambridge, Mass.: Harvard University Press, 1981).

Brown, D., J. Reid, H. Bluestone, D. McGranahan, and S. Mazie, eds., *Rural Economic Development in the 1980s: Prospects for the Future Rural Development Research Report No. 69* (Washington, D.C.: U.S. Department of Agriculture, September 1988).

Gillan, J. "Universal Service and Competition: The Rural Science," *Public Utilities Fortnightly*, May 15, 1986, pp. 22–26.

Miller, J. "Rethinking Small Businesses as the Best Way to Create Rural Jobs," *Rural Development Perspectives* 1, no. 2 (February 1985), pp. 9–12.

Moscovice, Ira. "Strategies for Promoting a Viable Rural Health Care System," *Journal of Rural Health* 5 (1989), p. 223.

Office of Technology Assessment. *Linking for Learning* (Washington, D.C.: U.S. Government Printing Office, 1989), p. 22.

Parker, Edwin. "Future Perspectives on Satellite Communication," *Telecommunications* 21, no. 8 (August 1987), pp. 47–48.

Parker, Edwin, Heather Hudson, Don Dillman, and Andrew Roscoe. *Rural America in the Information Age: Telecommunications Policy for Rural Development* (Lanham, Md.: University Press of America, 1989).

Rogers, E. *Diffusion of Innovations* (New York: Free Press, 1983).

Saunders, J., R. Warford, and Bjorn Wellenius. *Telecommunications and Economic Development* (Baltimore: Johns Hopkins University Press, 1983).

Schmandt, Jurgen, Frederick Williams, and Robert H. Wilson, eds. *Telecommunications Policy and Economic Development: The New State Role* (New York: Praeger, 1989).

Schmandt, Jurgen, Frederick Williams, Robert H. Wilson, and Sharon Strover, eds. *The New Urban Infrastructure: Cities and Telecommunications* (New York: Praeger, 1990).

Index

ABOUT THE EDITORS

The editors are all affiliated with the University of Texas at Austin. Their previous books include *Telecommunications Policy and Economic Development: The New State Role* (Praeger, 1989) and *The New Urban Infrastructure: Cities and Telecommunications* (Praeger, 1990).

DATE DUE			
AUG 1 5 1996			
MAR 2 2 1999			
MAY 0 3 2000			